Volume 1 of *A Traveller's Story of Vietnam's Past*
From Prehistory to 111 BCE
The Bronze Drums and the Earrings

© 2021 Tan Pham

All rights reserved. No part of this book may be reproduced or modified in any form, including photocopying, recording, or by any information storage and retrieval system, without permission in writing from the publisher, 315Kio Publishing.

First Edition (B) 2021
For any inquiries, please contact by email: nxb315kio@gmail.com

Edited by Anna Rankin, Paul Litterick   Designed by Son La Pham
Typeset in Fournier with Vietnamese language support provided by Seb McLauchlan

ISBN: 978-0-473-59804-4

THE BRONZE DRUMS AND THE EARRINGS

Volume 1 of *A Traveller's Story of Vietnam's Past*
FROM PREHISTORY TO 111 BCE

TAN PHAM

Contents

List of Figures	9
Chapter 1 – Rivers, mountains, and the Seas	23
A very large lake in the centre of China	29
Chapter 2 – 2500+ Years of History	33
Period I – Autonomy	33
Period II – Northern rule	34
Period III – Đại Việt (Great Viet) and Champa	35
Period IV – A divided land	36
Period V – One country and four Nguyễn kings	38
Period VI – French rule	39
Period VII – Division and war	40
Period VIII – A United Vietnam	40
Chapter 3 – A Summary of this book	41
Chapter 4 – The Hùng Kings and the Yue	45
Who were the Hùng kings?	46
100 eggs	49
The origin of the Vietnamese (Part I)	49
4.4.1 – The Lạc	51
Wet-rice cultivation	53
4.4.2 – The land the Hùng kings ruled	54
4.4.3 – Dragons and fairies	56
4.4.4 – The family tree of the first family of the Vietnamese	58
4.4.5 – Việt and Yue	59
Chapter 5 – The Four Immortals	65
God of the mountain - the first immortal	65
Genie on a horse - the second immortal	67
A naked fisherman - the third immortal	68
A timeless princess - the fourth immortal	70
5.5.1 – Gióng or Dóng ?	72
Chapter 6 – The Prehistory to the Hùng Kings	75

Chapter 7 – Flying Egrets and Plumed Warriors	79
Society	81
Bronze drums	82
Boats	84
Birds, houses and other animals	86
People	87
Music	91
Weapons	92
7.7.1 – Our ancestors made the first bronze drum	92
7.7.2 – Copper mines and trees	93
7.7.3 – The egret went to feed at night. Perched on a soft branch, it fell down to the pond.	94
7.7.4 – Weapons to kill from afar	95
Chapter 8 – The Last Hùng King and the 2000-year-old Fortification	97
8.8.1 – Cổ Loa citadel	100
8.8.2 – The man from Shu	102
8.8.3 – The kingdom of Âu	104
A possible connection to the Zhuang people (Zhuangzu)	105
Chapter 9 – The Magic Crossbow and the Tragic end of the Man from Shu	107
9.9.1 – The battle for Cổ Loa	112
Chapter 10 – A Time of War	117
10.10.1 – The invasion of the "Hundred Việt" or "Bai-yue"	119
Chapter 11 – The End of Autonomy	125
11.11.1 – The rise of Nan-yue	127
11.11.2 – A squatting old man	131
11.11.3 – The end of a dream	133
11.11.4 – Just one of the many commanderies in the empire	137
11.11.5 – A timeline of Nan-yue history	139
Chapter 12 – History Revisited	141
12.12.1 – Hero or villain	142
12.12.2 – Crossing over Cà pass – The commandery of Xiang	143
12.12.3 – A shifting land	145
12.12.4 – The 28-year gap	146
Chapter 13 – A Time to Trade	149
Of beads and earrings	152
Land of the golden sand	156
Chapter 14 – Conclusions	161

Appendices

1.	Key sources of early Vietnamese history in Chinese language	166
2.	Sources of Vietnamese history by Vietnamese authors written pre-19th century	169
3.	Names in Vietnamese, Pinyin Chinese and English	176
4.	Vietnamese urban and rural districts (Quận and Huyện)	181
5.	The kingdom of Văn Lang	184
6.	Other views of Việt and Yue	186
7.	Of stone axes and pottery jars	187
8.	The prefecture of Tây Vu	190

Endnotes	192
Bibliography	230

List of Figures

Figure 1 – Timeline showing eight periods of Vietnamese history. 16
Figure 2 – Topography of Vietnam showing select rivers and mountains that shape its history. 26
Figure 3 – Indicative clusters of the bronze and early iron sites (~1500 BCE-2nd CE, after Andreas Reinecke) that became cradles of Vietnamese civilization. 27
Figure 4 – A 19th-century gate at the top of Ngang pass that for many years marked the border between North and Central/South Vietnam. 28
Figure 5 – Contemporary China showing Dongting lake, the main rivers, southern mountains and provinces associated with Vietnamese history. 29
Figure 6 – Five mountains of the Nanling (or Wuling) mountain range. 30
Figure 7 – Gate through to Thiên Quang pagoda between the Hùng king's Lower and Middle temples in Phú Thọ province of North Vietnam. 47
Figure 8 – Phong Châu, Hùng temple, Mê Linh, Cổ Loa and other sites as mentioned in the text. 48
Figure 9 – An illustration of Lạc Long Quân and Âu Cơ and one hundred sons. 51
Figure 10 – Kingdom of Văn Lang within the solid line (7th century BCE). Âu Lạc kingdom (2nd - 3rd century BCE) occupied a similar terrain. 55
Figure 11– Sword of King Goujian at the Hubei Provincial Museum. 61
Figure 12 – Statue of a Yue man (bronze, 771-476 BCE [Spring and Autumn Periods]) from the State Museum of Zhejiang province, China. 61
Figure 13 – Yue states showing the kingdom of King Goujian near Kuaiji and Ba Shu where An Dương Vương was believed to originate. 62
Figure 14 – The forest along the steps to the Upper temple at Ba Vì mountain, where the first immortal resides. 66
Figure 15 – Gióng temple at Phù Đổng village. 68
Figure 16 – Statues of Princess Tây Sa, Chử Đồng Tử himself and Princess Tiên Dung at the Temple of Chử Đồng Tử. 70
Figure 17 – The annual Phù Dầy festival in remembrance and of gratitude to Princess Liễu Hạnh. 72
Figure 18 – Indicative clusters of the Stone Age sites (until ~1500 BCE, after archaeologist Andreas Reinecke). 77
Figure 19 – Sông Đà bronze drum, middle of the first millennium BCE. 82
Figure 20 – Hoàng Hạ bronze drum. 83

Figure 21 – Ngọc Lũ bronze drum, 2000-2500 BP. 83
Figure 22 – Cổ Loa bronze drum, 2000 BP. 83
Figure 23 – Boat on Ngọc Lũ drum. 84
Figure 24 – Boat and people on the Hoàng Hạ drum. 85
Figure 25 – Boat on top of Hoàng Hạ drum. 85
Figure 26 – Rubbing of the top of the Hoàng Hạ drum showing birds in full flight. 86
Figure 27 – Birds, crocodiles and warrior figures on Đào Thịnh bronze jar. 86
Figure 28 – Birds and deer on top of the Ngọc Lũ drum. 87
Figure 29 – A Đông Sơn dagger showing a bare-chested male figure wearing earrings, bracelets and breechcloth but no tattoos. 88
Figure 30 – Dagger showing a similar male figure similar to that of Fig. 29. 88
Figure 31 – A short sword (named Núi Nưa) showing a female figure. 88
Figure 32 – A close-up of the female figure on the Núi Nưa sword. 88
Figure 33 – Another female figure on the broken handle of a Đông Sơn sword; note her sarong. 89
Figure 34 – Lạch Trường bronze lamp (circa 3rd BCE – 1st century CE). 89
Figure 35 – Bronze leg ring. 90
Figure 36 – Đông Sơn bronze bells. 91
Figure 37 – Bronze ladle showing a man playing a khèn-like instrument (2500-2000 BP). 91
Figure 38 – Little Egret, note the two long plumes on the nape. 94
Figure 39 – Đông Sơn weapons. 95
Figure 40 – Cổ Loa citadel showing the outer, middle and inner walls. 99
Figure 41 – One section of the middle wall of Cổ Loa citadel near the display centre; the top of the wall is heavily covered by trees and vegetation. 100
Figure 42 – The headless statue of Mỵ Châu (or Mỵ Nương) at Cổ Loa Citadel. 109
Figure 43 – An Dương Vương killing his daughter, Mỵ Nương and the golden turtle. 109
Figure 44 – Bronze lock or trigger for the crossbow. 110
Figure 45 – Han crossbow trigger mechanism. 110
Figure 46 – Han crossbow trigger mechanism. 111
Figure 47 – A multi-arrow crossbow at Cổ Loa museum. 111
Figure 48 – Main invasion routes to the Red River Delta by adversaries from the North. 114
Figure 49 – Battleground between Zhao Tuo and An Dương Vương. 114
Figure 50 – Qin Shi Huang's imperial tour across his empire as depicted in an 18th-century album. 118
Figure 51 – Key locations in the conquest of Bai-yue. 121
Figure 52 – Qin terracotta army at Xi'an, Shaanxi, China. 122
Figure 53 – Qin terracotta soldier at Xi'an, Shaanxi, China. 123
Figure 54 – Northern mountain passes to Nan-yue. 127
Figure 55 – Jade burial suit of Zhao Mo at the Museum of the Mausoleum of the Nan-yue King in Guangdong, China. 129
Figure 56 – Former Han's invasion of Nan-yue. 135

LIST OF FIGURES

Figure 57 – Three commanderies established by the Qin in 214 BCE. 144

Figure 58 – Commanderies (Zhuya and Dan'er, not shown) under Former Han (108 BCE) (after Loewe). 145

Figure 59 – Indicative clusters of Sa Huỳnh sites. 151

Figure 60 – Po Nagar Champa Tower at Nha Trang. 151

Figure 61 – Burial jar, Sa Huỳnh culture, An Bằng site, Quảng Nam province, c. 2500-2000 years BP, National Museum of Vietnamese History, Hanoi. 155

Figure 62 – Cooking pots, Sa Huỳnh culture, National Museum of Vietnamese History, Hanoi. 155

Figure 63 – Tools and weapons. The dagger on the right is most likely a Đông Sơn weapon. 158

Figure 64 – Lingling-o penannular earring (Three node pendant), artefacts of Phú Hòa site (Đồng Nai province). 158

Figure 65 – Bicephalous agate earrings, 2,500-2,000 BP found at Giồng Cá Võ site, Cần Giờ district, Ho Chi Minh City. 158

Figure 66 – Earrings on a skull (bicephalous ear ornament), History Museum, Ho Chi Minh City. 159

Figure 67 – Beads (Agate), 2,500-2,000 BP found at Giồng Cá Võ site, Cần Giờ district, Ho Chi Minh City. 159

Figure 68 – Four main settlements that have expanded into Vietnam 164

Figure 69 – Hán, Nôm and Quốc Ngữ (Vietnamese language) 170

Figure 70 – Administration units in modern Vietnam 183

Figure 71 – List of prefectures under the kingdom of Văn Lang by different sources 185

PREFACE

Growing up in Huế, a sleepy city in Central Vietnam, I learned from my high school history teachers of the Hùng kings, the Trưng sisters, and the Mongol invasions as key characters and events in Vietnamese history. Residing abroad in my twenties and thirties, I read much of history in books, mainly those published in the West, and mostly encompassing the two terrible wars in Vietnam; both French and American.

In 1988 I returned to Vietnam from New Zealand and henceforth travelled there regularly throughout the mid-'90s for business. There, I visited many historical sites that had otherwise only existed in my school lessons: Cổ Loa citadel, Hoàn Kiếm lake, Đèo Ngang (Ngang pass) and so on. I began to collect Vietnamese history books; this time those written by Vietnamese rather than Western historians. I was looking for a simple book that could offer me a clear understanding of the stories, the meanings, and the interconnections between the historical events and the historical sites I had visited. Such information exists but is spread amongst many varied books. Some come in thick volumes written in Vietnamese, which are useful for scholars but not for an average Vietnamese speaker.[1,2] One is fairly concise but written some years ago and needs updating.[3] There are two recently published books which are very comprehensive but lengthy – over a thousand pages each.[4,5] Others are published in English but deal with either a specific period in history or are too brief for my needs.[6,7] The exception is historian Keith Taylor's two volumes which provide the most definitive treatise on the subject to date in English. But while his books, each around a thousand pages, may provide excellent reference material, it is likely hard going for the casual reader.[8,9] For those readers who prefer a briefer and more compact text on Vietnamese history in English, there is one such book, of around 250 pages, published in 2014 which covers the timeline from prehistory to approximately 2010.[10]

In light of my findings I decided to write a book on Vietnamese history, if merely to satisfy my curiosity and to help those who may share my interest. However, as is the nature of such an undertaking, time, work, family intervened and the project lay dormant until now, 25 years later.

During those months of challenging research, the ambition of the task became clear to me. Given the scope of the project and my free time to dedicate myself to such a task, it would take at least six years to complete (one book per year). Therefore, I decided to break the research down over several volumes in order to cover the first six out of eight periods of Vietnamese history. The eight periods selected pivot on major events that mark key turning points in the story of Vietnam, and which altered the course of its history. The selection of these eight periods is mine and not necessarily based on the historical timeline I was taught at school where one memorized the story of one king and one battle, following another king and another battle and so forth; stories often set against foreign invaders, and it was difficult to remember them all.

In broad terms, Period I covers the ancient times to 111 BCE (BCE=Before Common Era, equivalent to BC=Before Christ) when the people ruled themselves. In the following millennium, or Period II, the land of upper central and northern Vietnam was ruled by various Chinese dynasties, with the exception of a few years of Vietnamese autonomy. The country became independent at the beginning of the second millennium in the 10th century CE (CE=Common Era, equivalent to AD=Anno Domini, the year of the Lord). From then to the present time, barring a few episodes of foreign rule and much bloodshed, the country was once again autonomous, its land area double that of the previous millennium. Periods III to VIII cover this second millennium. The eight periods are summarized in Fig. 1. For easy reading, BCE will be used where applicable, but not CE.

The eight periods of Vietnamese history span over 2,500 years or so and there are myriad fascinating stories to tell. Given my love for travel, I decided to select and approach the stories from a traveller's perspective, which explains the title: *A traveller's story of Vietnam's past*. My aim is simply to fix a historical site in time and space: where it is located, why it is there and how it is connected to other historical locations. However, my books are not travel guides; readers will not find such details as where to stay and suchlike but where appropriate I have included notes of my visits to some of the sites mentioned in the books. In time, I plan to visit the remainder for a better appreciation of their stories.

Together with the timeline, the geography of Vietnam underpins my stories. I have simplified the stories where possible, but have included sub-sections, footnotes and appendices for those readers who seek further details; others may choose to ignore the sub-sections altogether and the stories should still hold.

Over the past few decades, interest in Vietnamese history has increased significantly, ranging from archaeological excavations, scholarly works, books, and translations of ancient texts; a large amount of this information is available on the Internet. I have relied heavily upon these sources of information alongside personal visits to historical sites and museums for my research.

Vietnam gained independence from China in the 10th century. Until then, all writings of its history were observed and recorded through a Chinese lens. As noted in Appendix 1, these works were consulted to study the three main historical characters and their kingdoms covered by this book. The oldest surviving works of Vietnamese history, written by its historians, were produced in the 12th century in Chinese script – by scholar Đỗ Thiện, now lost – (Classical Chinese or *Chữ Hán or Chữ Nho*) and not in the current form of Vietnamese written language, (National Language Script or *Chữ Quốc Ngữ*). A list of such works is shown in Appendix 2. *Chữ Quốc Ngữ* was introduced by a French Jesuit in the 17th century (Alexandre de Rhodes (1593 - 1660), an Avignonese missionary and lexicographer). The French colonial government made this form compulsory for all Vietnamese in the early 20th century, however, the Chinese script and its Vietnamese variation (*Chữ Nôm*) continued until the middle of the 20th century. During that time, three different written languages existed in Vietnam: Chinese, French, and Vietnamese scripts.

Other sources of information came from inscriptions on steles in Sanskrit and old-Cham scripts, found in central and southern Vietnam; the first of

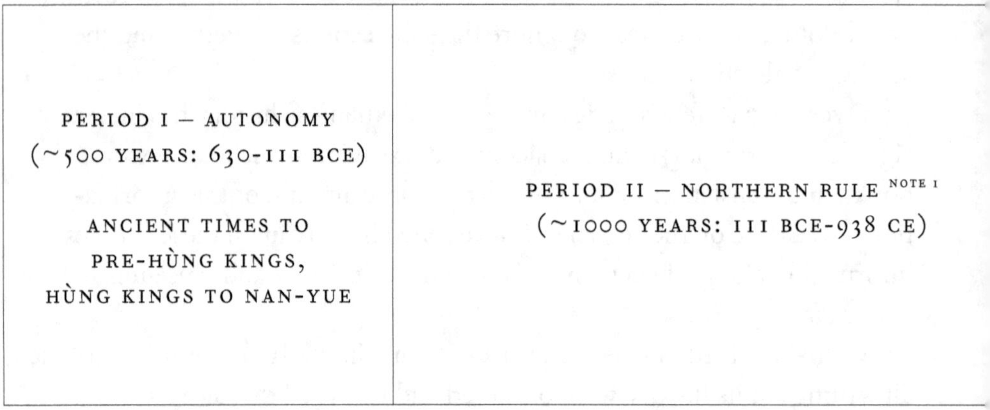

PERIOD I – AUTONOMY
(~500 YEARS: 630-111 BCE)

ANCIENT TIMES TO
PRE-HÙNG KINGS,
HÙNG KINGS TO NAN-YUE

PERIOD II – NORTHERN RULE [NOTE 1]
(~1000 YEARS: 111 BCE-938 CE)

Figure 1 – Timeline showing eight periods of Vietnamese history.

Note 1: The thousand-year period mainly covers the land north of Ngang pass (see Fig. 3). Immediately south, the territory became autonomous from around the third century; after which the southern border that marked the extent of northern rule shifted back and forth between Ngang to Hải Vân passes. But, effectively from the fifth century, it settled at Ngang pass.[11,12] The kingdoms to the south, Linyi/Champa and Funan/Zhenla ruled themselves.

PERIOD VII — DIVISION AND WAR
(21 YEARS: 1954-1975 CE)

PERIOD IV — DIVISION
(~200 YEARS: 1558-1802 CE)

| PERIOD III — INDEPENDENCE (~600 YEARS: 938-1558 CE) | IV | V | VI | VIII |

PERIOD V — ONE COUNTRY
(~60 YEARS: 1802-1858 CE)

PERIOD VI — FRENCH RULE
(~100 YEARS)

PERIOD VIII — UNITED VIETNAM
(45 YEARS: 1975–)

these appeared in the 4th century. These were neither Chinese nor Vietnamese sourced; and are not relevant to the period covered within this volume.

The adoption of *Chữ Quốc Ngữ* has meant millions of Vietnamese, myself included, are cut off from our own history as we are unable to understand books, records and inscriptions at temples or pagodas written in Chinese, Sanskrit, or old-Cham characters. The equivalent situation for English speakers who seek knowledge of their history is discovering that all sources prior to the 20th century are written in Greek.

Other than these sources listed, I have used Google Maps, without which it would have been difficult to construct my book: maps are the skeleton on which I build my story. Distances shown in this book are generally based on routes taken by car. I have also relied on images downloaded from Wikimedia Commons, and photos I have taken where appropriate.

In written form, Vietnamese language employs accents (or diacritics). For example: Long Thạnh (with a dot under the 'ạ') and Long Thành (with a grave above the 'à') are two differentplaces . Without accents they would be the same, so to avoid confusion I have used the full accents in Vietnamese names and locations. The translation from Vietnamese text to English, unless specified, is all mine. Furthermore, I decided to write this book in English rather than Vietnamese simply to make it more accessible for a wider audience.

As a matter of simple convention, I use local spelling for names for people and locations in their respective countries, and Pinyin Chinese instead of Wade-Giles Chinese. For example: Giao Chỉ instead of Jiaozhi, Zhao Tuo instead of Triệu Đà or Chao T'o, Guangdong instead of Quảng Đông, Champa instead of Chiêm Thành and so on. I have applied this convention where possible but there are exceptions, such as Vietnam instead of Việt Nam and Hanoi instead of Hà Nội given these names are familiar to readers in either language. Similarly, I use Western Ou instead of Xi Ou or Tây Âu and Linyi instead of Lâm Ấp. However, to assist those readers familiar with Vietnamese names, I have included a translation list in Appendix 3. As to references, I have included both English and Vietnamese sources; acknowledging that the latter means little to those unfamiliar with the language but it would be amiss to omit these altogether as there are readers who do and may find these helpful.

I have attempted to avoid using websites as references as these may be removed in the future, however this has proven difficult as the information is unavailable elsewhere, therefore I have limited their use where possible.

This first volume covers Period I. The title of the book, "*The bronze drums and the earrings*", refers to the two cultural artefacts produced in Vietnam during this period; the former from northern and the latter from central/southern Vietnam, respectively. My remaining volumes shall cover the ensuing five periods, until 1954 when the French finally departed the country after they first bombarded and landed in Touraine (Đà Nẵng) in 1858. I have limited my contribution to the years post-1954 as there exist many such history books covering these years.

ACKNOWLEDGEMENTS

I wish to thank my wife, Mỹ Thành, my son, Sonla Pham, and my daughter Mai-Linh Pham, who have each given me much encouragement and support for this book. I am grateful to Professor Michael Belgrave for his guidance and my Mitchong friends (a collective term for Vietnamese students who studied in New Zealand from 1957 to 1975, as coined by them): Biện Công Danh, Trần Quang Dương, Lê Thu Liễu, Trịnh Thị Sao and Nguyễn Văn Tư; my friends who have taken time out of their busy lives to read and comment on my draft: Nguyễn Thiên Nga, Nguyễn Lê Việt Dũng, Chris Hawley and Greg Szakats. I am also grateful for the editing by Paul Litterick, Anna Rankin; the comments and suggestions of Gillian Tewsley and the sharing of historical stories and books by Vũ Hồng Nam. My appreciation also extends to Google Maps for their permission of use.

CHAPTER I

RIVERS, MOUNTAINS, AND THE SEAS

Reaching Ngang pass – daylight was receding,
Grasses and trees mixed among the rocks, leaves jostled with flowers,
At the foot of the mountain, couched a few woodcutters
By the riverside, a hamlet with huts scattered.
Painful memory of the old country, the water hens sounded
Yearning for home, the francolins tired out
Stopped and gazed upon heaven, hills and water
Alone with my feelings on my own.

"Traverse Ngang Pass (*Qua Đèo Ngang*)" - Lady Thanh Quan, 19th century.[1]

Vietnamese children learn this poem as part of their school curriculum. I learned it many years ago and still remember its verses. I include it here not only because it is a lovely poem, but because it refers to a significant landmark in the history of Vietnam.

Vietnam is a north-south country; to travel from Hanoi, the capital in the north, to Ho Chi Minh City (or Saigon), the largest city, in the south, takes around two hours by air or 31 hours by car along Highway 1A, covering a distance of some 1,727 kilometres. Along the route, one has to cross many rivers. Until 1899, when the first bridge in Vietnam was built across the Hương (Perfume) river in Huế, one had to cross each of these rivers by boat. Conversely, if one wants to travel from east to west at the narrowest point of the country, Quảng Bình province in Central Vietnam, it is just 50 kilometres wide but one must make a rapid climb from sea level to around a thousand metres in this short distance.

Vietnam is an elongated S-shaped land running between the latitudes of 8° and 24°, bordered by China in the north, the Gulf of Thailand in the south, Laos and Cambodia in the west, and the East Sea in the east. It has a coastline of 3,444 kilometres long or 42 per cent of its total border length; the total area of the country is 331,123 square kilometres, of which only about 35 per cent is agricultural production land.[2]

The current border of Vietnam has been very much shaped by its geography, which has shaped its history. Rivers and mountains form natural borders and defensive positions; rivers provide water, food, transport and trading routes. Once humans learned how to grow crops and domesticate animals, they moved out of caves and settled on the plains and in river valleys. It is no accident that the major settlements in Vietnam (Hanoi, Saigon, Huế) are all on major rivers. Travelling by road would have been difficult. Then, Vietnam was covered in dense forests with a variety of animals including monkeys, tigers, snakes, elephants, rhinoceros and so on. People would have travelled by boat on the rivers across the country or along the relatively shallow coastline up and down the country. Rivers were where many major battles were fought throughout Vietnamese history as the armies used these waterways to move fightingships, troops, weapons and supplies.

The three main features of Vietnamese geography that have shaped its history are the mountains, the rivers, and the coastline. Fig. 2 shows the topography of Vietnam. On this map are marked the regions which are relatively flat, 0-500m above sea level. If one aligns this map with the archaeological sites for the Bronze and Early Iron Age periods, Fig. 3, they show quite clearly that most of these sites are located within the plains around the Red River Delta and other river valleys along central Vietnam. The history of Vietnam unfolds from the people who have settled in these places over the millennia.

The land of the country has not always been as today's map shows and has been called Vietnam only since the early 19th century. For the first millennium of the Current Era, the southernmost border of Vietnam was the Hoành Sơn mountain range, about 470 kilometres south of Hanoi, which runs northwest and forms a formidable natural barrier separating the north and the south of the country. Until 2004, when a tunnel was built, the only way to cross this range was to traverse a pass called Đèo Ngang or Ngang pass. The land to the north, in the first millennium, was called by different names – Văn Lang, Âu Lạc, Nam Việt, Giao Chỉ, Giao Châu, Vạn Xuân, Annam and Đại Cồ Việt. South of the pass was occupied by the Sa Huỳnh inhabitants who rose to become the Linyi, then Champa, civilizations.

Further south, the Mekong Delta formed the settlements of a people who developed a distinctive Indianized culture under the kingdom of Funan/Zhenla.

There were many wars and migrations over the following eight hundred years before the southernmost border of Vietnam shifted from Hoành Sơn to where it is today. Now there is a gate on top of Ngang pass built by King Minh Mạng in 1833 to mark the location, as shown in Fig. 4.

Rivers and mountain ranges form natural borders between regions, tribal groups or political states. However, over the centuries, rivers may change course, therefore using these as markers for historical events is not always reliable.

According to a report by FAO (Food and Agriculture Organization) on Vietnam, there are 2,360 rivers with a length of more than ten kilometres each crisscrossing the country.[3] Among these, three rivers in Central Vietnam flow east to the sea and have played a major role in Vietnamese history, forming the borders of a divided Vietnam for many years: Gianh, Bến Hải and Thu Bồn.

Further south from Ngang pass, two mountain ranges at Hải Vân and Cả passes (or Cape Varella) are significant landmarks in the history of Vietnam. Another prominent mountain range is the Annamite range (or Dãy Trường Sơn), which forms the backbone of the country from North to South and separates Vietnam from Laos. These locations are shown in Fig. 3.

In administrative terms, Vietnam is divided into provinces; each city has an administration centre and generally speaking, the borders encompass the rivers or mountain ranges. The province is further divided into a number of districts. Below the district level is the lowest official administration unit called communes or wards. Below this are hamlets, which are not officially defined; a pictorial representation of the arrangement is shown in Appendix 4.

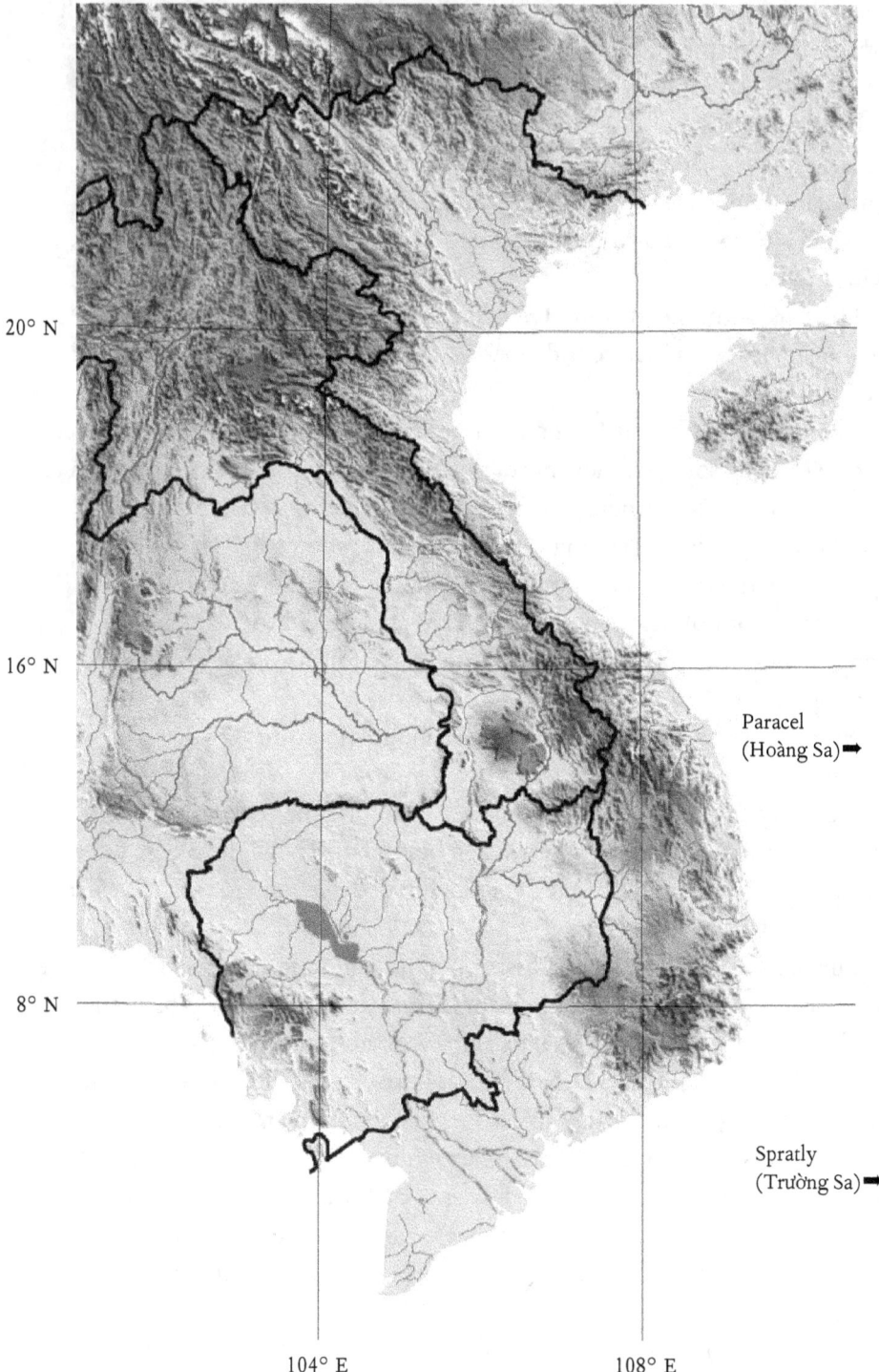

Figure 2 – Topography of Vietnam showing select rivers and mountains that shape its history.[4]

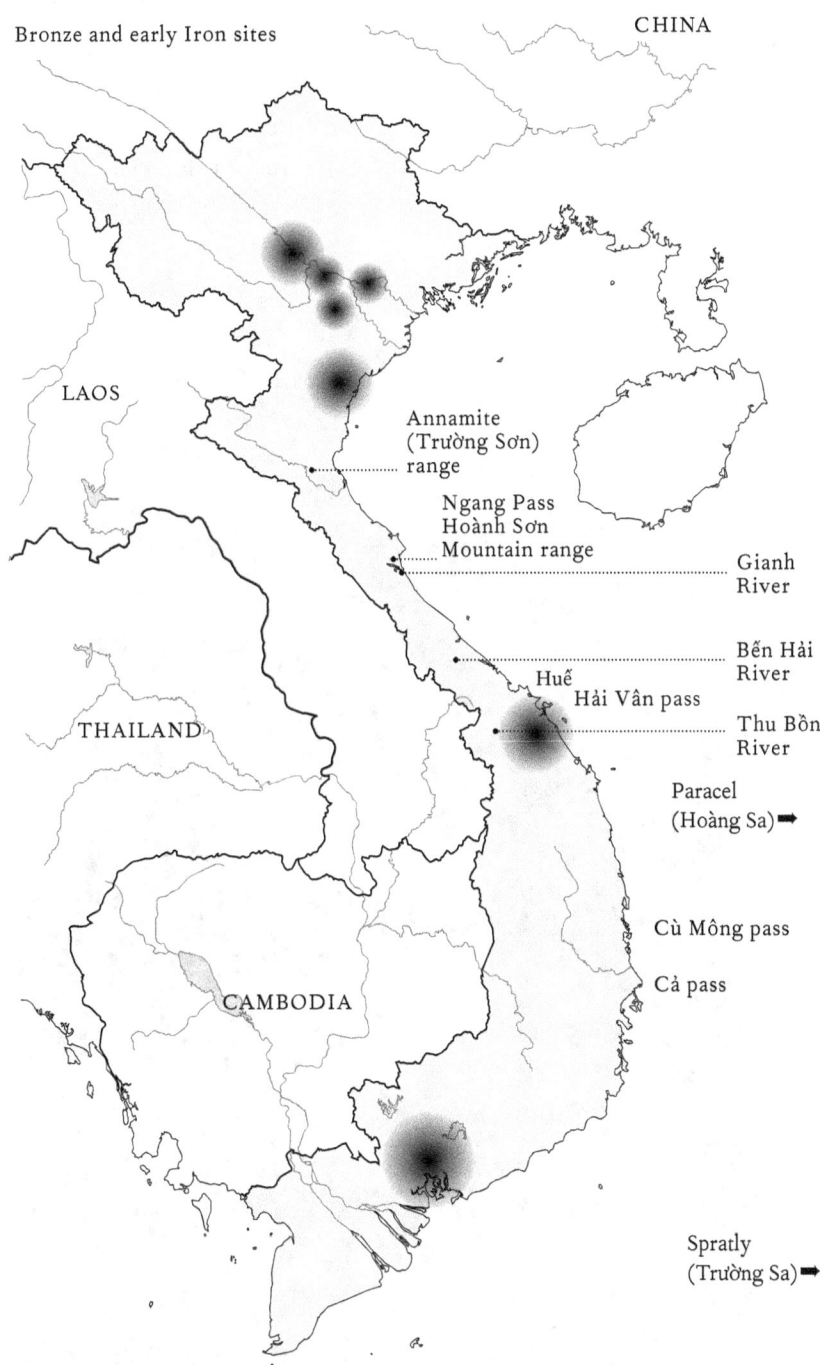

Figure 3 – Indicative clusters of the bronze and early iron sites (~1500 BCE-2nd CE, after Andreas Reinecke) that became cradles of Vietnamese civilization.

There are 76 sites north of Ngang pass, 17 in the central region and 13 in the south, a totalling of 107. While the number of sites could reflect the availability of research funding from the government, it may also represent the number of people who lived in these regions. Regions with a larger population tend to accrue and therefore leave behind more artefacts.[5]

Figure 4 – A 19th-century gate at the top of Ngang pass that for many years marked the border between North and Central/South Vietnam.[6]

A very large lake in the centre of China

Interactions between Vietnam and its neighbour in the north, China, have significantly shaped Vietnamese history. Many stories in early Vietnamese history refer to places in China, so it is helpful to briefly study its geography in order to identify certain locations. Fig. 5 shows the topography of China. One can see three major rivers flowing from its hinterland in the west to the sea in the east: the Yellow (Huang He) river in the north, the Yangtze or Yangzi river in the centre, and the Pearl (Zhu Jiang or Xujiang or Xi) river in the south.

Figure 5 – Contemporary China showing Dongting lake, the main rivers, southern mountains and provinces associated with Vietnamese history.[7]

The locations that predominantly feature in accounts of Vietnamese history are mostly located south of the Yangtze river. Those of interest are along the southeastern coast of China, and immediately north of the current border, as shown in Fig. 5.

In the centre of China near Yueyang on the right bank of the Yangtze in Hunan province is Dongting lake, which is about four times the land area of Singapore.[8] Around five hundred kilometres south of this lake is the Nanling (also known as Wuling) mountain range. Nanling means "Southern Mountains". The Nanling mountains effectively form the border of the two southern provinces of Guangxi, Guangdong and the northern neighbours of Hunan and Jiangxi. The mountain range stretches 1,400 kilometres from west to east, separates the Pearl River Basin from the Yangtze Valley and serves as the dividing line between south and central subtropical zones.⁹

Figure 6 - Five mountains of the Nanling (or Wuling) mountain range.

Vietnamese translation of Wuling is "*Ngũ Lĩnh*", *Ngũ,* which means five. The five mountains are Yuecheng (or Yuechengling) (Hunan-Guangxi border), Dupang (Hunan-Guangxi border), Mengzhu (Hunan-Guangxi border), Qitian (near Hunan-Guangzhou border), Dayu (Jiangxi-Guangdong, south of Ganzhou) and Wuyi mountain. These featured heavily in the expedition of the armies of China's First Emperor into the southern land as described in Chapter 10.¹⁰

There is another mountain range, Wuyi or Wuyishan in eastern China, south of Shanghai which runs north to south and forms the border between Jiangxi and Fujian provinces. Wuyi mountain range extends in the northeast direction into Zhejiang province. From the map, Fig. 6, one can see how these mountain ranges run along the border of the provinces mentioned above.

CHAPTER 2

2500+ YEARS OF HISTORY

Period I - Autonomy

Archaeological digs in Vietnam have found evidence of settlements as old as 500,000 BCE. The stories I will relay begin from the time in which historical annals recorded the first kings, the Hùng. This was the era when the people organized and ruled themselves in ways that suited them; thus I call it the autonomous period or Period I – from prehistory to 111 BCE, when the Former Han dynasty fanned out from Luoyang, absorbing north and central Vietnam into its empire (Fig. 5).

The first Hùng king came from a village near Mê Linh, located on the northern bank of the Red river. Eighteen Hùng kings followed, the last deposed by An Dương Vương in the 3rd century BCE. He built a great capital at Cổ Loa, just north of Hanoi, on the eastern side of the Red river. Most of the inner and outer walls of this oldest citadel in Vietnam still stand, over 2,000 years after they were built. Today, one can visit the museum and the temples, spend a quiet day wandering around the small, quiet village of Cổ Loa or climb one of the ancient ramparts (Figures. 8, 40).

Sadly, An Dương Vương did not rule for very long; he came to power at a time of great change in China and his downfall was a direct result of northern imperial ambition. By 221 BCE, Qin Shi Huang, whose tomb houses the famed Terracotta Warriors, had conquered the remaining six states, mostly north of the Yangtze river, and became the First Emperor.[1] He then turned his attention to the land south of the Yangtze and began his campaign with a massive invasion force, 500,000 strong. One of his generals, Zhao Tuo, led his army to Cổ Loa and drove An Dương Vương from the citadel. Zhao Tuo established the kingdom of Nan-yue (or Nam Việt) which includes Guangxi and Guangdong provinces (Fig. 5) as far south as Ngang pass.

His kingdom lasted for around 90 years before a Former Han emperor from the Yellow river; – his forefather had already deposed Qin Shi Huang's descendants – conquered Nan-yue and put an end to any independent aspirations of the southern states. This book covers this period.

Period II - Northern rule

Period II began with the Former Han rule in 111 BCE and lasted until 938 CE, over a thousand years. Numerous kingdoms and dynasties rose and fell in China. Except for brief periods of independence, the land north of Ngang pass, where the descendants of the Hùng kings and the majority of the ancestors of today's Vietnamese lived, was part of the northern empire. However, the local people did not accept northern rule passively and there were many uprisings. The most famous of these is that of the Trưng sisters in 40. The two sisters and their army expelled the local imperial ruler and established their reign at Mê Linh, the home of the first Hùng king. In 43, their revolt was brutally suppressed by the Later Han army. That same year, on the other side of the world, the Romans finally conquered Britain. The reign of the Trưng sisters was brief but for millions of Vietnamese down the centuries, they are heroines, revered and worshipped across the nation, irrespective of political beliefs, as a symbol against foreign invaders.

I learnt of the Trưng sisters at school many years ago, but I can easily recall their names and other key characters involved in this momentous event. There is a wonderful temple dedicated to the sisters at Mê Linh, where one can spend a lovely day wandering around the site amongst the shade of the trees in a cool breeze.

Vietnamese historians refer to this period as "*Bắc thuộc*" which loosely translates as "a colony of the north, or belonging to the north". Today's nation of China did not exist then; the land, now China, was occupied by various dynasties and kingdoms at differenttimessohistoricallyspeak ing, Northern rule is a more appropriate term than Chinese rule.

South of Ngang pass the situation developed differently. In the second century a revolt by the inhabitants at the southernmost district of the Later Han empire, just south of Hải Vân pass, spread north to Ngang pass and found a new kingdom. This kingdom, Linyi, is the forerunner of the kingdom of Champa (Vietnamese *Chăm*) who left behind many beautiful Champ towers along the central coast of Vietnam.[2] Linyi thrived from the second century to the eighth century. Champa continued from the ninth century to the 19th century before it was absorbed into Vietnam. However, from the third century; the land of Linyi, then Champa, was never again subject to northern rule. Further south to the Mekong Delta the land was part of another kingdom, Funan (Phù Nam) which became Zhenla; part of which also was absorbed into Vietnam.

Period III - Đại Việt (Great Viet) and Champa

The beginning of the 10th century saw the end of the Tang dynasty (618-907) in China and the dissolution of the country into what is termed a "Five dynasties and ten kingdoms" period (907-979), until a general from one of the dynasties (Later Zhou) conquered the others and established the Song dynasty (960-1279).[3]

In Giao Chỉ in 938, a local army led by Ngô Quyền defeated the Southern Han expedition force at the battle of Bạch Đằng river, which flows out to the Gulf of Tonkin at Hải Phòng (Fig. 48), finally ending the Northern rule. The man who would become the first king of independent Vietnam came from a small village on the south side of the Red river, not far from where the Trưng sisters raised their banners around nine hundred years earlier. This time the revolution was permanent and, barring a few brief periods of northern invasion, the Vietnamese again ruled themselves. I term this period Đại Việt (Great Viet) and Champa; the names of two independent kingdoms which existed at that time in the land of Vietnam. Today, one can visit the ancient village of Đường Lâm, 50 kilometres east of Hanoi, to sit in the village square among the old buildings, drink tea and watch the world goes by; one can also light a joss stick to offer one's respect at the tomb of Ngô Quyền himself, located near the village.

Some historians set the independent period as beginning thirty years later in 968 when Đinh Bộ Lĩnh united various warlords and declared himself

Emperor. However, I am of the ilk who prefer 938 given Ngô Quyền's victory provided the impetus for the local people to be free of the Northern rule.

Following independence, the land north of Ngang pass to the border with China, was named Đại Việt (Great Viet) by one of the kings during the Lý dynasty in the 11th century with its capital at today's Hanoi.[4] This name continued until it was changed to Vietnam in the 19th century.[5]

However, the northern dynasties were not about to relinquish their former colony easily and over the next few centuries they invaded several times, only to be defeated or driven out by the kings of Đại Việt. Two key existential events that happened to Đại Việt and Champa encompass the invasion of the fearsome Mongols in three separate expeditions in the 13th century and the occupation of the Ming dynasty of Đại Việt in the 15th century for around 20 years. There were also many wars between Đại Việt and its southern neighbour Champa; but throughout all these events, Đại Việt survived and expanded until the French arrived in the middle of the 19th century.

Period III lasted for around six hundred years to 1558, when a man by the name of Nguyễn Hoàng and his entourage, reportedly thousands in number, went south to lead the defence of the southern provinces situated between Ngang pass and Hải Vân pass.[6] In doing so, he started a dynasty and completely changed the course of Vietnamese history. Not only that, his surname Nguyễn has been taken up by millions of Vietnamese; those with this surname are spread across the world.

Period IV - A divided land

Period IV encompasses 1588 to 1802, and is referred to as "A divided land" to reflect the fact that for about two hundred years, Đại Việt, while nominally under King Lê, was ruled by two lords: Lord Nguyễn in the south (Đàng Trong [Inner Circuit or Cochinchina]), capital at Huế and Lord Trịnh in the north; (Đàng Ngoài [Outer Circuit or Tonkin]) capital at Hanoi. Dividing the two states was the Gianh river in Quảng Bình province, some thirty kilometres south of Ngang pass (Fig. 3).

While Period III was marked by the fledgling nation facing existential threats from foreign invaders, Period IV was noted for the southern expansion of Đại Việt at the expense of Champa. The northern border of Champa had shifted beyond Hải Vân pass to Cả pass, just north of Nha Trang, from 1611. By 1802, except for a few isolated locations and the Central Highlands, Đại Việt occupied much of the land of Vietnam as we know it today.

This period was also a time of division and civil wars; the longest of which came at the end of the 18th century, lasting thirty years (1771-1802). This war began with an uprising, known by historians as the Tây Sơn uprising, initiated by three brothers in Tây Sơn district, against the Nguyễn lord, then the Trịnh lord. Tây Sơn district is located about 50 kilometres east of Qui Nhơn city in Bình Định province, central Vietnam. Civil war raged across the length of Vietnam from Saigon, Huế to Hanoi. The brilliant Nguyễn Huệ (also known as Emperor Quang Trung) and his brothers also defeated invasion armies from the King of Siam (Thailand) in the west, and the Emperor of the Qing dynasty (China) in the north in several decisive battles. They also fought amongst themselves until Nguyễn Huệ united Vietnam, ruling from Huế for around four years before his death in 1792 at the relatively young age of 40.[7]

His reign did not last long: by 1802 his family members, descendants, generals and close relatives were hunted down, some killed by beheading, others had their bodies torn apart by horses or stamped upon by elephants, some were severely flogged and died.[8] The remains of Nguyễn Huệ and his brother were dug up and discarded, their skulls kept for 20 years at the armoury and later moved into a prison. The prison no longer exists, but its location is approximately the primary school of Tây Lộc, inside Huế citadel, at its western corner.[9] Nguyễn Ánh, a descendant of the Nguyễn lords and founder of the Nguyễn dynasty, was responsible for this savagery, apparently in revenge for what the Tây Sơn brothers had done to his ancestors.[10]

Together with the Trưng sisters, Nguyễn Huệ is one of the great Vietnamese heroes. Today, one can visit the Quang Trung Museum at Tây Sơn, Bình Định province, or view his large statue at Đống Đa, Hanoi. By contrast, for my generation through to the present time, Nguyễn Ánh is seen as a traitor, blamed for paving the way for the French colonization of Vietnam. The Vietnamese describe him in a phrase as one who *"Carries a snake to bite the family chickens"*.[11] He was also heavily criticized for the harsh treatment he inflicted upon his defeated foes. Within my study of history I now adopt a more sympathetic view and hope future generations are kinder to Nguyễn Ánh and his descendants, or at least the first four Nguyễn kings. Fortunately, historical accounts and positions are changing, and historians generally agree we ought to take a more balanced view of him.[12]

Today, one can visit his beautiful and quiet tomb in Huế, together with those of six other Nguyễn kings and nine Nguyễn lords, upstream of the Hương river. When there, spare a thought for Nguyễn Huệ and his family; their remains had been lost to history – the Nguyễn kings made sure of that.

Period V - One country and four Nguyễn kings

This period is relatively brief, at around sixty years, or two generations. It began in 1802 when Nguyễn Ánh defeated the remains of the Tây Sơn army and united the country under one rule from Huế as Emperor Gia Long, and one name of Vietnam, officially, the names of Đại Việt and Champa were no longer used. The French arrived in 1858, which changed everything. While the French was forced to leave in 1954, Vietnam was no longer able to rule itself in the same way that the Hùng kings, the Đại Việt kings, the Trịnh, Nguyễn lords and the four Nguyễn kings had done prior.

The long years of division and thirty years of civil war had left Vietnam weak and desperately poor.[13] The four Nguyễn kings were faced with the massive task of pacifying and rebuilding the country, and dealing with both internal rebellions and threats from the West. The citadels in Huế, the flag tower of Hanoi, and citadels at other major cities were built at this time. Many temples, pagodas and public works throughout Vietnam were repaired, and many irrigation canals were dug.[14,15]

The four Nguyễn kings continued the tradition of their forefathers, opening up new land and expanding their territory. By 1829, Vietnam occupied most of northern Laos and nearly half of Cambodia, possessing the largest land area in its history.[16] However, the borders between these countries and Vietnam were subsequently redrawn by the French under the Indochina Federation to the present borders.

In 1856 the French shelled Đà Nẵng, south of Hải Vân pass, and in 1858 troops landed. They attacked Saigon, taking most provinces in the Mekong Delta by 1862. By 1887, Cambodia and Vietnam were under French rule as Indochina which encompassed Tonkin (northern Vietnam), Annam (central Vietnam), Cochinchina (southern Vietnam) and Cambodia. Once again, Vietnam was broken up.[17]

Period VI - French rule

A thousand years enslaved by the Chinese,
A hundred years ruled by the French,
Twenty years of civil war,
A mother's legacy for her children,
A mothers' legacy is a sad Vietnam [...]
A mother's legacy, a jungle of dried bones.
A mother's legacy, a mountain covered with graves.

Trịnh Công Sơn's song from 1967 – "Gia tài của mẹ or A mother's legacy".[18]

Against overwhelming odds, the Vietnamese had previously defeated such foreign invaders as the Mongols, the Ming and the Qing, but in the late 19th century, the army of the Nguyễn kings, even with help from a warlord[19] in southern China, was no match for the combination of the French and the Spanish superior military technology. One lost battle[20] followed by a treaty[21] followed by another lost battle[22] and treaty[23]; they slowly ceded their sovereignty to the French. Hanoi citadel was mostly demolished by the French colonial government in 1882; Saigon citadel was completely destroyed in 1869 by the French expedition forces.

Resistance against the French began as soon as they set foot in the country and spread from the south to the north. It was not until the closing years of the 19th century that the colonial regime established its authority.[24,25] The first half of the 20th century saw a continuation of armed uprisings, peaceful protests, and economic exploitation.[26,27] For example, all private distillation of alcohol was banned. Alcohol production was a French monopoly sold to the locals at an enormous profit. World War II offered the Vietnamese opportunity for independence after the Japanese deposed the French in 1945. Under the Japanese occupation the Vietnamese suffered, what was possibly, the largest famine in their history where between 600,000 and 2 million people in northern Annam and Tonkin provinces starved to death.[28] In September 1945, under Hồ Chí Minh, Vietnam declared independence, soon after the Japanese surrender. This was not to last, and after lengthy but failed negotiations between the French government and the government of Hồ Chí Minh, the French army returned to Vietnam in 1946. The first Indochina war lasted nine years until 1954, when the French were finally defeated at the battle of Điện Biên Phủ, about 430 kilometres west of Hanoi, near the border between Laos and Vietnam.

Period VII - Division and war

When colonial rule ended in 1954 Vietnam was once again divided into two; this time, the border between North and South fell at Bến Hải river, north of Quảng Trị (Fig. 3). But peace did not last and the second Indochina war began soon after. It would be another 21 years before the country once again united when the tanks from the North Vietnamese army finally rolled into the Independent Palace in Saigon in 1975.

Period VIII – A United Vietnam

Since 1975, Vietnam has been united as one country. This period began with a mass exodus from the country by refugees in boats, followed by ten years of war and occupation of Cambodia, and a brief (27 days) but bloody war with China in 1979.[29] In 1989 Vietnam finally withdrew from Cambodia, and in 1994 the US Trade Embargo on Vietnam was lifted. Economic reform (named Renovation / *Đổi Mới*) was introduced in 1986 but it was not until the trade embargo was lifted that Vietnam was able to attract significant investments from developed countries, notably Japan, Singapore, Taiwan, and South Korea. Economic booms followed and the country became a gigantic construction site: many buildings, roads, houses, factories and bridges were built in the early 1990s.

   Listening to Trịnh Công Sơn's song "A mother's legacy' still brings tears to my eyes, but Vietnam is no longer a "sad country".[30] Many "dry bones" are still in the jungle and the mountain still has graves but the country has moved on.[31]

CHAPTER 3

A SUMMARY OF THIS BOOK

This book is about the Hùng kings, An Dương Vương and Zhao Tuo (or Triệu Đà), who are the main historical identities that shaped the events of Vietnam in Period I, and the kingdoms associated with them: Văn Lang (Fig. 10), Âu Lạc (or Ou luo) and Nan-yue (or Nam Việt) (Fig. 57). The land this book covers, extending from the south of the Yangtze to Cả pass (or roughly from the latitude of 13°N to 30°N) is shown in Figures 2 and 5 and described in Chapter 1.

Hùng were legendary kings of Vietnam, the first of whom and the eldest of 50 sons who travelled with his mother to the mountain believed to be Mt. Tản Viên, about 75 kilometres east of Hanoi. His father took the other 50 sons to the seas but history tells us little of their subsequent dispersal. The 100 sons from 100 eggs are at the heart of a lovely story relaying the meeting of the parents of the first Hùng king, as told in Chapter 4. In Vietnamese tradition, the Hùng kings are the ancestors of all Vietnamese, and they ruled over a kingdom called Văn Lang; believed to extend from southern China to central Vietnam.

According to the fable, these one hundred sons became the ancestors of the *"Bai-yue"* (A hundred Việt) kingdoms located south of the Yangtze river, among which is the *"Lạc Việt"* (or Luo-yue) tribe who inhabited the Red River Delta. The question of Vietnamese ancestry, the meaning of the *"Lạc"* people and the difference between *"Yue"* and *"Việt"* are discussed in Chapter 4.

During the reign of the Hùng kings, three stories were told of the legendary figures who became three of the Four Immortals *(Tứ Bất Tử)*. The fourth immortal, a princess, came later in the 16th century, but also occupies a special place among the Vietnamese. There are temples dedicated to the Hùng kings and the Four Immortals within a day's trip from Hanoi.

Most Vietnamese know about the Four Immortals: one man (a God), a couple, and a boy; each of whom existed during the time of the Hùng kings. Later, during the 16th and 17th centuries, the fourth, a princess descended from heaven three times. A traveller to Vietnam will undoubtedly come across one or several of these characters at temples, pagodas, and other historical sites. Given that three of these stories fall during Period I, they are included in Chapter 5.

The relatively flat region north of Mt. Tản Viên, where three rivers (Đà, Lô and Hồng [or Red]) meet and flow into the Red river, became the cradle of a civilisation that began around the 7th century BCE. Found artefacts of the civilization include bronze drums, musical instruments, agricultural implements and weapons. They painted a lively society with music, dancing and boat racing. The people lived in houses built on stilts, grew rice on paddy fields, wore beautiful bracelets and ankle rings, and made exquisite daggers. Another cradle of early civilization was found around Thanh Hóa, about 160 kilometres south of Hanoi, by the Mã rivers. There was where the first bronze drum was found at a village that has given rise to the name of this bronze age civilization: Đông Sơn. Historians refer to the people who lived in these times as the Lạc people. The bronze drums and other artefacts found during the time of the Hùng kings are described in Chapters 6 and 7.

Further south, beyond Ngang pass, different civilizations emerged. The *"Sa Huỳnh"* people, whose artefacts have been found at many sites in central Vietnam, did not make any bronze items but they made intricate beads, jewellery and pottery jars. Their lingling-o earrings are similar to items found in the Philippines and other parts of Southeast Asia. However, there is not much to tell as stories about those who lived there did not appear until the 1st and 2nd centuries, which is outside the timeline of this book. The archaeological finds in this region are discussed in Chapter 13.

Today, one can see these marvellous artefacts at museums in Hanoi, Ho Chi Minh City, and Thanh Hóa. Most provincial museums in Vietnam will have a few displays related to this era.

The historical events in this period happened during the reign of three ancient Chinese dynasties: the Zhou (1056-256 BCE), the Qin (221-207 BCE) and the Former (or Western) Han (202 BCE-9 CE) and the state of Chu (1030-223 BCE).

The reign of Hùng kings came to an end around the 3rd century BCE when the last Hùng king was defeated by An Dương Vương, a descendant of an ancient kingdom in China some 1,400 kilometres north of Hanoi.[1] He named his kingdom Âu Lạc and built a substantial fortification at Cổ Loa, which is still standing. One can visit the site, 20 kilometres north of Hanoi, wander around the village and climb one of the 2,000-plus-year-old earth ramparts. Unfortunately, one cannot walk far as there is no track or path through the overgrown vegetation and trees.

An Dương Vương's rule did not last long after a Qin general from China by the name of Zhao Tuo defeated him at the battle of Cổ Loa in the 3rd century BCE.[2,3] Zhao Tuo led the massive invasion of the Yue kingdoms south of the Yangtze river, on the order of the First Emperor of China, Qin Shi Huang, who gave us the famous Terracotta Army. Zhao Tuo fought An Dương Vương to a standstill, and finally had to resort to trickery and betrayal to capture Cổ Loa. He did so by getting his son, Trọng Thủy, to seduce An Dương Vương's daughter, Mỵ Nương, and stole the magic crossbow. In his rage the king beheaded his daughter. Trọng Thủy, burdened with guilt, jumped into a well and drowned. Today, one can visit the well and the headless statue of An Dương Vương's daughter at Cổ Loa. The tragic story of the couple, Trọng Thủy and Mỵ Nương, has been told many times down the centuries, taught at schools, and is the subject of many plays and songs. Cổ Loa citadel, the Battle of Cổ Loa and the story of the magic crossbow are told in Chapters 8 and 9.

Zhao Tuo then established an independent kingdom called Nan-yue which consisted of modern Guangxi, Guangdong, Fujian provinces in China, and the north and upper central of Vietnam with its capital at Panyu in modern Guangzhou, about 140 kilometres inland from Hongkong (Fig. 5). Nan-yue lasted over 90 years until the Former Han empire's expansion eventually engulfed it into its empire in 111 BCE. While Zhao Tuo's burial place is still unknown, his grandson left behind a massive tomb in all its imperial grandeur in Guangzhou. The rise and fall of Nan-yue are told in Chapter 11.

Intertwined with these stories are three battles which marked the transfer of power from one character to the next:

a. The battle of Cổ Loa (see 9.9.1), in the 3rd or 2nd century BCE, which ended the reign of An Dương Vương and his kingdom Âu Lạc. While the details of the battle are unclear, mapping it out has given us good insight into the strategic location of the citadel and the major battles in the same vicinity down the years.

b. The invasion of the Yue kingdoms by 500,000 strong Qin forces over seven years in the 3rd century BCE is vividly described in a number of ancient texts. Recreating the battle plans provides us with a glimpse into the scale and terror the rulers of the Yue kingdoms must have felt facing the might of the Qin empire. The invasion and the subsequent decline of the Qin empire gave rise to the formation of Nan-yue and elevated Zhao Tuo to emperor status. The invasion is described in Chapter 10.

c. The third battle took place at Panyu, Guangzhou; unlike the second battle it was swift but no less ferocious. Two emperors in China were one too many and Nan-yue was eventually vanquished by an army, far superior in number and most likely weapons, of the Former Han emperor. With their backs against the sea and facing four columns of somewhere between one to two hundred thousand Former Han troops and their allies, converging from the north and west along the various rivers, the defenders of Nan-yue had little chance. The citadel was burned in the winter of 111 BCE. This event is described in sub-section 11.11.3.

The battle of 111 BCE marked a major turning point in Vietnamese history, when the country became part of the Former Han empire. It would be a thousand years until when the people again ruled themselves.

CHAPTER 4

THE HÙNG KINGS AND THE YUE

THE WIFE SAID: *"I am a northerner by origin. I lived with you, the king, gave birth to one hundred sons but you left me and children, not bringing them up with me, became a person without wife and children, only loved yourself"*

THE HUSBAND REPLIED: *"I am of the dragon race, Head of the Water Underworld, you are of the fairies, live on earth. While negative and positive energy has fused to give birth to children, water and fire do not mix, different races make it difficult to live together and we have to separate. I will take fifty sons to the Water Underworld and you take fifty sons to the land, divide the land to rule. Up the mountains, down to the ocean, let each other know when needs arise, don't forget."*

A dialogue between the parents of the first Hùng king, from "A Collection of Strange Stories from Lĩnh Nam" (*Lĩnh Nam Chích Quái* [LNCQ]).[1]

The history of Vietnam begins in legends with the Hùng kings, from 680 BCE, according to one source, "Abridged History of Viet" (*Việt Sử Lược* [VSL]), and about 2,879 BCE, according to another, "Complete Book of the

Historical Records of Great Viet" (*Đại Việt Sử Ký Toàn Thư* [SKTT]).[2,3]

The earliest kings in Vietnamese history, the Hùng who ruled a kingdom called Văn Lang which, according to A Collection of Strange Stories from Lingnan (Lĩnh Nam Chích Quái) LNCQ, extended all the way from Nanling mountains in China to Hoành Sơn mountain range in Central Vietnam where Ngang pass is located.[4] There were 18 Hùng kings in a dynasty called Hồng Bàng.

Vietnamese historians agree the Hùng kings were historical figures, even if their kingdom was much smaller than described in history books. The dynasty is believed to have originated around the region of Phú Thọ, just north-west of Hanoi where rivers Đà, Lô, and Hồng meet (see 4.4.2).

Ancient texts did not refer to the Hùng kings directly but did mention *Lạc Vương* (Lạc king) (see 4.4.1) or the king of the Lạc, a people who practised wet-rice culture and lived in the same region as that of the Hùng kings. There has been intense debate among historians as to whether Hùng and Lạc kings are the same.[5] My position supports the proposition that the Lạc kings cited in ancient texts are the same as the Hùng kings mentioned in later sources, since they both refer to the chiefs of the tribes who lived in the region, now north Vietnam.

It is with the Hùng kings that I will begin the story of Vietnam. All Vietnamese school children learn that they are the descendants of the Hùng kings and "Children of dragons and grandchildren of fairies" (*con rồng cháu tiên*).

Who were the Hùng kings?

Unfortunately, the people who lived during the time of the Hùng kings did not leave behind any written texts. There are plenty of symbols among the artefacts but nothing resembling a written language. Recorded history did not appear until the arrival of the Former Han at around 111 BCE.[6] Written around two thousand years after the event, VSL (Việt Sử Lược), a 14th-century Vietnamese work, first mentioned Hùng kings here:

> "*During the rule of King (Zhuang of Zhou)*[7] *(696-682 BCE) a stranger from Gia Ninh used magic to conquer the various tribes, declared himself Hùng Vương (King Hùng), established the capital at Văn Lang, named his kingdom Văn Lang, with tolerant and honest customs, used tying knots*[8] *to record major events*[9]. *Reigned for eighteen generations, all of them called Hùng Vương.*"[10]

Gia Ninh is believed to be located in Phú Thọ province in northern Vietnam.[11]

Hùng in Vietnamese means 'strong' or 'heroic', but according to historian and archaeologist Hà Văn Tấn, it is the phonetic transcription of *Cun* in Mường, *Khun* in Thai and *Khàhuntz* in Munda; all mean 'leader' or 'chief'.[12] *Vương* means 'king', the same as another Vietnamese word, *Vua*. One can only speculate as to why all 18 Hùng Kings are all called Hùng Vương and not by different names for different kings. However, it makes sense if Hùng means 'chieftain', as there would be 18 chieftains of the Văn Lang kingdom over the centuries.

VSL continues to say that the Yue/Wu King Goujian (*Việt Câu Tiễn*) (reigned 496-465 BCE) sent an envoy to entice the Hùng king but he resisted. I mention this episode to illustrate two interesting observations: firstly, the king of Yue came from the Wu kingdom in modern Zhejiang province just south of Shanghai; there is no reason why he would bother with the Hùng king, thousands of kilometres south. Secondly, this event occurred around 200 years after the accession of the first Hùng king. If the two events cited by VSL were at the same time, the first Hùng king would begin his rule at about 496 BCE or later.

For years, the Vietnamese have celebrated Hùng kings on the 10th day of the third lunar month. The annual festival is held at Hùng temple, located in Phong Châu district, Phú Thọ province of North Vietnam (Figures. 7 and 8).

Figure 7 – Gate through to Thiên Quang pagoda between the Hùng's kings Lower and Middle temples in Phú Thọ province of North Vietnam.[13]

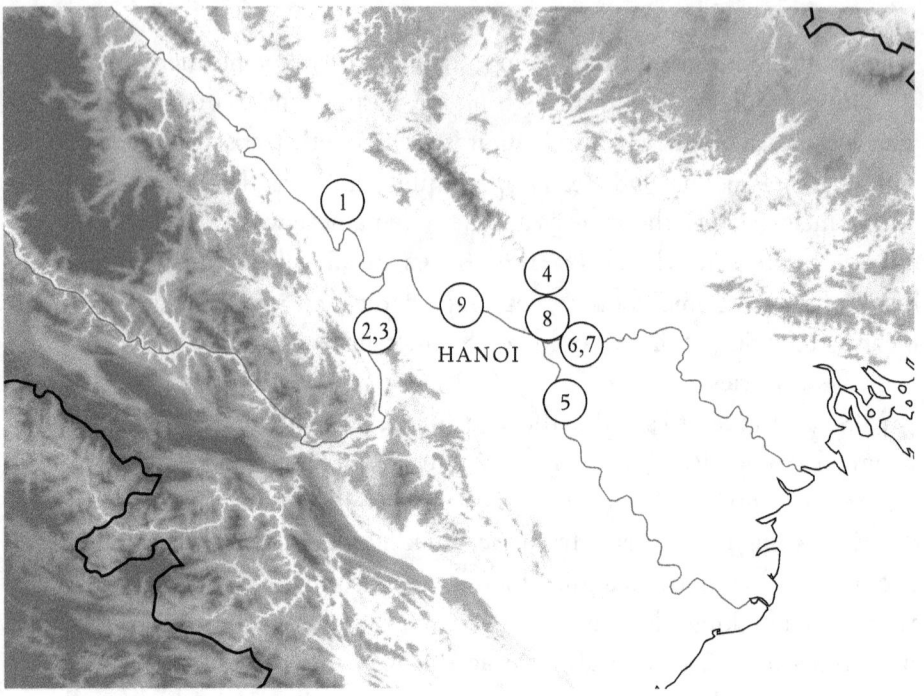

Figure 8 – Phong Châu, Hùng temple, Mê Linh, Cổ Loa and other sites as mentioned in the text. 1. Phong Châu, 2. Đền Trung, 3. Đền Thượng, 4. Sóc Sơn, 5. Đền Chử Đồng Tử, 6. Kiến Sơ pagoda, 7. Đền Gióng, 8. Cổ Loa, 9. Mê Linh.

Conversely, SKTT (Đại Việt Sử Ký Toàn Thư) dated the first king of Hùng Vương to 2,879 BCE. This date has given rise to the phrase "4,000 years of [Vietnamese] civilisation (or history)" (*4,000 năm văn hiến* [or *lịch sử*]) commonly used among the Vietnamese as an expression of pride.

I have adopted the dates in VSL, which coincide with the dating of the bronze drums and other artefacts which amply demonstrate the existence of an organised and civilised society in the region where the Hùng kings and their people lived. My Vietnamese history is thus around 2,500 years and not 4,000 years as is widely used, and what I was taught at school. My history aligns with current thinking among Vietnamese historians, whereby the figure of 2,700 years has been used.[14,15] Additionally, the Hùng king's rule ended in 257 BCE, therefore to have 18 kings over 2,622 years seems incorrect.[16]

100 eggs

Together with millions of Vietnamese over the centuries, I learned about Lạc Long Quân (*King Dragon of the land of Lạc*) whose mother came from Dongting lake, and his wife Âu Cơ, whose father ruled the land north of Nanling mountains (see Fig. 6). Lạc Long Quân, of the dragon race and Âu Cơ, of the fairy race, became the parents of the first Hùng king. They have been worshipped as the ancestors of all Vietnamese through the centuries. According to the story, Âu Cơ gave birth to a sac of 100 eggs which produced 100 handsome boys. However, as the boys grew, their parents decided to part ways, given they were of different races and could not continue to live together. So, 50 followed their father to the sea, 50 followed their mother to the mountain at Phong Châu, close to where the Hùng temple is now located (Fig. 8), and the eldest of her sons became the first Hùng king. This story is told in more detail in 4.4.3.

We also learned that these 100 sons are the ancestors of the Bai-yue (A hundred Việt). According to LNCQ, all Vietnamese down the generations are their descendants.[17] Among the Hundred Việt is a tribe called Lạc Việt (or Luo-yue) who lived in the Red River Delta region.

The Origin of the Vietnamese (Part I)

I grew up having learned the 100 eggs story and believed Vietnamese ancestors came from a Việt state in China, the Yue/Wu kingdom. I have now found that the story is not so simple. The Việt people are described by LNCQ as having short hair and tattooed bodies; these descriptions do not match those shown in the bronze artefacts found in northern Vietnam. Secondly, the ancient people who lived south of Ngang pass, the *"Sa Huỳnh"* certainly did not come from a Việt state in China. Part of the confusion is the translation of the Chinese term *"Yue"* as *"Việt"* by many Vietnamese historians; while linguistically correct, they are not always the same.

To avoid confusion, I will use the term *"Yue"* as in *"Bai-yue"* or *"Nan-yue"* to refer to non-Chinese people as described earlier, and *"Lạc"* to refer to the indigenous people living in North Vietnam during the Hùng king period.

It is clear there was an active and lively indigenous population living there, years prior to the arrival of the Yue, the Qin, or the Han from the regions around the Yangtze river. These were the *"Lạc"* north of Ngang pass and the *"Sa Huỳnh"* people to the south of this pass. However, over the millennium, a steady influx of people arrived to settle in this land and that mix of races produced the Vietnamese.

What of the 100 eggs legend? Is it a Yue or a Lạc legend? Now that I have an opportunity to study the tale closely, it seems strange that Âu Cơ would take her 50 sons all the way south to Phong Châu if she came from north of Nanling mountain, some 1,100 kilometres away. We should remember that by the time LNCQ was written in the 14th century, Vietnam had already been in China's cultural and political orbit for over 1,500 years. So, it is possible that the writers of LNCQ, who would have been well-versed in Chinese studies, may have tried to fit the local legend (Lạc Long Quân and Âu Cơ) to Shen Nung, a revered character in Chinese mythology.[18]

While the legend was told in a number of Vietnamese historical texts such as LNCQ and SKTT, it was not mentioned in VSL, which predated LNCQ and SKTT, even if it first mentioned the Hùng king. In fact, one of those historical texts made some rather acerbic comments:

> *"One hundred sons" is a social saying to wish someone to have sons... but to give birth to eggs... no different from birds, not humans... so this story is absurd"*.[19]

One historian made it clear that the connection between the Vietnamese ancestors to Shen Nung cannot be treated as history.[20]

The other possible explanation is that LNCQ covered the stories south of Nanling mountains where the Bai-yue tribes lived. Among those were the Yue, who came south and lived in "Lạc Việt" (Luo-yue or contemporary North Vietnam); the legend travelled with them.

Alternatively, the story of how the ancestors of the Vietnamese came to be could be a hybrid between the 100 eggs legend by the indigenous Lac people, combined with the underwater world and fairy myth by the migrant Yue. There is a similar legend told by the Mường, a minority group living around contemporary Hòa Bình, about 75 kilometres west of Hanoi. In this legend, two birds gave birth to 100 eggs, after 50 days, 97 eggs hatched and produced 97 people of different races, 50 went to live in the delta and 47 went to the highlands and became Mường, Mán, Mèo, Thổ Đen, and Thổ Trắng.[21]

Whatever the myth, I like the story. I'd rather be a grandchild of fairies than of frogs or birds – which appear frequently on the bronze drums as made by the Lạc people under the Hùng kings.

More details of *"Việt"* and *"Yue"* can be found in 4.4.5.

Figure 9 – An illustration of Lạc Long Quân and Âu Cơ and one hundred sons.[22]

4.4.1 – The Lạc

Page 427 of Volume 37 of "Additional Explanation of Commentary of the Water Classic" (*Thủy kinh chú sớ* [TKCS] quotes a passage from "Records of the Outer Territory of Giao Châu" (*Giao Châu ngoại vực ký*), a Chinese work (which no longer exists): [23]

> "*In the past, when Giao Chỉ (Jiaozhi)* (roughly North Vietnam) *did not have any prefectures or counties, of the land, there were Lạc điền (Lạc fields) which followed the rising and lowering of tides. People planted crops on these fields to harvest. These people were called Lạc dân (Lạc people). They had Lạc vương (Lạc kings) and Lạc Hầu (Lạc marquises) to watch over the urban and rural districts. In rural districts, mostly the position was called Lạc Tướng (Lạc general) who had bronze seals and green ribbons.*"

Most historians have quoted this passage to prove the existence of the Lạc people in northern Vietnam. Much ink has been spilt to analyse this passage so I will summarise my selection of key points as follows:

Firstly, the expression "*There were no prefectures and counties (quận huyện)*" refers to the time when the land was not organised as it would have been under the Han or Qin rule.

Secondly, what is the meaning of Lạc? There are several interpretations; from the name of a river, to a type of horse, to the name of a bird. [24,25] researcher Nguyễn Kim Thản believed *Lạc* means *water*. I tend to agree with him as it is related to the wet-rice culture, but rather than trying to extract its exact meaning, I use it simply as the name of the indigenous people who practised wet-rice culture at the time of the Hùng kings.[26] Wet-rice cultivation encompasses planting seeds in a nursery on dry land, and once the seeds grow into small plants, moving them to a deliberately flooded field, for example, rising tides, for them to fully grow.

Thirdly, the use of rising tides for rice farming was not only possible but indeed evidence of the practice has been found in ancient Lạc fields near Lake Lãng Bạc, which, according to historian Đinh Văn Nhật, is approximately the area north of the Cầu and Thương rivers, extending as far as Bắc Ninh and Bắc Giang cities. [27,28]

Fourthly, an earlier version in Records of Guangzhou (*Quảng Châu Ký*) did not mention *Lạc Vương* at all. On the other hand, later historians provided more titles and additional connections between them: *Lạc Hầu* as the civilian chief, *Lạc Tướng* as the military chief, and *Bố Chính* (subaltern officials) to support the king, *Lạc Vương*.[29] The king's son and daughter were called *Quan lang* and *Mị nương*.[30,31] Vietnamese historians also suggest that there were three classes in a Hùng king society: the aristocrats (*Lạc Hầu, Lạc Tướng, Phụ Đạo* [tutor of the prince]), the people (*Lạc dân*) and the servants (*Nô tì*).[32]

I am not convinced by such interpretations, and would suggest that the *Lạc Vương, Lạc Hầu* and *Lạc Tướng* terms were used by the original author of the passage to describe the chief of different regions of different sizes. This is clearly indicated by the last sentence of the above passage regarding the position of *Lạc Tướng*. Similarly, under the Han, *Hầu* or marquis, is the chief of a marquisate; a prefecture-size administration unit under a commandery and *Vương* or king is the head of a kingdom equivalent to but separate from a commandery (see 11.11.4). *Quan lang* is a term to refer to local administrators among the ethnic people, like the Mường. *Mị (Mỵ) nương* is a Tai term for princess.[33] I have not found any references to *Nô tì* (servants) in any ancient text.

Finally, having a bronze seal and a green ribbon is a Qin and Han idea as a symbol of investiture and unlikely to be an indigenous practice.[34] I have not seen any reference to a bronze seal among the Đông Sơn artefacts; further, a seal would be used only on papers or scrolls when one uses written language and there is no evidence the *Lạc* people developed one.

Be that the case, the passage clearly refers to the existence of an organised society which practised wet rice culture in the region of north Vietnam before the Han arrived in 111 BCE.

WET-RICE CULTIVATION

The method of wet-rice cultivation in the Red River Delta was practised before the Han arrived in the 2nd century BCE and recorded in the above passage in TKCS. It was likely to be the same as that described below in the 20th century:

Talking about wet-rice-cultivation, Mr. Hien, a farmer in Hai Duong province in the Red River Delta, explained in 2008:[35]

"To start a crop, we have to prepare the land. We empty the water from each field. Then we plough deep and rake it carefully with the help of the buffalo . We put down fertiliser, either natural or chemical, water is constantly needed too.

Normally we select the best species from previous crops, using techniques passed down through generations. In order to germinate it we put the paddy in a jute sack and soak it in water for 24 hours. We then take it out of the water and arrange it in a dark, damp place to facilitate germination. After 12 hours we repeat the process. In cool winter weather, straw ash is mixed with the paddy in order to keep it warm. When the roots reach two to three centimetres you can sow rice in a small prepared area.

During this period the young rice plants need water, but not too much. After one month you pick the young shoots and transplant the rice seedling to another field. Working the fields requires diligence, During the three-and-a-half months of rice development you have to constantly watch your field. You need to pull out any weeds growing with the rice. There has to be water in time for each period of development of the rice.

When the rice is mature the whole family has to work. We cut the rice with sickles and bring it home by ox cart. Fortunately, machines are now used for separating the paddy and straw."

4.4.2 – The land the Hùng kings ruled

LNCQ tells us the Hùng kings ruled over a kingdom called Văn Lang, a large country with the northern border at Dongting lake, the western border near Ba Shu (Sichuan, see Fig. 13), the southern border to Hồ Tôn (Champa, south of Ngang pass), and the eastern border to Nam Hải (East China).[36,37]

Vietnamese historians under the Nguyễn dynasty doubted the extent of the kingdom, noting that both Dongting lake and Ba Shu region are a long way north of Vietnam.[38] These historians went so far as to suggest that the old history text on this subject was a little overblown.

Modern Vietnamese historians tend to agree, and set the northern border of Văn Lang kingdom only to the southern region of Guangxi and Guangdong provinces and the southern border to Ngang pass.[39] They also adhere to LNCQ's description of Văn Lang as the land of the Bai-yue, and not only that of the Hùng kings.[40]

Vietnamese works such as VSL, SKTT, cited the names of 15 counties under the kingdom of Văn Lang and there are different sets of names as shown in Appendix 5. Since VSL was written prior to the others, I will use the names as they appear in VSL. In VSL, there were 15 prefectures, two of which were in the south of contemporary Guangxi, China; Văn Lang then covered southern Guangxi, northern Vietnam to Ngang pass and, according to historian Đào Duy Anh, it would equal the kingdom of Âu Lạc.[41]

As a place, the name of Văn Lang was not mentioned in LNCQ and SKTT among the 15 regions. However, the name first appeared in TKCS which referred to a Văn Lang man and a Văn Lang Cứu stream.[42,43] However, these references are likely irrelevant given the location cited (*Chu Ngô*) as assigned to it, is near Quảng Trị province, south of Ngang Pass, which is too far south from Gia Ninh where the Hùng king first appeared.[44] Furthermore, the Văn Lang man, according to TKCS, lived in the wilderness and ate raw meat, which does not fit the profile of a people with the technology to make the bronze drums, and who lived in houses built on stilts. The reference to Văn Lang in the Old Book of Tang is closer to the position Vietnamese historians have agreed upon:

> "Gia Ninh was the administrative centre of Phong Châu, land of Mê (Mi) Linh district during the Former Han dynasty, belong to Giao Chỉ, which was the land of ancient Văn Lang."[45]

Văn Lang river was also mentioned in relation to Gia Ninh.⁴⁶ Today, there is a Văn Lang commune at Hạ Hòa district, Phú Thọ province. It is on the left bank of the Red river, some 50 kilometres north-west of the Hùng king temple.

According to historian Trần Quốc Vượng, Mê Linh as a district under the Former Han dynasty was much larger than Mê Linh, which is located about 30 kilometres north-west of Hanoi on the northern bank of the Red river.⁴⁷ It would basically cover the region where the three main rivers, Đà from the south, Lô from the north, and Hồng (or Red) rivers from the northeast meet. The region is a plain between Ba Vì and Tam Đảo mountains of some 80 kilometres between them. Hùng temple is located in Việt Trì in this region, also where archaeological sites of the Phùng Nguyên and Gò Mun periods were excavated. It could be that Văn Lang only covered this region (see Fig 8.)

For now, in the absence of concrete evidence, I take the conventional view of Vietnamese historians and map it as shown in Fig. 10 in a solid line. However, based on archaeological evidence, it could be argued Văn Lang would include only the region around Mê Linh, Cổ Loa and possibly the Thanh Hóa regions.

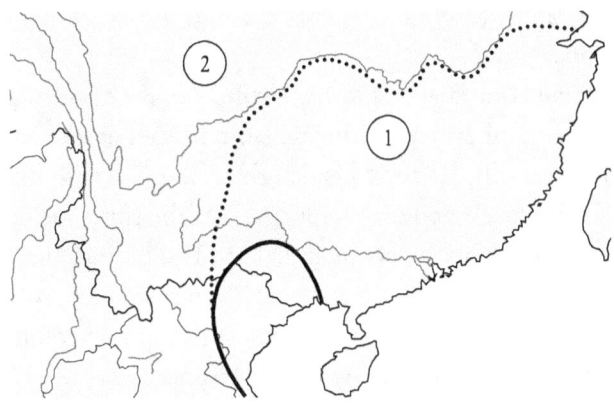

Figure 10 – Kingdom of Văn Lang within the solid line (7th century BCE).⁴⁸ Âu Lạc kingdom (2nd - 3rd century BCE) occupied a similar terrain.⁴⁹

Notes: 1. Dongting lake, 2. Ba Shu (contemporary Sichuan). The kingdom border is marked as the solid line according to Đào, the dotted line is the interpretation of the northern and eastern borders as based on SKTT. I have not included the mountainous region in the west of north Vietnam in this figure as these regions were not mentioned in VSL.

4.4.3 – Dragons and fairies

LNCQ told a number of stories, among which is the story of the first Hùng king. The term *Lĩnh Nam* in the book title literally means 'south of Nanling mountains'.[50] It is from this story that I, together with millions of Vietnamese over the years, learned about Lạc Long Quân and Âu Cơ, the parents of the first Hùng king who are worshipped as the ancestors of all Vietnamese.

LNCQ told us that the first Hùng king's great grandfather, Đế Minh, travelled in the southern region to Nanling mountains and married the daughter of Vụ Tiên.[51] Đế Minh was the third generation from Shen Nung (*Viêm Đế Thần Nông*), a Chinese mythical deity in the 28th century BCE (or 2695 BCE). Đế Minh's first son, Đế Nghi continued his father's reign and ruled the north (there is a place associated with Shen Nung called Shen-nongjia, in Huben province, about 500 kilometres north-west of Dongting lake).[52] Đế Minh's second son ruled the south of Nanling mountains as Kinh Dương Vương (or Lộc Tục); his kingdom was called Xích Quỷ (Kingdom of the Red Devils) and he had a special talent for travelling in the Water Underworld. LNCQ did not explain the meaning of this term but one might imagine that Water Underworld is a world underwater in a lake or a river. He married the daughter of Long Vương at Dongting lake; they had a son named Lạc Long Quân (King Dragon of the land of Lạc) who too travelled in the Water Underworld.[53]

Lạc Long Quân continued his father's rule, and in the north, Đế Lai, Lạc Long Quân's cousin, inherited the throne from his father, Đế Nghi, and decided to tour the south. He took his daughter, Âu Cơ, with him but left her behind while he continued on his journey. At the time, the people in the south were harassed by the north and asked Lạc Long Quân, who was in the Water Underworld to return to help. Upon his return, he met Âu Cơ and was so captivated by her beauty that he magically turned himself into a handsome young man surrounded by many servants living in a magnificent castle. Âu Cơ was pleased to follow him. When Đế Lai returned, he ordered a search for Âu Cơ but Lạc Long Quân used his magic and turned into many shapes and forms such as devils, dragons, snakes, tigers and elephants. Đế Lai's people were afraid, unable to find him. Đế Lai returned to the north, Lạc Long Quân then married Âu Cơ. She gave birth to a sac of eggs, but thinking this abnormal, threw the sac into a field.

After seven days, the sac broke and presented 100 eggs; each produced a handsome boy, Âu Cơ brought them up; they needed no mother's milk but grew by themselves. They were handsome, strong, intelligent and universally respected as extraordinary children. Lạc Long Quân spent much time in the Water Underworld, but Âu Cơ and the children wanted to return to the north. The Yellow Emperor, who defeated Đế Lai, ordered his troops to the border so Âu Cơ and her children could not pass, and were forced to return to the south. [54] Âu Cơ called out to Lạc Long Quân,

"Father, where are you, leaving me and my children lonely, sad and miserable for days and nights?" [55],[56]

Lạc Long Quân appeared and they met at Đất Tương.[57] Âu Cơ said to him:

"I am a northerner by origin. I lived with you, the king, gave birth to one hundred sons but you left me and children, not bringing them up with me, became a person without a wife and children, only loved yourself".

Lạc Long Quân replied:

"I am of the dragon race, Head of the Water Underworld, you are of the fairies, live on earth. While negative and positive energy has fused to give birth to children, water and fire do not mix, different races make it difficult to live together and we have to separate. I will take fifty sons to the Water Underworld and you take fifty sons to the land, divide the land to rule. Up the mountains, down to the ocean, let each other know when needs arise, don't forget." [58]

LNCQ went on to convey that these 100 sons are the ancestors of the *Bai-yue* (Hundred Việt or Bách Việt) and that all Vietnamese down the generations are their descendants. All the characters within this story are summarised in 4.4.4.

4.4.4 – *The family tree of the first family of the Vietnamese*

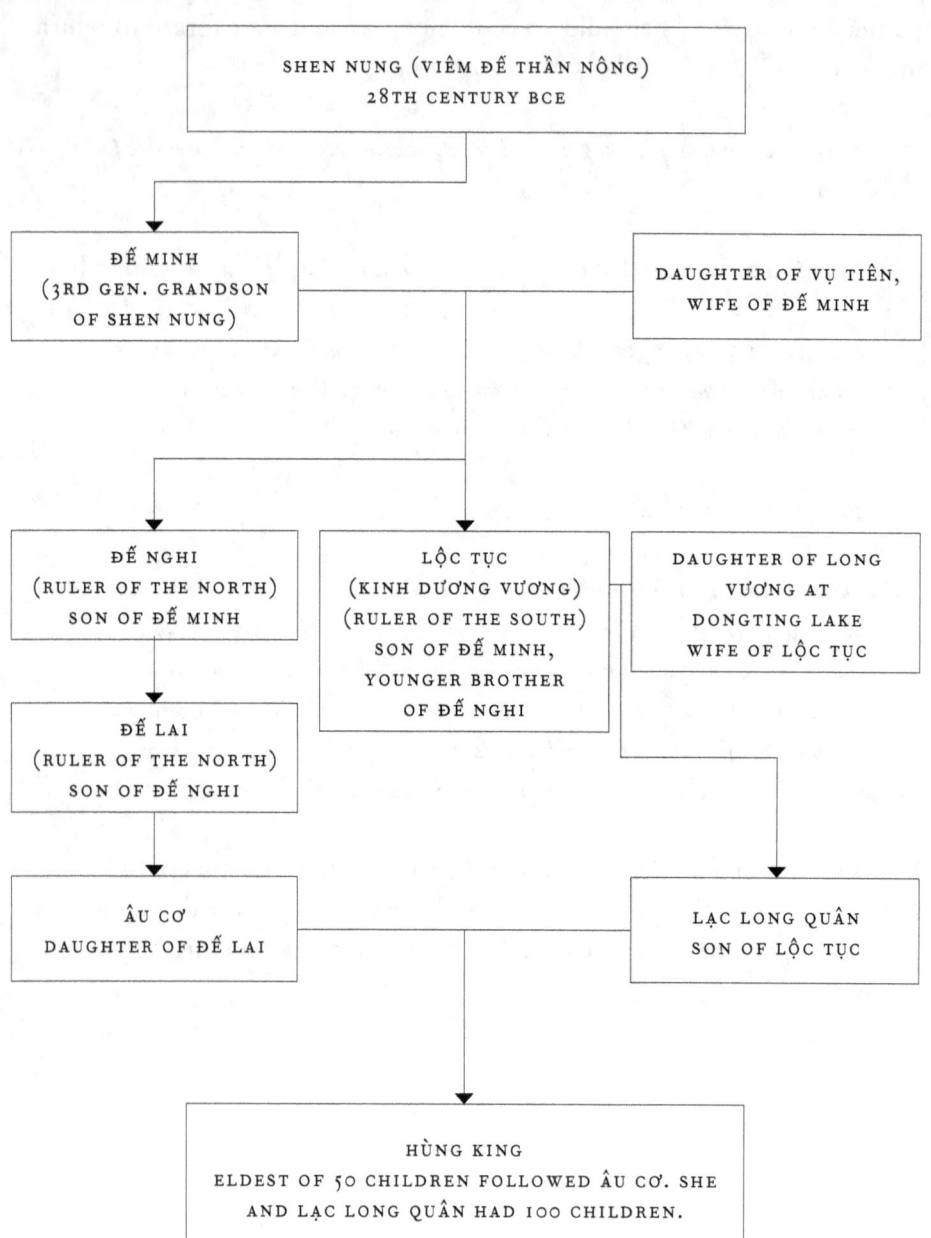

4.4.5 – Việt and Yue

So, what is the origin of the word *Việt* ? According to historian Erica Brindley, the author of a detailed book on the Yue, the term *Việt* is a Chinese phonetic pronunciation of the modern Mandarin Yue.[59] This term is the same applied to the name of Vietnam (or *Yue nan*), the reverse of the historical Nam Việt (Nan-yue or Southern Yue).[60] However, as shown below, Việt and Yue peoples are not the same. Việt refers to those who are Vietnamese whereas Yue people is a collective and historical term referring to people who lived, generally, south of the Yangtze river.

Most Vietnamese historical texts refer to the Yue as Việt which is correct linguistically, but not from the perspective of location, as the Yue in Nan-yue or Min-yue were not the same as the Việt in the Red River Delta. For example, SKTT mentioned that a Vietnamese administrator (or official) captured Lu Jia in the battle of Panyu (see 11.11.3) but according to a Chinese work, "The Records of the Grand Historian", abbreviated as Shiji, a Yue palace attendant caught him. This Yue person was more likely a Nan-yue person from Panyu than someone who came from the Red River Delta. Other Vietnamese historians did make the distinction, and used the terms "Phi Hoa" (non-Chinese) and "Hoa Nam" (Southern China) to refer to those who came from south of the Nanling mountains.[61]

The translator of Shiji explains:

> "The term Yue 越 was probably an attempt to reproduce the name the people called themselves, but it also reflects one of the basic meanings of the term: "To cross over, beyond,.. since these peoples lived beyond the pale of Han Chinese influence." " Yue may also refer to the area in which these people lived." [62]

Historian William Southworth suggests *Yue* is a pejorative term for "outer barbarians."[63] In Brindley's book, this term was used by the Sinitic people to

> "Designate a wide array of coastal and southern indigenous peoples inhabiting areas south of the Yangtze river." [64]

It is first used to designate a Yue people in the Annals of Lü Buwei (*Lü shi chun qiu*), compiled around 239 BCE.[65,66]

However, at the time of the Yue, the people of Sichuan, Guizhou, and Yunnan provinces in the west and south-west China were called Ba, Shu, Yelang and Dian but not Yue (Fig. 13).[67] It could be that because they were on the western side of the Nanling mountain range. Interestingly, the area covered by the Hundred Yue as given in various sources seems to match the description by LNCQ (see 4.4.2).[68]

The state of Yue was first mentioned in Shiji.[69,70] According to Shiji, the second son of King Shao Khang of the Xia dynasty, the first dynasty in ancient China (2070-1600 BCE),[71] was to:

> "Tattoo his body, cut his hair, cut the grass to establish a hamlet"

at Mt. Kuaiji near the city of Shaoxing of Zhejiang province (see Figures. 5, 13), and found the state. Twenty generations later, Goujian, mentioned in VSL as Việt Cầu Tiến in relation to the first Hùng king, in the 5th century BCE, became the king of the Yue state.[72] North of Yue was the kingdom of Wu. The two countries fought each other over several years until 473 BCE, where Yue troops under King Goujian surrounded and defeated the king of Wu at Mt Gusu, a district of Suzhou on the eastern shore of Lake Taihu. Yue was conquered by the Chu in 333 BCE and ceased to exist. Shiji continues:

> "And as a result of this, the Yue (ruling class) dispersed. The sons of many clans vied for positions, some became kings and other rulers. They banked south of the Yangtze, along the coast and attended court in the state of Chu."[73]

The dispersal of the Yue southward appears to be the explanation for the terms "Bai-yue" used by subsequent historians.[74] The Yue states of interest to this story are Min-yue, Nan-yue and Luo-yue, plus Eastern Ou and Western Ou.[75] The term Eastern Yue

> "Refers alternately to those Yue people who traced their ancestry to the pre-Qin state of Yue and lived in the area now southern Zhejiang and northern Fujian, to the state of Min Yue, and to the region itself."[76]

While there are other Yue states, they add up to less than 15, so "A hundred Yue" seems a misnomer but for its contemptuous meaning.

In 1965, a sword was found in Hubei province in central China. Detailed studies have concluded that it belonged to King Goujian (496-465 BCE); the inscription on the scabbard reads "Sword of Goujian, King of Yue".[77]
The sword (see Fig. 11) is now housed in Hubei Provincial Museum, some 820 kilometres west of the city of Shaoxing in Zhejiang province where the king once ruled.

THE HÙNG KINGS AND THE YUE

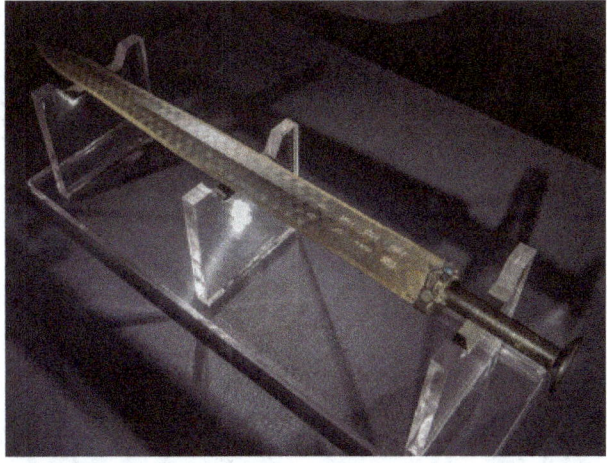

Figure 11– Sword of King Goujian at the Hubei Provincial Museum.[82]
The inscription is translated as 'Yue-king-Gou-Jian-self-made use sword'.

Figure 12 – Statue of a Yue man (bronze, 771-476 BCE [Spring and Autumn Periods])
from the State Museum of Zhejiang province, China.[83,84]
Note the tattoos and the short hair of the Yue man.

Figure 13 – Yue states showing the kingdom of King Goujian near Kuaiji and Ba Shu where An Dương Vương was believed to originate.[85]

Interestingly, LNCQ described the people who lived during the time of Lạc Long Quân as follows:

> "Used tree bark for clothing, kept hair short to make it easier to travel in the forest, tattooed body to be the same as the monsters of the Water Underworld, got salt from ginger roots, grew things by using fire, built houses out of timber to avoid tigers, wolves, cooked rice in bamboo sticks."[78]

Which seems to match those described in Shiji:

> "As for cutting the hair and tattooing the body, piercing the arms and buttoning lapels on the left, these (are the practices of the) Ou-yue people (of the South west)."[79,80]

The statue of a man (see Fig. 12) from Yue, in the State Museum of Zhejiang province in Hangzhou, matches the description in LNCQ; one can see the short hair and the tattooing quite clearly. These features seem to confirm the accuracy of Shiji's description of the Yue people of King Goujian and the strong possibility that LNCQ simply copied it.

However, the description of the people who made the bronze drums as obtained from archaeological artefacts paints a different picture: they wore their hair either short, in a bun or ponytail, the men had loincloths and the women wore long skirts.[81] They liked jewellery: bracelets, beads, rings. The bracelets were made from nephrite, amphibolite and bronze. Both men and women wore earrings; no gold or silver jewellery had been found (see Figures. 31 to 33).

It becomes clear that the Yue people of LNCQ, while translated into Vietnamese as *Việt*, are not the same as the ancient Vietnamese or the *Lạc* of the Đông Sơn bronze artefacts.

So, were the Hùng kings Yue people? The answer is yes in that they lived in the land of the *Bai-yue* as members of the Lạc Việt (Luo Yue) tribe. But the answer is no, if the question is related to the original Yue of King Goujian's Yue. Even if VSL mentioned King Goujian in relation to the Hùng kings, it is difficult to imagine that he would send an envoy 2,300 kilometres south to entice the Hùng king to give up his kingdom. The enemies of King Goujian were the Wu to the north and the Chu to the west, not a state 2,300 kilometres away in the 5th century BCE.

CHAPTER 5

THE FOUR IMMORTALS

God of the mountain - the first immortal

South of Hùng temple and east of the Đà river is Ba Vì national park, about 70 kilometres east of Hanoi; it is a nice place for a day trek where one can climb 1,320 steps up to Núi Vua (King Peak, 1296 m). The national park is also where one of the four immortals lived. Vietnamese know of the Four Immortals (*Tứ Bất Tử*); the Spirit of Mt. Tản Viên (*Tản Viên Sơn Thánh*) is the most famous. There are three temples dedicated to him and his brothers at the National Park. Đền Hạ (Lower temple or Đền Tản Viên Sơn Thánh) by the Đà river bank, Đền Trung (Middle temple) further up the mountain, are both on the western side of the park and can be visited at the same time. However, Đền Thượng (Upper temple) is at the top of the mountain and can only be reached from the eastern side of the park.

The story of Tản Viên Sơn Thánh (the Spirit of Mt. Tản Viên) is popularly known as the story of Sơn Tinh (the mountain spirit) and Thủy Tinh (the water spirit). A 14th-century Vietnamese work, Compilation of the Departed Spirits in the Realm of Việt (Việt Điện U Linh (VDUL)) first told us Sơn Tinh and Thủy Tinh were friends from Gia Ninh.¹ The Hùng king had a beautiful daughter named Mỵ Nương and the king of Shu (see Chapter 9) sent an envoy to offer marriage, which would have been around the third or fourth century BCE. His Lạc Hầu (Lạc marquis) advised against the proposition and suggested he should instead look for a talented person with magical power for his daughter. Sơn Tinh applied and demonstrated his powers to the king by walking through gemstones and rocks, Thủy Tinh also applied and showed he could walk through water and fire. The king was delighted and on advice from his Lạc Hầu told the two candidates to return with wedding gifts; whoever came first would marry his daughter. Sơn Tinh worked through the night and returned early the next morning with gold, silver, precious gems, horns of rhinoceros, elephants and rare birds. The king was pleased and married him to Mỵ Nương. Thủy Tinh arrived in the afternoon with precious pearls, corals, and rare fishes, but it was too late. He became enraged and chased after Sơn Tinh with his troops but Sơn Tinh and Mỵ Nương had already left for Tản Viên in the Ba Vì mountain range. Hence-forth, each autumn, Thủy Tinh returned to raise the water against Tản Viên mountain, but the local people used timber to build fences to protect the foot of the mountain and stop Thủy Tinh from reaching its peak.²

Autumn in the northern hemisphere begins in September and ends in November while in northern Vietnam the rainy season starts a little sooner, with the highest rainfalls in Hanoi during the months of July, August and September.³ So, autumn is the rain and flood season for those living near Tản Viên, when Thủy Tinh returns to seek his revenge. Over the years, this story has inspired many plays, songs, paintings, and in recent years, computer games and films.

Figure 14 – The forest along the steps to the Upper temple at Ba Vì mountain, where the first immortal resides.⁴

Genie on a horse - the second immortal

Downstream of the Red river, where it branches off to the Đuống river, just north of Hanoi, there is an ancient village called Phù Đổng and there one finds a temple for the second immortal. He is called by several names: Saint Gióng (*Thánh Gióng*), Heavenly King of Phù Đổng (*Phù Đổng Thiên Vương*), Sir Gióng (*Ông Gióng*) and, a less known name of Soaring-to-Heaven-King (*Xung Thiên Thần Vương*). Today, one can find many statues of him on a horse with an iron whip or a bamboo staff. [5]

His story is that of a boy born at midday on the seventh day of the first lunar month to a wealthy sixty-year-old man in Phù Đổng. Until he was three years old, he could not talk or stand but lay flat on his back. When the country was invaded by the Ân from the north, the Hùng king[6] sent out emissaries to the villages everywhere to look for a person with the talent to lead the fight on the advice of a three-metre-tall old man with a yellow face, big belly, white hair and beard who had appeared at court three years earlier (who turned out to be Lạc Long Quân). [7] The boy heard the news from his mother, and to her amazement, asked to see the emissary. When the emissary arrived, the boy sat up and said,

> "Please tell the king to make me an iron horse, 6m tall, an iron sword, 2.1m long, an iron whip and an iron helmet. I will mount the horse, wear the helmet and attack, the enemy will be massively defeated, the king will have nothing to worry about."[8]

He then asked his mother to bring rice and wine; the neighbours also brought betel nuts, wine, cakes and fruits; he consumed them all. On hearing the news of Ân forces arriving at Mt. Trâu Sơn at Vũ Ninh, he stretched his legs and stood over three metres tall, sneezed over ten times, shouted *"I am the heavenly general"*, put on his helmet and mounted his horse. They galloped, and within the bat of an eyelid, arrived at the front of the Hùng king's troops and charged the enemy. The king of Ân was killed, his soldiers fled or surrendered on this 9th day of the fourth lunar month, and the heavenly general who arrived at Sóc Sơn dismounted, disrobed, and flew to heaven. Ân is the name of the Shang, also known as Yin, a dynasty that ruled China from 1,600 to 1,046 BCE with the capital at Yinxu in Anyang of Henan province; the dynasty preceded the Zhou dynasty.

There are several versions of this story, as discussed in 5.5.1, but I prefer the story above for the sight of a giant on an iron horse with an iron whip, flying about beating up the invaders. There are three places of interest for travellers: one is Gióng temple at Phù Đổng village where he was born, the other is another Gióng temple at Sóc Sơn where he flew to heaven and the last location is Mt. Trâu Sơn where the battle was believed to have taken place. This is the same mountain that Zhao Tuo retreated to (see also 9.9.1).

Figure 15 – Gióng temple at Phù Đổng village[9]

A naked fisherman - the third immortal

Sailing down the Red river to the coast, rather than taking the left turn to the Đuống river, one continues for another thirty kilometres or so, where one will reach a low-lying region where two temples of Chử Đồng Tử (Young boy Chử), the third immortal is located. One is Đền Chử Đồng Tử, easily accessible from the river and the other is Đền Hoá Dạ Trạch, which is some three kilometres south, inland and adjacent to Triệu Việt Vương temple. Most tourists visit the first; the second is on the site of the marsh that Chử Đồng Tử and his wife created before they flew to heaven. This fairy tale with a happy ending is told in LNCQ as follows:[10]

The Hùng king of the third generation had a beautiful daughter by the name of Tiên Dung Mỹ Nương (Princess Tiên Dung, divine beauty).[11] At eighteen years of age, she did not wish to marry, preferring to travel and have fun. Meanwhile, in the village of Chử Xá, along the eastern bank of the Red river, a father-and-son peasant family fell into hard times when their house and belongings were destroyed in a fire, leaving one piece of loincloth for them both.[12] The father died and told his son to bury him naked but his son could not bring himself to do so, so he buried the loincloth with his father and remained naked. Standing in the water by the riverbank, he, Chử Đồng Tử, would fish and beg for food from the boat travellers.

One day, Tiên Dung's royal barge appeared with gongs, bells, music, and many servants. Chử Đồng Tử panicked and hid in a sandy bank, covering himself with sand. A little later, Tiên Dung's barge anchored at the same beach. She told her servants to assemble a curtain around the reeds, remove her clothes, and clean herself. Unfortunately, the water cleared away the sand and revealed Chử Đồng Tử. Tiên Dung was frightened but collected herself and said, *"I do not want to get married but now I found you, both of us naked in the same spot, it must be the work of heaven."* She wanted to marry him but he refused; she persisted, explaining it was arranged by heaven, so eventually, he relented. On hearing the news, her father, the king, was not pleased, thinking she had abandoned him, so Tiên Dung decided not to return. Together with Chử Đồng Tử, they established the Thám market (contemporary Văn Giang market, Hưng Yên) and prospered doing business with many foreign merchants who treated them as lords.[13]

On the advice of a merchant, Tiên Dung told her husband to take gold with him to meet with a merchant in order to buy goods overseas. While visiting a shrine at Mt. Quỳnh Vân, Chử Đồng Tử met a boy monk, Ngưỡng Quang[14], who passed onto him some magic, and he decided to stay and study until his fellow traders returned. The monk gave him a staff and a conical palm hat and told him: *"The supernatural in these things."* Chử Đồng Tử returned to his village and began teaching Buddhism, Tiên Dung was enlightened, sold their house, business, and together they travelled to seek out teachers of the religion.

On one occasion the darkness was falling, and there were no houses nearby. Chử Đồng Tử planted the staff and used the hat for shelter. After midnight, they found themselves in a castle, which appeared out of nowhere, surrounded by servants, soldiers, officials and all the riches as a separate kingdom.[15] Hùng king heard this news and thought his daughter had rebelled, so he gathered his troops to attack, camped at Tự Nhiên. Tiên Dung did not want to fight her father. Overnight, a strong wind started, blowing the sand, trees and castle, together with her and her husband and servants to heaven. The land caved in and became a marsh called Nhất Dạ Trạch (one-night marsh). Here, a 6th-century Vietnamese king, Triệu Quang Phục, held out and successfully fought against the troops of the Liang dynasty (502-557), with help from Chử Đồng Tử, according to the story. Over the centuries, the marsh has drained as there is little to see, except a terrain of very flat ground.

The third Hùng king would have been in the sixth century BCE counting the first Hùng king in the seventh century BCE. However, in the story, Chử Đồng Tử became a Buddhist but Buddhism did not come to Vietnam until the second century CE, so the timing is a little confusing. There is presently a Quỳnh Vân pagoda located at Thạch Bàn commune, Thạch Hà district, Hà Tĩnh province. This pagoda is believed to be the beginning of Buddhism in central Vietnam. It is north of Ngang pass and is a long way south (about 360 kilometres) from Chử Đồng Tử village. Tự Nhiên, which means natural, is a commune in Thường Tín district, on the western bank of the Red river, and opposite Dạ Trạch on the other side of the river, the river bank at Tự Nhiên was when Chử Đồng Tử first met Tiên Dung.

Figure 16 – Statues of Princess Tây Sa, Chử Đồng Tử himself and Princess Tiên Dung at the Temple of Chử Đồng Tử. In the version at the temple, Chử Đồng Tử married a second wife, Princess Tây Sa, so at the temple, the statue of him is flanked by two wives as shown.[16]

A timeless princess - the fourth immortal

The fourth immortal is a woman; a fairy who came to earth from heaven three times. Princess Liễu Hạnh appeared much later in Vietnamese history but her presence is felt across the entire country, with many temples dedicated to her: the main temple is at Phủ Dầy, about one hundred kilometres south of Hanoi in Nam Định province, the other two are related to her subsequent appearances on earth, at Phủ Tây Hồ and Sòng Sơn.[17,18]

While there are many books and papers written on her, I will refer to a story by a female writer, Đoàn Thị Điểm (1705-1748)[19] from the early 18th century, called Vân Cát[20] Thần Nữ Truyện (Story of Vân Cát Goddess)[21,22] since virtually all existing accounts of Princess Liễu Hạnh are based on this version.[23]

To summarise, in around 1557 a man named Lê Thái Công in Vân Cát district dreamed that he witnessed a young lady drop a jade offering cup at the Heaven Palace (Thiên Cung) of the Jade Emperor (Ngọc Hoàng Thượng Đế), and she was expelled from heaven to earth *[first time]*.[24,25] After he woke, his wife delivered a daughter whom they named Giáng Tiên (Fairy Who Came Down). Sadly, she died at the age of 21 after three years of marriage. She ascended to heaven and persuaded the Jade Emperor to let her return *[second time]*, this time as Princess Liễu Hạnh, a title conferred upon her by the Emperor. On earth, she visited the capital where her husband, Đào Lang, and children lived, stayed one night and disappeared; later she disguised herself as an older woman or a beautiful young woman playing the flute under the moon. She wandered around the country after her parents and husband died and her children had grown.

She met a scholar by the name of Phùng Khắc Khoan (1528-1613), first, at Lạng Sơn, a northern border town with China when he was on his way to China and then at West Lake in Hanoi, and impressed him with her poetic abilities. From there, she appeared in Nghệ An, about 300 kilometres south of Hanoi where she met and married Sinh, a poor orphan student, whom she identified as an incarnation of her previous husband. One day, she told him she was a fairy and had to return to heaven. She missed her husband and again persuaded the Jade Emperor to let her return to earth. This time *[third time]* she was accompanied by two other fairies, Quế and Thị; they arrived at Phố Cát in Thanh Hóa province, just sixty kilometres southwest of her original home. By now, *"The princess was supernaturally powerful: good people received blessings, evil people were punished with disasters."*[26] During the Cảnh Trị (1661-1671) reign, her temple was reduced to ashes by the king, who believed she was an evil spirit. Soon after, the region was affectedb y an epidemic, which wiped out the flocks and herds. She appeared and told the people to ask the dynasty to rebuild her temple, then she would eliminate all calamities. Princess Liễu Hạnh is one of a number of mother goddesses the Vietnamese worship in Đạo Mẫu (Mother Goddess).[27]

Figure 17 – The annual Phù Dầy festival in remembrance and of gratitude to Princess Liễu Hạnh.[28] The sign reads: "Group 6 – Carriage for the First Mother", presumably in reference to her first appearance on earth.

5.5.1 – Gióng or Dóng ?

There are several versions of this story; the version in another Vietnamese work, Abridged Annals of An Nam (An Nam Chí Lược [ANCL]), written before LNCQ, in which someone with honour and moral standing from Phù Đổng village, with the support from the people, led the fight to defeat the rebels, then flew to heaven after the victory.[29] There was no mention of the Hùng king, Ân invaders, a three-year-old boy nor iron horse or whip. Similarly, there was no boy-grown-into-a-giant nor iron horse/whip in the version in SKTT.[30]

Historian Trần Trọng Kim doubted the Ân invaded, because their kingdom was too far north (over 2,000 kilometres) and there was no reason as to why they should invade the Hùng king, not to mention the timing difference if the first Hùng king appeared in the seventh century CE, about four hundred years after the end of the Ân dynasty. However, there are two other stories in LNCQ where the Ân invaders also feature.[31,32]

The version at the temple explained how Thánh Gióng's mother stepped on a giant footprint in her garden and became pregnant. The iron whip was broken during the battle and Thánh Gióng replaced it with a bamboo staff.

There is also a version in VDUL in which the boy ate a lot of rice and became a giant, and a story about a local earth spirit at Kiến Sơ pagoda –

behind Gióng temple in Phù Đổng. One study suggests "Gióng" should read "Dóng" and the shrine is for the god of storms.[33,34] The Dóng festival tradition of praying for and worshipping the rain has become a belief in heroes fighting against enemies. In Trần's words:

> *"Genie Dóng was a character of folk mythology constructed long before the fourteen and fifteenth centuries [stories collected by VDUL and LNCQ], a multidirectional character (a genie of trees, rocks, storms, thunder and lightning etc.) assembled gradually ... he acquired the comprehensively synthesized figure of a three-year-old boy suddenly grown up to become a giant."* [35]

Trần may well be right and the story may yet change again; but for now, the hero figure is embedded in Vietnamese culture among other stories of immortals.

CHAPTER 6

THE PREHISTORY TO THE HÙNG KINGS

THE ORIGIN OF
THE VIETNAMESE PART II

In this chapter, I will briefly outline the archaeological evidence and not discuss the other origin theories based on language and DNA research as these two subjects take us beyond the scope of this book.[1,2] Further, I believe there is a sufficient body of knowledge from historians and archaeologists to paint a convincing story of Vietnamese ancestry.

In the summer of 1926, a sixty-year-old French archaeologist, Madeleine Colani, initiated the excavation of several caves around Hòa Bình province, about eighty kilometres south west of Hanoi, in North Vietnam. By 1926, Colani (Strasbourg 1866-1943 Hanoi) had lived in Vietnam for nearly thirty years, having come to Hanoi in 1899 and joined the Geological Survey of Indochina (GSI) in 1914.[3] She explored more than 20 sites, notably Sào Đông, Xuân Khắm, Mường Khang (Khển) and Triêng Xeng. In these caves, she found many artefacts including flakes made from cobbles and adze-like tools. Her work was the beginning of many studies in what is now known as Hoabinhian culture. To date, around 150 Hoabinhian sites, predominantly caves and rock-shelters, have been identified in Southeast Asia with a chronological age ranging between 30,000 and 6000 BP and a geographical distribution that covers 4.5 million square kilometres from Burma to Vietnam and from southern China to Sumatra, (BP = before present, where present is AD 1950, to convert BCE to BP, simply add 1950).[4]

Colani died in Hanoi in 1943. Hà Văn Tấn grew up in Hà Tĩnh, 363 kilometres south of Hanoi and became Head of the Institute of Archaeology (established in 1968) and a renowned Vietnamese archaeologist and historian. Since the departure of the French in 1954, Professor Hà Văn Tấn and many of his colleagues, both Vietnamese and foreign, have undertaken many archaeological excavations across the entirety of Vietnam.[5,6] These excavations show that humans have lived in Vietnam and Southeast Asia for a long time; in fact, a homo erectus site, Thẩm Khuyên, was recently dated at 401,000 to 543,000 years ago.[7] Thẩm Khuyên cave is now a tourist attraction, 174 kilometres northeast of Hanoi, in Lạng Sơn province.

Archaeologists generally classify Hoabinhian culture as belonging to the New Stone Age (Neolithic) in contrast to the Old Stone Age (Paleolithic). They also describe the Bronze Age and the Iron Age following the Stone Age as humans evolved and learned how to make tools from metals.[8,9] Appendix 7 shows cultures other than Hoabinhian and their locations at different ages excavated by archaeologists in Vietnam.[10] For these stories, I am interested in the Bronze, and the beginning of the Iron Ages, as this period overlaps with the story of the first kings of Vietnam; the Hùng kings and the makers of the bronze drums and the earrings. Of particular interest is the Đông Sơn civilization.

To gain an understanding of how humans came to Vietnam, I refer to archaeologist Peter Bellwood:

> *"The first Homo sapiens population arrived in Vietnam from an ultimate African source around 70,000 to 50,000 years ago, as part of the population that spread as far eastwards as Australia and New Guinea. The modern Australomelanesian descendants of these pioneer sapiens populations still occupy Australia and New Guinea today, but East Asia underwent additional cultural and biological changes at the start of the Neolithic, around 2,500 to 2,000 BCE in the case of Vietnam."* Bellwood believed *"2,000 BCE was the point from which the existing modern populations of Vietnam were created in ancestral form... South Chinese Neolithic populations pressed southwards, settling alongside the indigenous hunter-gatherer population represented by the Hoabinhian, Bacsonian and Đa Bút complexes."*[11]

Archaeologist Nguyễn Lân Cường, in an excellent paper on human origin studies with its description of ancient skulls, craniums, and teeth found in

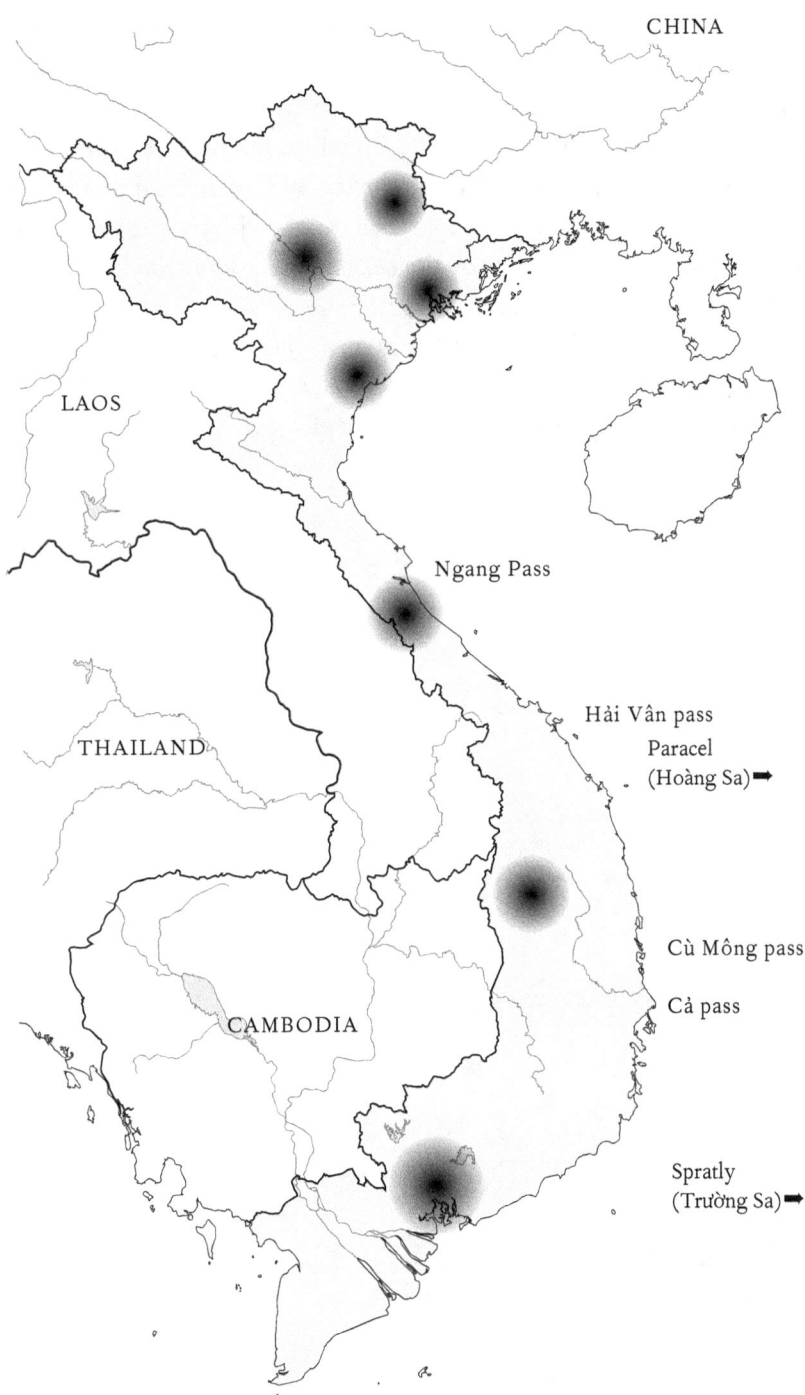

Figure 18 – Indicative clusters of the Stone Age sites (until ~1500 BCE, after archaeologist Andreas Reinecke).[13,14]

various archaeological sites in Vietnam, has a similar view. He suggests a movement of three groups of people during the Neolithic age. The first group moved from the caves in Bắc Sơn region to the coastal area of Hải Phòng, the second spread out from the west of Thanh Hóa to the sea and their remains were found at Đa Bút, the third fanned out from the west of Nghệ An (south of Thanh Hóa) to the sea and left behind their traces at Quỳnh Văn. These coastal people then mixed with people coming south from China, the Philippines by the sea and up from Malaysia and Indonesia.[12] They were the forebears of the Vietnamese.

The 2,000 BCE (or 3,950 BP) ties in with the beginning of the Bronze Age in Vietnam (see Appendix 7) when many artefacts from the sites excavated in this period were evidence of a well-developed society.

CHAPTER 7

FLYING EGRETS AND PLUMED WARRIORS

The indigenous people in northern Vietnam during the Bronze age made many beautiful bronze items; the most famous are the bronze drums. In 1924, a bronze drum was found by a French customs official, Louis Pajot, at the village of Đông Sơn on the eastern bank of the Mã river, near the Hàm Rồng bridge in Thanh Hóa province. Léonard Aurousseau, the Director of the École française d'Extrême Orient (EFEO) had asked Pajot to investigate the location and distribution of archaeological sites through interviews with villagers at Đông Sơn, having heard many antiquities, including bronze items, were found and sold to museums and private collectors. Subsequently, many such drums have been found in Guangxi, Yunnan provinces in southern China, northern Vietnam, Thailand, Malaysia and Indonesia – with many in Java.[1]

To date, 355 bronze drums have been discovered in Vietnam, and 415 in Southeast Asia,[2] among which some 140 were Đông Sơn drums[3] (a list of 114 bronze drums found in Vietnam can be found in a book by historian Nguyễn Duy Hinh).[4] The most famous of the Đông Sơn drums are Ngọc Lũ (discovered in 1893), Hoàng Hà (found in 1937), Cổ Loa (found 1982) and Sông Đà (about 1889).

The dating of Đông Sơn drums indicates they were likely to have been produced from the 5th to the 3rd centuries BCE, the Late Bronze Age overlapping with the Iron Age. The origin of the bronze drums has been fiercely debated between Chinese and Vietnamese scholars (see 7.7.1). While the debate will continue, the Vietnamese, understandably, are very proud of the Đông Sơn civilization and in recent years have used the Đông Sơn drums and associated design images, particularly the birds in full flight, as symbols to represent the country.

The name of Đông Sơn village became the name of a bronze age culture as more bronze artefacts were found (and continue to be found) throughout Vietnam and nearby countries. This culture thrived from 700 BCE to 200 CE, following three other bronze age civilizations with sites found in the region where the Hùng temple is located (see Fig. 8) in Phú Thọ and Vĩnh Phúc provinces on the bank of the Red river.[5] There are about four hundred sites, mainly concentrated in the three river deltas of the Red, Mã, and Cả rivers that flow through the cities of Hanoi, Thanh Hóa and Vinh respectively. Based on the location and age of the finds, Vietnamese historians identify the people who made the Đông Sơn artefacts as those who lived under the Hùng kings. They appeared in ancient Chinese text as the Lạc people, as part of the Bai-yue tribes (see 4.4.1).[6]

Archaeological finds from these sites include weapons (spears, arrowheads, harpoons, halberds, tridents, daggers, breastplates, swords, cleavers), agricultural implements (axes, hoes, shovel hoes, ploughshares, shovels, sickles), daily use items (jars, vases, baskets, kettles, dippers and spoons, incense burners, lamps), jewellery, decorations (bracelets, wrist and ankle rings, hairpins, belt-buckles, statues), bells and the famous bronze drums and *thạp* (jars).[7]

Today, one can see many of these artefacts at the National History Museum[8] in Hanoi, where one can see the Hoàng Hạ[9], Ngọc Lũ[10] and Cổ Loa drums[11] (Figures 20, 21, 22 respectively), the Museum of Vietnamese History[12] in Ho Chi Minh City and Thanh Hóa Provincial Museum[13], which houses the largest number of bronze drums (35 out of 129 catalogued)[14] and Cổ Loa citadel at Đông Anh district - Hanoi. Other provincial museums also display them.[15] Outside Vietnam, the Musée Guimet in Paris is where the Sông Đà drum (see Fig. 19) is displayed.[16] Musée Barbier-Muller in Geneva also has an excellent collection of Đông Sơn bronze items.[17]

Looking at the drums and other Đông Sơn artefacts, one cannot help but marvel at the great skills and artistic perfection of the people who made them at the time. However, while the people of Đông Sơn culture were capable of making these beautiful and exquisite bronze items, they did not leave behind any written language, despite attempts to interpret the symbols.[18] Luckily, they produced wonderful and vivid images on the drums, axes, halberds and jars; these images have given us a glimpse into what their society was like.

Society

The people at the time of the Hùng kings and Đông Sơn culture first appeared in ancient texts as the Lạc who practised rice cultivation based on the tides. Archaeological findings of many agricultural implements including hoes, ploughshares, shovels, sickles and axes supporting an active production of food. The images on the drums reveal that they were living in houses built on stilts. They had a governing system with a chief at the head of the tribe; the people knew how to grow rice, catch fish, hunt, build houses and boats, and weave clothes.

Lac society under the Hùng king must have been relatively prosperous. They produced daily use items: jars, vases, baskets, kettles, dippers and spoons, incense burners and lamps. People wore jewellery made from bronze, glass, and stone – bracelets, wrist and ankle rings, hairpins, belt buckles, statues. They made music, danced, and raced on long river boats. They took time to produce elaborative images of animals, people, and decorative patterns on such mundane items as axes and bells. There must have been demand or appreciation of such items among the ruling class for these items:

> "This civilization was organized into rice-growing villages of significant size, apparently linked according to a confederation of tribes. Such drums testify to a solid organization of commercial and political networks allowing their leaders to obtain the materials necessary for their development." [19]

Finally, they knew how to fight, judging by the abundance of weapons found among their artefacts.

Bronze drums

THE CHIEF OF THE MAN (BARBARIANS) TRIBE CRIED: *"The big drum is the most valuable, can exchange thousands of buffaloes, the next size can be exchanged for seven to eight hundred buffaloes. Whoever gets three drums can call himself a lord. Beating the bronze drum at the mountain village and the Man people will gather, now that the drums are gone, the fate of the Man people is sealed."* [20]

Given the amount of work required in making a bronze drum (see 7.7.2), it would not require too much guesswork to associate ownership with wealth, high social standing, and power.[21] Bronze drums were used for funeral rites, preparation for battles, praying for rain, storage of sacred items and burying the dead.[22] There is even a temple dedicated to the ancient bronze drum as a divine entity at Đồng Cổ.[23]

Figure 19 – Sông Đà bronze drum, middle of the first millennium BCE.[24]

The first thing that strikes an observer is the star shaped in the centre of the top of the drum, with 12, 14, or 16 rays; 12 being the most common. I do not have any explanation for the numbers other than the idea that it may have been easier for the makers to divide a circle into an even rather than an odd number of segments. Some researchers have suggested that it represents 12 months of the year. Around it, images of the boats, people, and birds are seen as moving from left to right in a counterclockwise direction. Colani suggests this rotation reflects the direction of movement of the sun during the day relative to the drum maker looking up from his village.[25] Others suggest the star shape represents either the northern Polar star or is in fact a design feature, however most agree with Colani that the star is a symbol for the sun.[26]

Figure 20 – Hoàng Hạ bronze drum.[27]

Figure 21 – Ngọc Lũ bronze drum, 2000-2500 BP.[28]

Figure 22 – Cổ Loa bronze drum, 2000 BP.[29] There is an inscription in Han characters on the Cổ Loa bronze drum: *"The 48th drum of the Tây Vu set, which weighs 218 jins"* (nearly 72 kg).[30,31]

Boats

The image that appears most frequently on the drums and jars is a boat. Some researchers have identified seven different uses for the boats from the images found on the drums and other bronze artefacts: fishing, transport, fighting, ceremonies, racing, recreation and seagoing.[32] Others suggested these boats were designed to take the dead into the afterlife,[33] as practised by the Dayaks of Borneo,[34] whom some researchers believe to be the descendants of the Đông Sơn people.[35,36] I would suggest that this interpretation is a little far-fetched, based on the sheer distance from Borneo to Phú Thọ.

Figure 23 – Boat on Ngọc Lũ drum.

Whatever the interpretation, boats must have played an important role in the life of Đông Sơn (or Lạc) people. These were most likely designed to be river boats: long, narrow boats are more suitable for river traffic. They can be made from tree trunks and handle better when the river flows fast. At sea, the waves render these boats difficult to manoeuvre, and they easily get capsized. The design shows that one end of the boat is elevated to accommodate the length of the rudder, and the other end is also high to help reduce the water drag on the boat. Such design is common to other Vietnamese river boats. In fact, the design of a boat during the Nguyen dynasty in the 19th century is strikingly similar to the Đông Sơn boat.[37]

The people who made these drums were likely to settle along the rivers and not by the sea, as some historians have indicated.[38,39] They extracted salt from ginger roots[40] not from the ocean, as one would expect, were they living closer to the coast. There is plenty of salt in the sea.

Most of these figures wear headgear which appears to be made from peacock feathers, and a matt-like shape, some believe to be made from reeds.[41,42] From left to right of Fig. 23: one holding the rudder, a dog, one standing on a platform, playing a gong, with a drum below; one playing what appears to be a drum made from water buffalo skin, and holding a child or a prisoner; one holding a spear. The scene shown on the boat appears to represent a celebration or ceremonial occasion.[43]

Figure 24 – Boat and people on the Hoàng Hạ drum.

Figure 25 – Boat on top of Hoành Hạ drum. From left to right: One boatman holding the rudder; one stands on a platform, apparently playing a gong, with a drum below; two wear skirt-like costumes. The scene shown on the boat appears to represent a celebration or ceremonial occasion.

Birds, houses and other animals

Besides the boats, there are many different images of birds; the most common is the long neck and beaked bird in full flight, likely to be little egret[44] with legs tucked behind. The others resemble spot-billed pelicans[45], black-faced spoonbills[46], Chinese pond herons[47], peacocks[48], parakeets[49], partridge[50], western swamphen[51], coucals[52], pheasants[53], and ducks common in the Red River Delta.[54]

Figure 26 – Rubbing of the top of the Hoàng Hạ drum showing birds in full flight. Note the long plumes behind the nape which resemble Little Egrets. Moving down from the top left corner, one can see a house on stilts with a curved roof and two people sitting, a male and a female figure pounding rice, another house on stilts with a dome roof and one person inside.[55] There are also images of animals, such as deer, water buffalo, humped cattle[56] crocodile, fish, tiger, leopard, fox and dog.

Figure 27 – Birds, crocodiles and warrior figures on Đào Thịnh bronze jar.[57]
Note the pair of crocodiles in the centre between two boats.

Figure 28 – Birds and deer on top of the Ngọc Lũ drum. Note the house with a round roof on the upper left, and one with the curved roof in the centre. Both are believed to be communal houses; the figure on the first house is playing a set of gongs, the two figures on the second house are playing a game. Between the two houses are a male and a female figure pounding rice, four figures are sitting on the right corner playing the drums below them through the floor. The bird in front of the deer is likely to be a parakeet; the little egrets are at the bottom.

People

The images on the boats show us only an outline of a person; to get a clear picture of what they would look like, one would need to look at the Đông Sơn daggers and swords. These lethal bronze weapons are beautiful, particularly at the handle with both male and female figures exquisitely made. The best example would be the sword found at Thanh Hóa, called Núi Nưa, and treated as one of Vietnam's national treasures (Figures 31, 32). Đông Sơn daggers and short swords are collector's items.

According to Dr Nguyễn Việt, Đông Sơn daggers and short swords appeared about the 5th or 4th century BCE.[58] He divided them into three types: one with a T-type handle, one with a garlic shape instead of the flat bar of the T, and one with a human or animal figure; the last kind was made at a later time, after the 2nd century BCE.

He also notes that the daggers with female figures tended to be found in Thanh Hóa, Nghệ An provinces, a region around the Mã and Cả rivers, whereas those with male figures were all found around the Red River Delta further north.

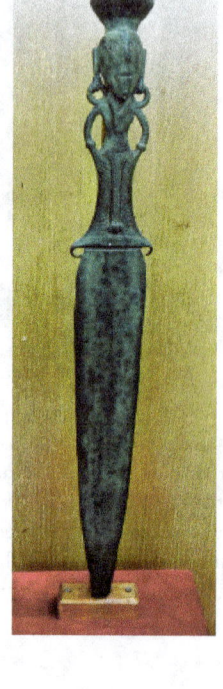

Figure 29 – A Đông Sơn dagger showing a bare-chested male figure wearing earrings, bracelets and breech-cloth but no tattoos.[59]

Figure 31 – A short sword (named Núi Nưa) showing a female figure.[61]

Figure 30 – Dagger showing a similar male figure similar to that of Fig. 29.[60]

Figure 32 – A close-up of the female figure on the Núi Nưa sword. This shows her wearing earrings, bracelets, a skirt (or sarong) and possibly a necklace. Her skirt could have been made from woven flax and hemp fibres, grown on the hills and still used by ethnic minorities in Vietnam.[62,63]

Figure 33 – Another female figure on the broken handle of a Đông Sơn sword; note her sarong.[64]

Figure 34 – Lạch Trường bronze lamp (circa 3rd BCE – 1st century CE).[65]

The following description is based on that of the National Museum of History in Hanoi: the lamp is crafted in the shape of a male figurine whose upper body is bare and wears a loincloth. He is kneeling, and his two hands hold a plate. The figurine has an oval face, his eyes are wide open, and he is shown with a faint smile. He wears a crown and his hair is tied in a topknot. Three S-shaped branches are attached to his shoulders and back, each holding a dish for the lamp oil, but the dishes are missing. On each branch, at about halfway, there is a kneeling figure in a praying position. There is also a figure holding each branch connecting it to the shoulder and back.

There are four figures at the base; musicians, with two playing flutes. The main figurine wears ornaments on his arms and wrists, and has earring holes in the earlobes. His shoulders and waist are decorated with bands of lotus petals.[66]

The lamp was found during the excavation of a brick Han grave at Lạch Trường harbour, Thanh Hóa province, by archaeologist Olov Janse in 1935. He found 20-nine Han graves which led some historians to believe that these belonged to those Han soldiers who accompanied Ma Yuan in his expedition against the Trưng sisters in 41-44.[67] While the graves were Han's, Olov Janse suggests that the lamp figure may be of Indian origin and not Han. On the other hand, researcher Phạm Quốc Quân, having studied a number of bronze lamps of a similar period, categorises it as a latter Đông Sơn piece.[68]

Figure 35 – Bronze leg ring.[69]

Music

The Lạc people played a variety of musical instruments including the drums, the gongs, bells and khèn.[70] The gongs and the khèn are still played by ethnic people in the Central Highlands and the North West.[71]

Figure 36 – Đông Sơn bronze bells. Missing is the dead weight suspended from the top of the bell to create sound by impacting against the wall of the bell when it is shaken from side to side.[72]

Figure 37 – Bronze ladle showing a man playing a khèn-like instrument (2500-2000 BP).[73]
Note his headgear and breechcloth, which would seem to match that of one of the dagger handles.

Weapons

Weapons are the most found items among the Đông Sơn artefacts, constituting over half the bronze items.[74] These people had battle axes, spears, arrowheads, harpoons, "ge" type halberds, tridents, daggers, swords and cleavers. They also produced bronze breastplates and locks for crossbows (for an explanation of these items, see 7.7.4) but apparently no personal shield or helmet.

It is interesting to note that there is no image of anything on the Đông Sơn artefacts that resembles tattooed bodies or short hair. There are also no dragons, snakes, or fairies as per the legend of the Hùng kings, but there are plenty of birds, deer, toads, and frogs. Even the geometric patterns on the drums bear little resemblance to the tattoos on the statue from the Bai-yue time (see Fig. 12).

7.7.1 – Our ancestors made the first bronze drum

The origin of the bronze drums has been fiercely debated between Chinese and Vietnamese scholars, both claiming the drums were first made by their own ancient people. The Chinese refer to them as Shizaishan drums, the Vietnamese as Đông Sơn drums.

Shizaishan drums are named after a hill by Dianchi lake in the city of Kunming in Yunnan province, southern China. If one takes the boat upstream of the Red river from Hanoi, one arrives at the border into China at Lào Cai; from there, continuing for another 267 kilometres, one will reach Yuanjiang. Approximately 200 kilometres north is the city of Kunming. Shizaishan bronze drums were found in 1960 in 20 tombs nearby and the site turned out to be the cemetery of the Kingdom of Dian (see Fig. 13). Dian people were not referred to as a Yue tribe in Chinese texts; prior to absorption into the Former Han empire, Dian societies were *"Highly stratified and militaristic"*.[75] They produced many bronze drums and weapons.

The scholars will continue to debate for some time yet but as for me, China and Vietnam are recent nationalistic concepts with no bearing on those people who made beautiful drums, which were distributed widely along the Yunnan and the Red River Delta to the rest of southern China and southeast Asia.[76,77] They made and traded them because they had the know-how and access to the copper mines in Kunming (China) and Lào Cai (Vietnam), (see 7.7.2). A few minority groups still play bronze drums, including the Mường of Vietnam, the Karen people of the mainland Southeast Asian mountains, and tribes on the Indonesian island of Flores (near Australia).[78] Most Karen bronze drums were used to entice the spirits of ancestors to bring rain, funerals, marriages and housewarming ceremonies. One can find a good summary of the debate in a paper by scholars Xiaorong Han, and Keiji Imamura's papers.[79,80]

7.7.2 – Copper mines and trees

Bronze is produced by melting copper with tin (normally in a 9:1 ratio) or some other metals. To make bronze, one would need to melt the copper at a temperature of 1083°C; to reach this temperature, one requires plenty of firewood and charcoal. Based on author John Perlin's estimate, nearly three hundred pine trees would be needed to produce the Cổ Loa bronze drum.[81] So, one would need to have access to trees.

One would also need access to a copper mine and a foundry to melt and mix the metals. In 1970, Vietnamese archaeologists found the remains of a bronze foundry complete with furnaces, and moulds for axes and spearheads which dated to 1500 to 2000 BCE at Thành Dền, in Tự Lập village, Mê Linh district, on the east side of the Red river, about 35 kilometres northwest of Hanoi. It has since been excavated many times. Thành Dền is considered by Vietnamese archaeologists as the largest bronze foundry in ancient Vietnam.[82]

It happens that the site is downstream from the largest copper deposit complex in Vietnam at Sin Quyền, Bát Xát District, Lào Cai. Copper can be easily transported from there down to Thành Dền on the river. Similarly, close to where the Shizaishan bronze drums were found (see 7.7.1), there is a large copper mine at Dayao, north west of Kunming.

Thành Dền is near Phong Châu, the reported capital of the Hùng king. It is also located in the valley between Tam Đảo National park on the north side and Ba Vì mountain range on the south. There are now many trees on these mountain ranges and one might imagine there must have been plenty over 2,000 years ago. Conversely, the decline of bronze manufacturing could be tied to the unsustainable use of trees for fuel.

The existence of a large coal mine in Sin Quyền may explain the rise of the Bronze Age in Vietnam around the area where the Hùng kings first emerged. Sin Quyền is now an open-cast copper mine. It is located upstream of the Red river, on the west side some 300 kilometres northwest of Hanoi and less than a kilometre from the Vietnam-China border.

Figure 38 – Little Egret, note the two long plumes on the nape.[87]

7.7.3 – *The egret went to feed at night. Perched on a soft branch, it fell down to the pond.*

Cò is a familiar bird in Vietnamese society; together with pigs, chickens, and water buffalo, *Cò* forms part of the rural scene.[83] Flocks of white *Cò* in flight over the rice fields is a common sight in many parts of Vietnam and has inspired many poems and songs.[84,85]

In Vietnam, *Cò* is a term used for the egrets, smaller herons and bitterns in the Ardeidae family, but the herons are known as *Diệc*. The Black-crowned Night Heron (*Nycticorax nycticorax*) is called *Vạc*. So which are the birds on the Đông Sơn drums and other artefacts?

Checked against the World Bird Database for the Red River Delta of Vietnam, I believe the little egret is the most likely when compared with the bird on the drums with its two plumes on the nape (see Fig. 26).[86]

7.7.4 – Weapons to kill from afar

Many bronze spearheads were found among the Đông Sơn artefacts; the spear poles, which would have been made of wood, have long since perished. Scholars have classified spearheads as longer than 15 cm; those between 7 cm and 15 cm are harpoon and javelin heads, those shorter than 7 cm are arrowheads.[88] Spears are thrusting weapons, whereas javelins and harpoons are throwing weapons; generally, a javelin once thrown is not expected to be retrieved but a harpoon is to be retrieved: it has a barbed shape which would remain in the body it penetrates. A few trident heads, or three-pronged spear heads, were also found; tridents are generally used for spearfishing rather than for fighting.

Interestingly, not many bronze swords were found, presumably because as an attacking weapon, a bronze sword is not as effective as a cleaver or battle axe and as a thrusting weapon, a spear or a dagger would be more lethal. Quite a few *ge* halberds, a two-handed pole weapon, were found; these were Chinese weapons which continued to be used until the Han dynasty. The *ge* weapon is used in a swinging motion like a long scythe; later, a spearhead is added to the blade which creates the thrusting motion. This weapon is known as a *Ji*- type or dagger-axe halberd; the *Ji* effectively replaced the *ge*- type. I have not seen any bronze *Ji*- type ⊦ head among the Đông Sơn artefacts.

Figure 39 - Đông Sơn weapons. Seen here are two breastplates, upper left and centre, and the Ge type halberd head (the head would have been attached to a wooden pole, where the exhibition stand is, which has long perished) at the upper right. On the display counter, the arrowheads are on the lower left and a harpoon head is on the lower far right of the front row.[89]

CHAPTER 8

THE LAST HÙNG KING AND THE 2000-YEAR-OLD FORTIFICATION

THE LAST HÙNG KING TOLD THE SON OF THE KING OF SHU: *"I have divine power, is Shu not afraid? Then the king neglected to repair his weaponry, only wanted to eat, drink and have fun. The Shu army drew near [to the palace], still drunk, half-conscious, coughing up blood, the king jumped into the well and died. His soldiers turned their spears and surrendered."*[1]

And this is how the reign of the Hùng kings ended. Around 257 BCE, having defeated the last Hùng king, the prince of Shu by the name of Thục Phán declared himself An Dương Vương, established his capital at Phong Khê, now identified as Cổ Loa, and named his kingdom Âu Lạc.[2] The origin of Thục Phán is a subject of debate among historians; some believe he came from the kingdom of Shu (Sichuan province in China), while others suggest he was a local king from the province of Cao Bằng, near the northern border between Vietnam and China. Having reviewed the arguments, I support the theory that he was a descendant of the Shu kings (see 8.8.2). If anything, the technology and knowledge needed to build Cổ Loa citadel are unlikely to have come from local indigenous people, and no one has found any earthen fortification of similar size anywhere in Vietnam. The citadel was built as a defensive fortress for war and the people who built it knew what they were up against. A war machine from the north was far more destructive than anything the local people had previously experienced.

As for the naming of the kingdom, I believe Âu Lạc is a combination of two kingdoms: Western Ou and Lạc, which extends all the way from south of Guangxi to Ngang pass (see 8.8.3).

Cổ Loa, located on the eastern side of the Red river, is about ninety-five kilometres downstream from Phong Châu, the capital of the Hùng kings, and is north of Hanoi, just eighteen kilometres by car across Nhật Tân bridge. It is the oldest capital in Vietnam, built more than a thousand years before Thăng Long, the ancient capital of Hanoi, and two thousand years before Huế, the imperial capital of the Nguyễn kings. Ancient texts mention its nine walls, but now only three remain and there is little evidence of the other six. The site stretched over roughly 600 hectares and within it, archaeologists found a bronze foundry, some ten thousand arrowheads, and various weapons and agricultural implements; many of these are displayed at the exhibition centre near the entrance to the citadel (See Fig. 40).[3]

Archaeologists believe Cổ Loa, particularly the outer and middle walls, was built between 300 and 100 BCE over two to three generations, on an existing fort dated to 500 BCE. The inner wall was likely built at a later date, the time of the Later Han (25-220 CE) with further addition and repairs of the citadel in the 15th century. It was occupied by the Han and became the capital once again in the 10th century, after which its role declined when Thăng Long (or Hanoi) was chosen as the new capital in the 11th century.

Today, one can visit the site, including the display centre to view some Đông Sơn artefacts, climb one of the walls, wander around the village, and make an offering to the Guard God at the Northern Gate Shrine (*Miếu Cửa Bắc*) by the north gate of the middle wall. More details of the citadel are provided in 8.8.1.

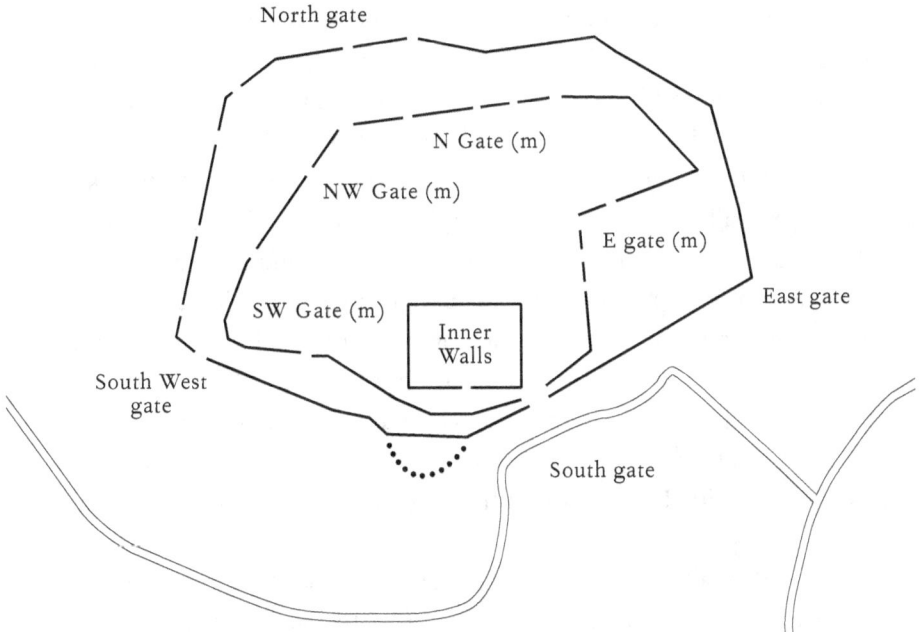

Figure 40 – Cổ Loa citadel showing the outer, middle and inner walls. Today, it is difficult to locate each of the walls but some sections of the two outer walls can be easily identified. N=North, S=South, E=East, W=West, m=middle.[4]

Figure 41 – One section of the middle wall of Cổ Loa citadel near the display centre; the top of the wall is heavily covered by trees and vegetation.[5]

8.8.1 – Cổ Loa citadel

Cổ Loa, located on the eastern side of the Red river, is north of Hanoi, just 18 kilometres by car across Nhật Tân bridge. Standing over two thousand years, the two outer walls (or ramparts) are between 3 to 10 m high and 12 to 25 m at the base;[6] the total length of all three walls combined is 16.15 kilometres,[7] with the inner wall estimated at 1.65 kilometres, the middle at 6.5, and the outer wall at 8,[8] about the same as the perimeter of Huế citadel.[9] Each wall has a ditch or moat on its outside with a width of about 12 m wide in some places and 4.8 m in depth. The site stretches over roughly 600 hectares.[10]

The outer wall has four gates; the northern and southwestern gates are more of a break in the wall where the road goes through. The southern gate of the outer wall shares the same access as that of the middle wall, the eastern gate is a river gate; there is little sign of it now as the area has been filled for use as a paddy field. The section of the outer wall on the northeast corner over the railway line is mostly flattened.

The middle wall has five gates, the eastern gate is also a river gate, and little sign of it remains. The width at the top of the wall is about 10 m on average, with a base of about 20 m. The tallest, Gò Ông Voi, is in the northeast, with a height of about 10 m.

The inner wall is rectangular; it has just only one entrance at the southern side, which is on the same route as the southern gates of the middle and outer walls. The height of the wall is around five metres.

Since 2007, Nam C. Kim, a United States-based archaeologist, in conjunction with the Vietnamese Institute of Archaeology, has undertaken three excavations at the outer, middle, and inner walls.[11] The location of the excavation at the middle wall is just east of the northern gate and that of the outer wall approximately north of it.[12] The inner wall was also excavated near the north west corner.[13] From the findings, Kim suggests the construction of the middle rampart occurred in five phases.[14]

- PHASE 1 (500-300 BCE) featured a clay wall and platform with a maximum height of about 1 m and a width of 1.8 m.

- PHASE 2 (300-100 BCE) involved dump earth with a maximum height of 2 m and a width of 17 m.

- PHASE 3 (300-100 BCE) used thick stamped earth with a maximum height of 2.5 m and a width of 24 m.

- PHASE 4 (300-100 BCE) used dumped earth with a maximum height of 3 m and a width of 24-25 m.

- PHASE 5 (POST-100BCE) involved thin stamped earth with a maximum height of 4 m and a width of 26 m.

Kim suggests:

> *"The bulk of the rampart was probably built continuously over a relatively quick time frame, within two to three generations at most. Phases 2-4 constitute the bulk of the original rampart, dating to between 300 BCE and 100 BCE."* [15]

He also estimates a volume of earthen materials for three ramparts to be about one million cubic metres;[16] it would take a workforce numbering a few thousand over two to three generations to build it.[17]

This time period coincides with both kingdoms of Âu Lạc and Nan-yue being cited in historical texts (see 8.8.2, 11.11.1), however Kim is reluctant to take a definite position linking these kingdoms to Cổ Loa settlement, citing insufficient evidence, and would thus rather use a "Cổ Loa Polity" as the entity that existed at the time of the citadel's construction.[18]

Archaeologist Trịnh Hoàng Hiệp, who worked with Kim on the excavations, had no such hesitation; his view is that An Dương Vương of Âu Lạc kingdom built Cổ Loa over an existing fort of an earlier local tribe,[19] and both agree that the bulk of the construction took place well before Han annexation in 111 BCE.[20,21] Trịnh also reports that the construction of the inner wall was entirely different from the outer and middle walls.[22] However, some of it may have been built at the same time as the middle and outer wall.[23] Others suggest the inner wall was mostly built during the Later Han era (25 BCE-220 CE) when both the middle and outer walls were also raised and repaired.[24]

The site Trịnh excavated in the inner wall included a bastion-like feature (*Ụ hỏa hồi*) where a mound of earth taller than the wall and extending beyond the wall at between ten to 50 metres was built; there are eighteen of these placed around the perimeter of the rectangular wall.[25] A bastion allows defenders to provide fire support to others on the wall, and other bastions during an attack on the fortification.

Between the outer and inner walls on the northern side there are two mounds; Đồng Chuông and Đồng Dân; it is not clear what they were used for. At the excavation site on the outer wall archaeologists also found platform mounds for watchtowers.[26]

Cổ Loa was occupied by the Han during the northern rule period. After independence in 938 CE, Ngô Quyền set his capital there for 10 years, but few artefacts of his reign have been found.[27] There were, however, a number of artefacts discovered from the 15th century Lê dynasty period.[28]

8.8.2 – The man from Shu

The paragraph that follows the citation of the Lạc on page 427 of Volume 36 of TKCS reads:

> "After that, the son of the king of Shu (Thục) brought 30,000 soldiers to fight the Lạc kings and Lạc hầu (Lạc marquises), conquered the Lạc tướng (Lạc generals). The son of the king of Shu then called himself An Dương Vương."[29]

There are two interesting points made within this paragraph. The name of Thục Phán is not mentioned, and the Lạc kings are referred to in the plural, not only one king, as is cited in later sources such as VSL, when the name Thục Phán appears. This fits the explanation that there were many chieftains at the time of An Dương Vương's conquest. The question of where An Dương Vương came from is still not settled by historians and to obtain an answer to this question, we must briefly review the situation in China at that time.

During the era of Hùng kings, ancient China was ruled by the Zhou dynasty (1046-256 BCE) over a territory mainly north of the Yangtze river with its capital at Luoyang, by the Yellow river and north of Nanyang (see Fig. 5), some 2,300 kilometres northeast of the capital of the Hùng kings at Phong Châu. The people who lived on the land south of Zhou territory were considered barbarians by the Zhou. The land was ruled by various kingdoms, which ancient Chinese historians called Bai-yue (A hundred Việt) (see 4.4.5). Towards the end of its reign, the Zhou dynasty was broken into a number of warring states. Until that time, Hùng kings reigned relatively unscathed but the turmoil of China was about to reach the land of the Lạc. One state, Qin, conquered the others and unified China under the First Emperor, Qin Shi Huang (259-210 BCE). He continued the construction of the Great Wall of China and also left behind the famous Terracota Army at Xi'an.

Among the states conquered by Qin in 316 BC were Ba and Shu in the Sichuan province (see Fig. 13). It was from Shu that the son of the king by the name of Thục Phán defeated the last Hùng king in 257 BCE or 59 years later, according to VSL.

Some Vietnamese historians have doubts about this story, since Cheng Du, the capital of Sichuan, is some 1,420 kilometres north of Phong Châu and it would therefore seem unlikely that Thục Phán would travel all this way with the remnants of his army to attack the Hùng king.[30] Additionally, 59 years after the fall of Ba and Shu to the Qin is too great a distance in time for one generation from father to son. SKTT offers a different story in which the grandson of Thục Vương took revenge over the last Hùng king because the king refused to marry his daughter to Thục Vương father. While the king wanted to, his aides advised against it: "*They want to occupy our land, the marriage is just an excuse.*"[31] A grandson makes more sense from the perspective of time but SKTT also repeats the VSL story that Thục Phán came from Shu.

Vietnamese historians have several theories for which to explain the origin of Thục Phán; one is that he came from Cao Bằng, thought to be the capital of Nam Cương kingdom.[32,33] Another is that he came from Ai Lao, an ancient kingdom located in Yunnan, west of Kunming and the upper reach of the Lancang river.[34,35] One can find a detailed analysis and discussion of the various theories by historian Kiều Thu Hoạch, who agrees with the Shu theory.[36] Kiều cites four reasons in support of his conclusion: one is that in the history of Sichuan the ancient citadel at Chengdu was built with the help of a turtle, similar to that of Cổ Loa's golden turtle story.[37] Two, is the use of crossbows: the Shu people were renowned in Chinese history as crossbow makers and sharpshooters. Three, is horse breeding: the Shu people bred small horses called Shu horses that suited narrow and difficult roads, and horse breeding in Vietnam began in the time of An Dương Vương. Four, is dressmaking: which the Shu brought to northern Vietnam.

I support the proposition that An Dương Vương was a descendant of the Shu kings for reasons explained previously. I note further that during the attack on the capital of Nan-yue in 111 BCE (see 11.11.3), the Han transported the convicts from Ba Shu as reinforcement by ship, therefore it was possible for the royal refugees from Shu to use this same route to access the area around Nanning, which was later identified as most likely to be Western Ou, and from there to the Red River Delta.

8.8.3 – The kingdom of Âu

Âu in Vietnamese is Ou in Chinese. In Zhejiang province there is a river called Oujiang (*jiang* means river) flowing by the city of Wenzhou to the East China Sea. This river is south of Shaoxing where the first Yue people settled (see 4.4.5). In ancient texts, this region is called Eastern Ou, named after the river Ou, as it is located east of the capitals of the Qin and Han dynasties in central China.[38]

Immediately south of Zhejiang is Fujian province where a river, named Minjiang, flows through the main city of Fuzhou. In Han and Qin times, Fujian was the kingdom of Min-yue, which was also named after the river.

South of Fujian is Guangdong, and the west is Guangxi; these two provinces make up the bulk of ancient Nan-yue. The present capital of Guangxi is Nanning, which is located on the Yong river, east of Nanning. Two rivers, Zuo and Youjiang, flow into the Yong river (see Fig. 48). If one follows Zuo upstream, one reaches Chongzuo, the seat of the Qin commandery Xiang (see 12.12.2). Continuing from there eastward on the river, one reaches Cao Bằng and Lạng Sơn in Vietnam, located at the border with China.

The kingdom of Western Ou first appeared in Huainanzi (See 10.10.1); while scholars have not explained whether there is any relationship between Eastern and Western Ou.[39] Most agree Western Ou (or Xi Ou) is located in Guangxi province, just northeast of the Vietnam-China border.[40,41] Referring to Figures. 5, 13 and 48, one sees relatively flat areas along the Zuo, Youjiang and Yong rivers extending to the foot of the Nanling mountains. I suggest this area is Western Ou, and most likely within the commandery of Xiang, given it is on the invasion route the Qin army marched in 221 BCE (see 12.12.1 and Fig. 13), and where they killed the Lord of Western Ou (see

10.10.1) early in the war.[42] Note Zuo river in Vietnamese is *Tả Giang* or West river.[43] Âu Lạc (or Ou Luo) territory was thus a combination of Western Ou (southern Guangxi) and Lạc Việt (northern Vietnam) as shown in Fig. 10.

A POSSIBLE CONNECTION TO THE ZHUANG PEOPLE (ZHUANGZU)

In 40, Trưng sisters, based in Mê Linh, revolted and people from Hepu commandery in southern Guangxi together with those from Giao Chỉ, Cửu Chân and Nhật Nam joined her.[44] In 178, the people of the same commandery also rebelled and mobilized thousands from the other commanderies to participate in the rebellion.[45] The rebels of Hepu were not Han and could well be the ancestors of today's Zhuangzu; the largest ethnic group who live in Guangxi Zhuang Autonomous Region of Southern China. During the Former Han, they were known as Wuhu (Ô Hử), which became Li under the Later Han, Lao or Liao during the Three Kingdoms and Lang under the Jin dynasty. Their close relatives on the Vietnamese border are the Tày, the Nùng who live around Lạng Sơn, Cao Bằng and Hà Giang provinces.[46]

Given their record of rebellion against the northern dynasties, the Zuangzu could well be the Yue people of Western Ou who put up such a fierce resistance against the Qin centuries earlier. It should be noted that Zhao Tuo referred to Western Ou as a kingdom located on the west of Panyu (see 11.11.2), which is east and south of Guangxi province.

CHAPTER 9

THE MAGIC CROSSBOW AND THE TRAGIC END OF THE MAN FROM SHU

An Dương Vương's reign lasted fifty years, until 180-179 BCE.[1] His demise is another legend most Vietnamese know: the golden turtle story. I learned it in my history lessons at school; it is frequently retold as part of the legend of the magic crossbow one finds at Cổ Loa. In this story, An Dương Vương has the help of a golden turtle in building his citadel at Cổ Loa. The turtle also gives the king his claw to make a lock, or a triggering device, for the crossbow.[2] This became the magic crossbow, and with it An Dương Vương was able to defeat the invading Qin army led by Zhao Tuo.

The magic crossbow was such an effective weapon that Zhao Tuo plotted to steal it. He proposed a marriage between his son Trọng Thủy to the king's daughter, My Nương (or My Châu).[3] Trọng Thủy then sweet-talked My Nương into letting him see the magic crossbow; he swapped the crossbow's turtle claw lock for an ordinary lock then lied to his wife that his filial piety required him to visit his father. My Nương cried, telling him she usually wore a goose feather jacket and would use the feathers as markers so he would know where to find her in the event they were separated on his return. Trọng Thủy took the magic crossbow's lock to his father. Zhao Tuo was pleased, and promptly attacked An Dương Vương. The king continued playing chess at the news of the attack believing his magic crossbow would repel the enemy, but the magic crossbow no longer had the turtle claw lock.

The king lost the battle and fled with his daughter on horseback. Heading south, they reached the coast but there was no boat. The king cried out for help, the golden turtle appeared and shouted:

> "*The person sitting behind you is your enemy*"

upon hearing this the king drew his sword and killed his daughter. Before she died, she said,

> "*By fate, I am a girl, if I had conspired to betray and harm my father, turn me into dust when I die. But if I am a loyal daughter but betrayed by others then turn me into pearls to cleanse the disgrace.*" [4]

She died by the sea, her blood was washed away by the waves and consumed by the oysters, turning her blood into pearls. The golden turtle parted the water and led the king who held a rhinoceros horn to the sea.[5] Trọng Thủy followed the goose feathers and found his wife's body; he took her back to Cổ Loa and buried her there where her body turned to alabaster. He was deeply mournful, seeing his wife whenever he bathed; eventually he jumped into a well and drowned. From that day on, legend has it that pearls washed by the water of this well will shine brightly.

The "pearl" well is still at Cổ Loa, there are also statues of An Dương Vương, the golden turtle, and Mỵ Nương at the ancient citadel. Mỵ Nương statue is a stone covered with a woman's dress but without her head (see Fig. 42), it was disconcerting and sad when I first saw it.

The crossbow is a powerful weapon and at the time of An Dương Vương in the 3rd century BCE, it was widely used by the soldiers of the Qin and Han dynasty in China. An ideal army's proportions were 10,000 infantry, 6,000 crossbowmen, 2,000 halberdiers with shields, and another 2,000 spearmen with shields.[6] Such weapons would form part of An Dương Vương's arsenal: bronze locks and thousands of arrows have been found at Cổ Loa (see Fig. 44). Recent efforts to reconstruct a magic crossbow using local materials have produced a crossbow that can shoot five arrows between eighty to one hundred metres at the same time (see Fig. 47).

Figure 42 – The headless statue of Mỵ Châu (or Mỵ Nương) at Cổ Loa Citadel.[7] A comparable story is told in VDUL with different characters set in the 6th century.[8] The similarity of the two stories may have given Ngô Sĩ Liên, a 15th-century Vietnamese historian and the compiler of SKTT, doubt on the magic crossbow and the goose feather legend.[9] But Trọng Thủy and Mỵ Nương's tragedy is one of the Vietnamese famous love stories and has inspired many plays, books, and songs.

Figure 43 – An Dương Vương killing his daughter, Mỵ Nương. Note the golden turtle. Trọng Thủy is the shaded figure on the black horse.[10]

Figure 44 – Bronze lock or trigger for the crossbow; note the gap for the arrow between the two small curved plates acting as the cock hook and the groove leading from there to position the body of the arrow.[11]

Figure 45 – Han crossbow trigger mechanism showing the two pins, the frame (top of photo), the trigger (lower left). The hook and the trigger rest are in the centre.[12,13]

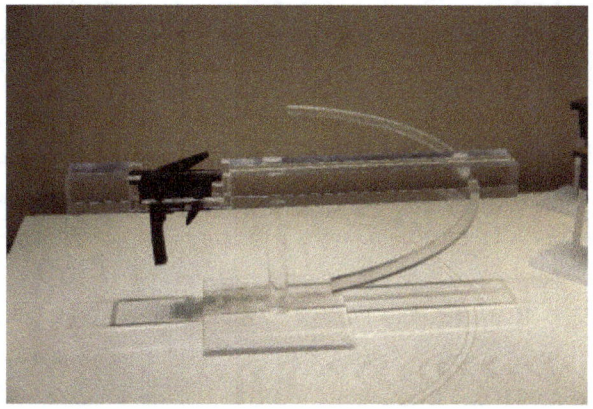

Figure 46 – Han crossbow trigger mechanism.[14]

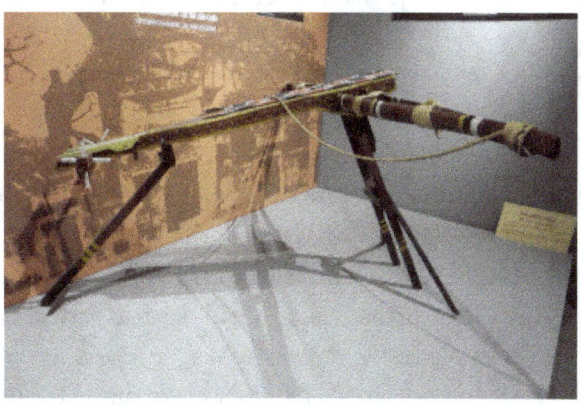

Figure 47 – A multi-arrow crossbow at Cổ Loa museum.[15] Note the bow string winding mechanism. During An Dương Vương's time, the bow string was likely to be pulled back by hand, and not by a winder as shown.

9.9.1 – The battle for Cổ Loa

The story above is told in LNCQ which may have copied it from TKCS, where it first appeared hundreds of years earlier on page 427 of Volume 36:

"The king of Nan-yue, Commandant-Governor Tuo, led an army to attack An Dương Vương..... An Dương Vương had a holy man by the name of Cao Thông [or Cao Lỗ in Vietnamese sources] helping him, and made him a magic crossbow, one shot can kill 300 men.[16] The king of Nan-yue knew he could not win and withdrew his army to the district of Vũ Ninh[17],[18]. .... He then sent his son, a prince, named Thủy to surrender and worship the king. An Dương Vương did not know Cao Thông was a holy man, did not treat him properly, Cao Thông left and told the king: "If you can keep this crossbow, you'll be the king of all under heaven, if not, you'll lose it all." Thông left, An Dương Vương had a daughter called Mị [spelling Mị in TKCS but My in LNCQ] Châu. Châu saw Thủy as decent and serious, they spent time together. Thủy asked Châu to see her father's magic crossbow. He stole it, used the saw to cut it off then ran off to tell his father. When the king of Nan-yue attacked, An Dương Vương used the magic crossbow but it broke. An Dương Vương escaped to the sea by ship. Now, behind the district of Bình Đạo there were old signs of the king's palace."[19,20]

There was no mention of the golden turtle, the killing of My Châu, nor the suicide of Thủy.

The battle for Cổ Loa was a decisive battle in Vietnamese history, and a major turning point as significant as the battle of the Bạch Đằng river in 938 where the Vietnamese regained their independence from the Southern Han dynasty or the battle of Điện Biên Phủ in 1954, when French colonial rule finally came to an end.

Unfortunately, there is not much information on this battle other than a short paragraph in TKCS and archaeological finds such as arrowheads and locks. In fact, some writers even suggest that it never happened and An Dương Vương did not exist, but this view is not shared by other historians.[21] In an attempt to understand of how Cổ Loa fell, I turned to geography and an 18th-century Vietnamese history work, A Brief History of Việt (*Việt Sử Tiêu Án* [VSTA]).[22]

The position of the Red River Delta relative to its northern neighbour, China, is such that invasion usually took one or two of three different routes: from the north west via the Red river crossing Lào Cai (the Sui in the 7th century, the Mongols in the 13th century), from the north-east via Lạng Sơn (the Ming in the 15th century) or from the east via the Bạch Đằng river at the coastal of Hải Phòng (the Later Han in the first century, the Southern Han in the 10th century). The first and third allow easy transportation of troops by ship and the second is the shortest and easiest route for troops to travel from the staging area near the northern border to the Vietnamese capital (see Fig. 48).

From the limited information cited in historical texts, the enemy An Dương Vương faced would most likely come from the second route via Lạng Sơn. This is because by 180 BCE, after the First Emperor of China died, Qin armies had reached as far south as Chongzuo, the seat of a Qin commandery (an administrative unit (or a district) under a military commander) 90 kilometres northwest of Lạng sơn. An Dương Vương's nemesis, Commandant-Governor Zhao Tuo, had already been stationed in Panyu (see Fig. 56).

Qin armies had tower ships and used them in the southern invasion, travelling along rivers and man-made canals (see 10.10.1).[23] Therefore, it is reasonable to assume they would continue to use rivers as means of transport to head further south. Qin sailors could take their ships all the way from their commandery at Panyu to Lạng Sơn or Cao Bằng (see Fig. 48).[24]

The builder of Cổ Loa certainly expected enemy attacks from the northern direction, judging by the layout of the citadel (see 8.8.1). The two outer walls are further from the innermost wall in the northern direction than in the southern walls, which would have given the king and his entourage additional time to escape via the southern gates to the Hoàng Giang river. This river is connected to the Đuống river and from there to the Red river flowing to the Gulf of Tonkin.

Similarly, the citadel can be supplied from the south via the same rivers, as the Hoàng Giang river forms almost a semi-circle around the citadel, and so provides additional protection from attacks from the eastern and southern directions.[25] An Dương Vương chose the location of his capital well, in fact, (see Fig. 49), one can see the logic of Cổ Loa defence against a northern invader, who would have to cross the Cầu river at some 20 kilometres northwest of Cổ Loa, the king's first line of defence. It is about 60 kilometres long, anchored on the left flank by the mountain range of the Tam Đảo mountain and on the right flank by Yên Tử national forest. Any invaders to Cổ Loa from the north via Lạng Sơn would be forced to cross the Cầu river between these two mountain ranges; the alternative is to go over or around mountains, quite an undertaking.

The king's troops stationed on these mountains could easily see the enemy coming. Down the years, the Cầu river was the scene of a number of famous battles between the Vietnamese and the northern invaders. The Viet-namese under Lý Thường Kiệt defeated the Song troops along Như Nguyệt

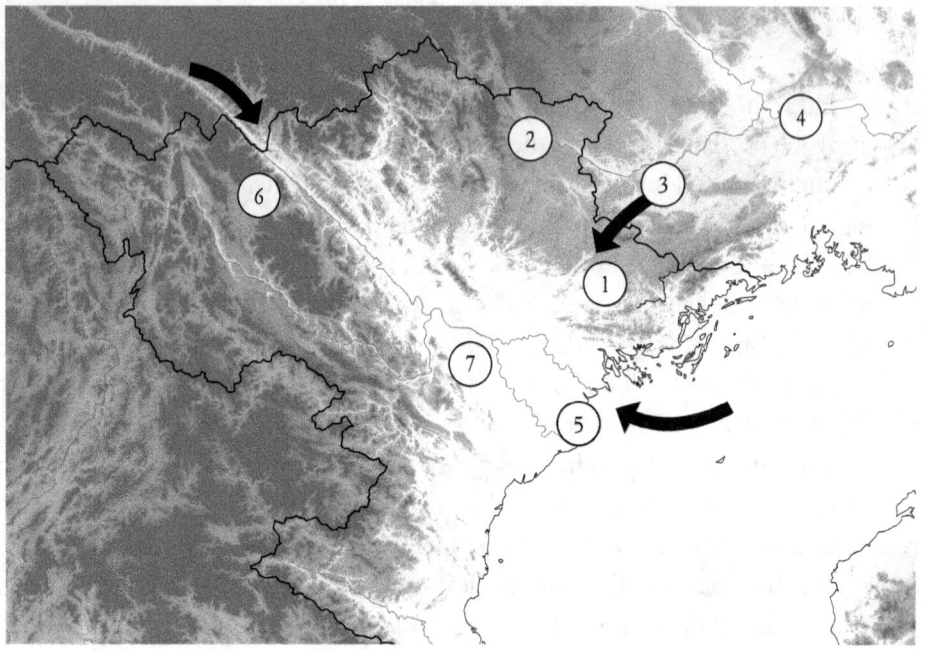

Figure 48 – Main invasion routes

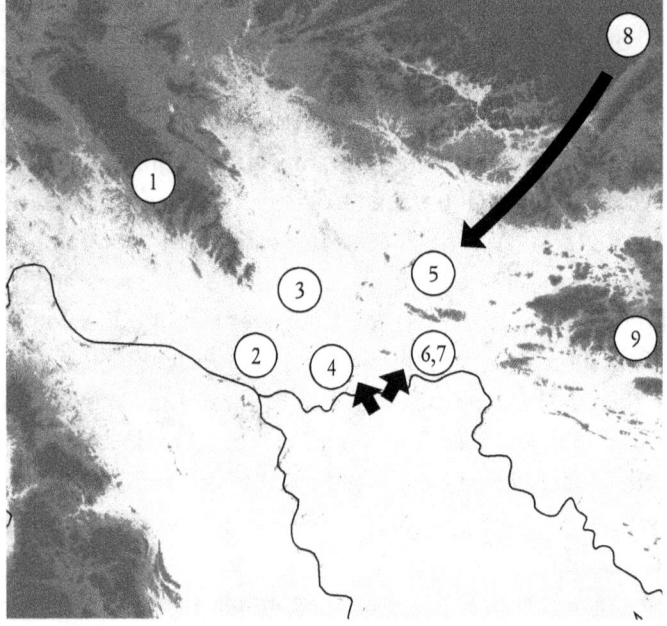

Figure 49 – Battleground

in 1077 near Cà Lỗ,[26] the Cầu river intersection by Tam Đảo mountain range. In 1285, the Vietnamese defeated the Mongols at Vạn Kiếp, near Chí Linh, by the foot of the Mt Yên Tử range.[27]

Taking Cổ Loa would not have been a walkover for Zhao Tuo. Armed with crossbows and other weapons behind tall and strong walls, An Dương Vương would have put up a strong resistance. If the legend is to be believed, it was a cunning betrayal by Zhao Tuo of a seemingly over-confident king that led to the downfall of the citadel.

According to VSTA, two Qin commanders, Ren Xiao and Zhao Tuo, led their army to Âu Lạc and camped at Bắc Giang with Ren Xiao's ship anchored at the Tiểu Giang river.[28,29] If the Terracotta Warriors guarding Qin Sin Huang's tomb found outside Xi'an, China are anything to go by, An Dương Vương was facing a battle-hardened and formidable army. Zhao Tuo's troops were likely to wear body armour and carry swords.[30] They would have had crossbows, bows, spears, *"ge"* halberds and, in all likelihood, would have been supported by tower ships.

Apparently An Dương Vương was not deterred; he attacked at Mt. Tiên Du (where Phật Tích pagoda is).[31] Using his magic crossbow, the king defeated Zhao Tuo who retreated to Mt Võ Ninh (Mt Trâu Sơn at Ngọc Xá, Bắc Ninh). Zhao Tuo sued for peace. Both sides agreed that the land of Bình Giang would belong to Zhao Tuo and the king would continue to rule the land south of it.[32] VSTA tells us Ren Xiao became sick and returned to Nan-hai, the war reached a stalemate until Zhao Tuo's son seduced An Dương Vương's daughter and stole the magic crossbow to defeat An Dương Vương, entering Cổ Loa sometime in 180-179 BCE. Âu Lạc was no more, absorbed into Nan-yue.

Left top: Figure 48 – Main invasion routes to the Red River Delta by adversaries from the North, through Lạng Sơn (1), Lào Cai (6) or Hải Phòng (5).

Lạng Sơn is by the Kỳ Cùng river on the Vietnam side. On China's side, it becomes the Ping'er river. Cao the Bằng is by the Bằng river; it retains the same name, or the Shuikou river, on China's side. Both flow into the Lijiang river, which becomes the Zuo river flowing by Chongzuo (3) before it joins the Youjiang river just east of Nanning (4).

Key: 1. Lạng Sơn, 2. Cao Bằng, 3. Chongzuo, 4. Nanning, 5. Hải Phòng, 6. Lào Cai, 7. Hanoi

Lef bottom: Figure 49 – Battleground between Zhao Tuo and An Dương Vương in 3rd century BCE.

The map shows Như Nguyệt ferry on the Cầu river (border between Hanoi and Bắc Giang provinces) between the two mountain ranges, Tam Đảo on the left, Yên Tử on the right, protecting the entrance to Cổ Loa at the lower left of the map. Zhao Tuo's troops' movements are shown by arrows.

Key: 1. Tam Đảo district, 2. Cổ Loa, 3. Như Nguyệt ferry, 4. Lạn Kha mountain, 5. Bắc Giang, 6. Ngọc Xá (Mt. Châu Sơn), 7. Mt Non Vua, 8. Lạng Sơn, 9. Yên Tử National Forest.

An Dương Vương killed his daughter at Diễn Châu, a district in Nghệ An province.[33] There is now a beautiful temple dedicated to the king and his daughter called Đền Cuông, about 20 kilometres south of Diễn Châu and seven kilometres inland from Cửa Hiền beach, where the king and his daughter were believed to have met their tragic end. Cửa Hiền beach is some 300 kilometres south of Cổ Loa, so the king and his daughter must have fled for weeks to travel that far; the distance indicates that the land the king travelled through must have been friendly territory, presumably part of his domain. In SKTT, the first year of An Dương Vương's reign was 257 BCE. His reign came to an end in the 50th year in 208 BCE.[34]

CHAPTER 10

A TIME OF WAR

"*The Yue people fled deep into the mountain and bushy forest; it was not possible to fight them. We kept the troops in the garrison to keep watch over abandoned territories. It lasted for many days. The troops became weary. Then the Yue came out and attacked them. The Qin soldiers suffered a great defeat. Subsequently, condemned men were sent to protect the garrison against the people of Yue.*"

From a passage in the "Book of Former Han" *(Han shu)*[1,2] translated from a French translation by Aurousseau.[3]

By 221 BCE, the state of Qin under Qin Shi Huang had conquered the remaining states north of the Yangtze river (see Fig. 13). He now turned his attention to the south and decided to send the bulk of his army, 500,000 strong, into Bai-yue land. The poor kingdoms of the Bai-yue were soon to experience the massive upheavals and terrible sufferings that Qin soldiers were to set upon them. It was one of Qin's generals, Zhao Tuo, who was at the head of one of the invading armies that put an end to Âu Lạc and the tragic death of its king, An Dương Vương.

Figure 50 – Qin Shi Huang's imperial tour across his empire as depicted in an 18th-century album.[4]

A record of this event was noted in Huainanzi by a Former Han Prince, Liu An (179-122 BCE), some eighty years later. According to Liu An:

> *Qin Shi Huang was interested in the horns of rhinoceros, the tusks of elephants, the plumes of the kingfishers and the pearls (round and irregular) of the land of the Yue; so he sent the military governor Tu Sui as the head of 500,000 men divided into five armies to conquer these countries.* [5,6]

The army proceeded in five columns: one to the east, one to the south east and three in the middle in the southern direction. The staging areas were approximately in Hunan and Jiangxi provinces and possibly included Anhui province, effectively north and east of the Nanling and Wuyi mountains respectively.

The eastern invasion was, by all accounts, smooth, and the Qin armies managed to subdue Min-yue and Nan-yue in a relatively short time, but the southern attack into Western Ou ran into difficulties. North of the Yangtze river, where the Qin defeated other states in previous years, was relatively flat but the south was mountainous and the Yue put up fierce resistance.

However, Qin armies were eventually able to conquer the Yue territory and established three commanderies at Kwelin (around Guilin), Nan-hai

(Guangdong) and Xiang (around Guangxi). According to Aurousseau, the Director of the École française d'Extrême Orient (EFEO), the campaign lasted at least seven years, from 221 to 214 BCE (see Fig. 51).

Aside from the sufferings, two aspects of the campaigns are striking: the practice of sending settlers considered to be "*socially undesirables*" and the transport of single women from the home population to the occupied territories, a practice not limited to ancient China but to continue across the world until colonial times in the 19th century. More details of the invasion are provided in 10.10.1.

10.10.1 – The invasion of the "Hundred Việt" or "Bai-yue"

The invasion of Yue was described by Shiji as:

> "*In year 33 (214 BCE), Qin Shi Huang sent the inveterate vagabonds, men who lived with their wife's family and merchants to attack the land of Lou-leang or Luliang and establish three commanderies: Guilin (or Kwelin), Xiang, and Nan-hai and deported the condemned men there to hold the garrison and in year 34, sent the corrupt prison wardens to build the Great Wall and to exile in Nan-yue.*"[7,8]

There is a prefecture in Yunnan called Luliang, but this is too far to the west of the invasion route. Aurousseau translates this as the 'land of the southern barbarians' which makes sense. Guilin is a city in Hunan, Nan-hai is in Guangdong province. Shiji also mentions the man leading the invasion:

> "*Then, [the Emperor] sent Commandant [Zhao] Tuo to cross the Wu-ling (Five Mountain] ranges and attack the hundred [tribes of] Yue. Commandant [Zhao] Tuo knew that the central states toiled under extreme hardship, so he stopped there, made himself king, and did not come back; he sent a man to submit a memorial requesting thirty thousand unmarried women in order to mend the clothes of the officers and men. The August Emperor of the Qin allowed him fifteen thousand.*"[9]

Until then, the southern states in modern Vietnam and China were spared from the bloody warfare up north. But now Qin Shi Huang, having defeated the other northern states, wanted more, and would not allow the Nanling mountains to stop him from fulfilling his imperial ambition.
Historians agree that 221 BCE was the year Qin Shi Huang finally brought the kingdoms of Han, Wei, Zhao, Yan, Qi, and Chu under his rule as one dynasty,

Qin. Shiji explains that in 221 BCE, (or Qin year 26), his dynasty extended north to the Yellow river, west to Sichuan province, east to Korea and the east China sea and south to the *"Region where the houses with doors facing north."*[10,11] In the northern hemisphere, during the summer solstice, the sun is directly overhead and a gnomon (or stick) planted at the Tropic of Cancer latitude ($23°26'12.0"$ or $23.43666°$) north of the Equator would cast no shadow at midday. If one moves it north of this latitude, the shadow falls to the north, but south of this latitude, the shadow falls to the south. Thus, to get the sun on this day, the doors of the houses, located south of the Tropic of Cancer, would need to face north.

The Nanling mountain range is just north of the Tropic of Cancer (Guilin is at $25.2345°$ N) and Hong Kong (at $22.3193°$ N). This may explain why the southern border of the Qin empire in 221 BCE was the Nanling mountain range. Aurousseau also reached the same conclusion.[12] This makes sense, because by 223 BCE, the state of Chu had already fallen to Qin, which would thus extend the Qin southern boundary to the south of Changsha in Hunan province. By then, Eastern Ou or Zhejiang and most of Jiangxi provinces, were already in the Qin empire.[13] The climate south of the Tropic of Cancer was and is, tropical, which explains the various references in Shiji to the southern region as hot and wet. From the passage in Huainanzi and the work by Aurousseau, I have mapped the campaign as follows: [14]

1. The first army occupied the mountain pass near Mt Yuechengling.

2. The second army guarded the border pass south of Lingling, north of Mt. Mengzhuling.

3. The third army was stationed at Panyu in Guangzhou of Guangdong province.

4. The fourth army covered the border of Nan-yue near Mt Dayuling.[15] These locations are all in the Nanling mountain range.

5. The fifth army was concentrated by the Xinjiang river flowing into Poyang lake near Yugan county.

These locations are based on the above text in Huainnazi and are interpreted by a number of historians.[16,17,18] In this book, I use Aurousseau's version. The positions of the first and second armies would be consistent with the canal the Qin troops dug.

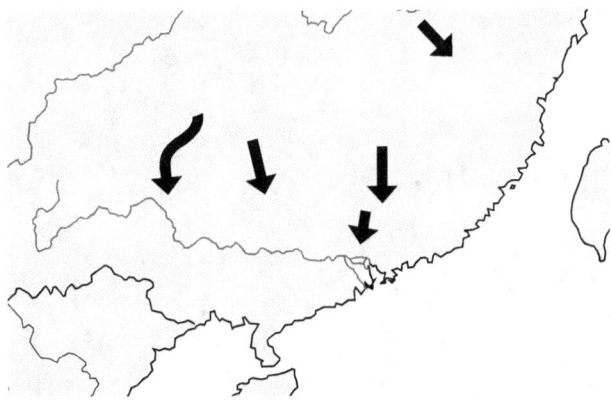

Figure 51 – Key locations in the conquest of Bai-yue; the invasion took place via five separate routes.

By all accounts, the eastern invasion of Nan-yue and Min-yue states went smoothly and the third, fourth and fifth armies reached their designation with the fifth army occupying Min-yue (Fujian) by 221 BCE.[19] However, the southern invasion by the first and second armies ran into fierce resistance and the situation was grim, as described by Huainanzi:

> "For three years, we were not able to stop wearing the cuirass (body armour) and stretching the crossbow. Superintendent Lou was sent. There were no means to assure the transport of rations so he made the troops dig a canal for the grain to be sent this way."

The canal the Qin troops dug is Lingqu canal, about 36 kilometres long and connecting the Xiangjiang (at Xing'an) and the Liudong (Lijiang) river (at Rongjiangzhen).

With the canal complete, the Qin armies continued south but the war did not go as expected, Huainanzi continued:

> "We could then fight the Yue people. We killed I Hsu Sung [Yi Song], the Lord of the Western Ou. So, the people of Yue went deep into the bush and lived with the animals. None consented to become a slave to the Qin; The Yue chose among themselves the men of valour whom they made their chiefs. Then they attacked the Qin at night; they inflicted a great defeat and killed Military Governor Tu Sui. The dead and wounded were many. After this, the Emperor sent the deportees to hold the garrison to protect against the Yue people." [20]

Figure 52 – Qin Terracotta Army at Xi'an, Shaanxi, China.²⁶

Shiji told the story of the Bai-yue invasion as follows:²¹

"He ordered Commandant Tu Sui to attack the Bai-yue people in the south in tower ships.²² He also sent Inspector Lu to dig the canal to transport the grain. The [Yue] people fled, the army wasted many days and food ran out, the [Yue] people attacked and Qin soldiers were defeated. Qin then sent Commandant Zhao Tuo. At the time, Qin suffered misfortune in the north by the Hu and was tied down by the Yue in the south. After ten years of [fighting], men still wore their armour and women transported provisions. Then the Qin Emperor died and the world rebelled."

However, Qin armies prevailed and were able to conquer the Yue territory. Shiji reports:

"The prestige [of Qui Shi Huang] made the four seas tremble. In the south, he occupied the territories of the Bai-yue, of which he made the commanderies of Kwelin and Xiang; the princes of the Bai-yue, their heads bowed with ropes around the neck, delivered their destiny to junior officers." ²³

Other than Kwelin (around Guilin) and Xiang, the Qin found another commandery, Nan-hai (Guangdong). After a detailed analysis, Aurousseau concludes that the campaign lasted at least seven years from 221 to 214 BCE when these commanderies were established (see Fig. 57). I summarised his findings below: ²⁴

221 BCE	Five armies of the Qin dynasty assembled, roughly 100,000 each on the north of the Nanling and west of the Wuyi mountain ranges, which was at the time the border between the Bai-yue and the Qin dynasty. The army was led by Military Commander Tu S'ui.
221 BCE	The fifth army attacked Min-yue and made it a Qin command called Minzhong. Nan-yue was taken soon after, but the invasion of the first and second armies faced fierce resistance that delayed their advance for three years. Superintendent Lou was called to dig the canal at Lingqqu.
219 BCE	
218-214 BCE	With the completion of the canal, the campaign continued. The Lord of the Western Ou, I Hsu Sung, was killed but the Qin Military Governor, T'u Sui, of the invasion forces was also killed in 220 BCE.[25] Commandant Zhao Tuo was sent as the new leader together with the deportation of the undesirables to be attached to Qin soldiers, or to colonise the Yue.
214 BCE	The campaign was over, Bai-yue land south and west of the Nanling and Wuyi mountain ranges was divided into three Qin commanderies: Guilin, Xiang and Nanhai.

Four years later, in September of 210 BCE, the First Emperor of China, Qin Sin Huang, died at the relatively young age of 49. The Qin dynasty continued for another three years to 207 BCE, which historians consider the end of the Qin empire.

Figure 53 – Qin terracotta soldier at Xi'an, Shaanxi, China. Note the body armour protecting the shoulders and the chest. [27]

CHAPTER 11

THE END OF AUTONOMY

REN XIAO, GRAVELY ILL, SAID TO ZHAO TUO: *"I have heard that Chen Sheng and others have made rebellion, that Qin has done many immoral deeds and that the world is suffering ... the Middle Kingdom is in turmoil, uncertain when peace will return ... Panyu*[1] *is surrounded by dangerous mountains, blocked by Nan-hai which from east to west is several thousand li*[2]*; there is also support by people from the Middle Kingdom*[3]*, furthermore Panyu is the key centre of an entire region so it could be used to build a country. There is no one among the senior officials in the commandery I can tell; therefore, I invited you to inform you."* [4,5]

Ren Xiao died soon after this utterance and Zhao Tuo succeeded him as the new Commandant of Nan-hai, (Guangdong province in China, a commandery that the Qin established sometime in 209 BCE). He promptly annexed the other two commanderies to create Nan-yue and declared himself the king. His capital was around Panyu, some 150 kilometres northeast of Hong Kong.

The year prior, the Emperor had died and the country was in turmoil until a new dynasty, the Former Han, arrived on the scene. The Qin dynasty ended in 207 BCE but it was not until 202 BCE that the First Emperor of

Han consolidated his power. Meanwhile, Nan-yue continued to exist as an independent kingdom; according to Shiji's account, so too did Âu Lạc under An Dương Vương. The Former Han Emperor died and his wife became the first Empress (see 11.11.1). Apparently, she did not much like Zhao Tuo and issued a decree to stop the Han from exporting iron and steel implements, along with mares, female oxen, and goats to Nan-yue.[6] Zhao Tuo's reaction was to declare himself an emperor, attacking the neighbouring western kingdom, while bribing and intimidating his northern, Min-yue, and southern kingdoms of Western Ou and Luo (or *Lạc*). This event is recorded in ancient Chinese texts and marks the end of Âu Lạc's independence, which historians set at around 179 BCE. While Âu Lạc was absorbed into Nan-yue, Zhao Tuo left it to rule itself as two districts: Giao Chỉ (north Vietnam) and Cửu Chân (Thanh Hóa, Nghệ An, Hà Tĩnh) down to Ngang pass (see Fig. 58)

Zhao Tuo died in old age in 137 BCE and his grandson, Zhao Mo, became the next king and emperor of Nan-yue. Zhao Mo's grand tomb in Guangzhou was discovered in 1983 and now is a large museum with various artefacts, including a Đông Sơn bronze jar and bells.

The Han dynasty continued its imperial expansion and soon their fighting ships and soldiers arrived at Panyu. With an overwhelming force, Han troops burned Panyu, killed Zhao Tuo's descendants, and put an end to Nan-yue as an independent kingdom. North and Central Vietnam were absorbed into the Han empire as three commanderies: Giao Chỉ, Cửu Chân (under Zhao Tuo's time) and Nhật Nam (provinces of Quảng Bình, Quảng Trị, Thừa Thiên-Huế). According to some sources the empire may have also included three provinces south of Hải Vân pass to Cả pass (see Fig. 58); the end of Nan-yue also spelt the end of all of Bai-yue states.

The year was 111 BCE and it was a major turning point in Vietnamese history: from that time for over a thousand years, minus a few brief periods, the Lac people were no longer able to decide their future; decisions were thrust upon them by northern kings and emperors located far beyond the Red River Delta and Hải Vân pass.

Those symbols from Đông Sơn drums would soon disappear to be replaced by four Chinese-derived holy beasts: Dragon (*Long*), Quilin-Chinese unicorn (*Lân*), Turtle (*Quý*), and Phoenix (*Phụng*) and would not be rediscovered for 2,000 years, well into the 20th century. One thousand years is a long time in human history; Vietnam could very easily have been part of China now, like other Yue kingdoms and those of Ba, Shu, and Dian (see Fig. 13). So how did they manage to emerge from this protracted period and restore their independence? That is another story, and I will recount it in a later book.

11.11.1 – The rise of Nan-yue

The conversation between Ren Xiao and Zhao Tuo took place sometime after 209 BCE, five years after the invasion of Bai-yue states ended and a year after the death of Qin Shi Huang in 210 BCE. Ren Xiao was the Commandant of Nan-hai, the new commandery established by the Qin after the war, which covered much of Guangdong province in China. Zhao Tuo was the Commandant General of the Qin army who led the expedition force after the death of the original commander, Tu Sui. At the time of this conversation, Zhao Tuo was the Magistrate of Long Yuan in Nan-hai (the original town is now called Tuocheng in Long Yuan County, Heyuan district, Guangdong province).

Zhao Tuo came from Zhengding near Shijiazhuang, the capital of Hubei province in China, some 1,900 kilometres north of where he ended up as a Magistrate. Before he died, Ren Xiao forged an imperial edict and appointed Zhao Tuo as the new Commandant of Nan-hai. Immediately following Ren Xiao's death, Zhao Tuo ordered the closure of the three border passes: Heng-pu, Yang-shan, and Huang-hsi. He eliminated other leaders appointed by the Qin and replaced them with his supporters (see Fig. 54).[7,8]

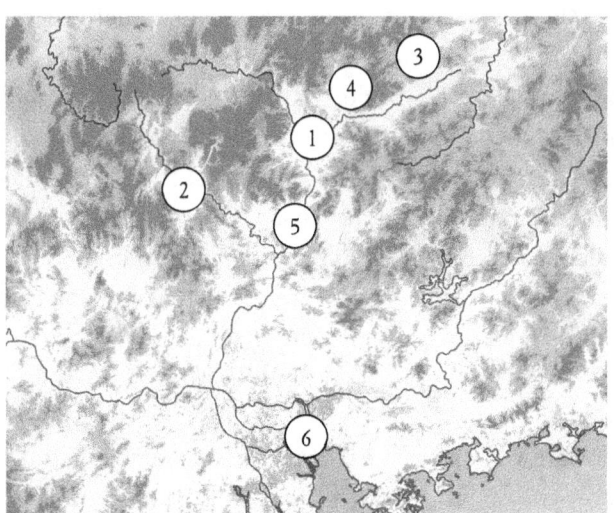

Figure 54 – Northern mountain passes to Nan-yue.
Key: 1. Shaoguan 2. Yangshan County 3. Dayuling 4. Zhoutianzhen 5. Yingde , 6. Panyu

Heng-pu is somewhere between Zhoutianzhen and Dayuling, Yangshan is in Yangshan county and Huang-hsi is in Yingde. By closing these passes, Nan-yue would be protected from the northern attacks.

In 207 BCE, the Qin dynasty was finally destroyed. Seizing the opportunity, Zhao Tuo promptly attacked and annexed the other two commanderies at Guilin and Xiang (See Fig. 58) into Nan-hai and declared himself King Wu of an independent Nan-yue which extended beyond Guangdong into Guangxi province.

The Qin court surrendered to the future Han ruler, Liu Bang in November/December 207 BCE. Liu Bang became the Emperor Gaozu of the new dynasty, Former Han, on 28 February, 202 BCE.[9] He established his capital at Luoyang in Henan province, near the heartland of the ancient Han state, by the Yellow river (See Fig. 5). The Han dynasty lasted for around four hundred years to 220 CE, and was divided into two different periods; the first as Former (or Western) Han and the second as the Later (or Eastern) Han. The Qin dynasty under Qin Shin Huang lasted for barely 15 years.

Emperor Gaozu decided to leave Zhao Tuo to run Nan-yue independent of the Former Han, and in 196 BCE he sent an envoy named Lu Jia to confirm his position with a seal and a message that Zhao Tuo should keep the peace in Bai-yue, not pillage the neighbouring states, and share the border with Changsha of Hunan province.

A year later, Emperor Gaozu died. Zhao Tuo and Nan-yue were left to themselves without interference from the Han until 184 BCE, when Empress (Dowager) Lu Zhi, the widow of Emperor Gaozu, issued a decree that Nan-yue was not allowed to buy iron implements, mares, female oxen, and goats at the border pass to Nan-yue.[10] Zhao Tuo thought this edict was a plot by the king of Changsha, so he declared himself Emperor Wu of Nan-yue and sent his army across the border into Changsha (now the name of the provincial capital of Hunan), destroyed a few border towns, and returned to Nan-yue. In retaliation, Empress Lu Zhi dispatched Zhou Zao, a general and Marquis of Lung-lu to invade Nan-Yue; but the Former Han army suffered from heat, humidity, and plague, and was unable to cross Nanling mountain into Nan-yue.[11] Over a year later in 180 BCE, Lu Zhi died and the campaign was abandoned.

Empress Lu Zhi was the first Empress of China and a ruthless woman. Shiji tells us how she had the limbs of one of the Emperor's favourite concubines, Lady Qi, chopped off, her eyes gouged out, her ears burnt off and made her mute by forcing her to drink poison. The Empress then kept Lady Qi in a toilet and called her a "human swine". Then she called to her son, Emperor Hui, and showed him the horribly deformed Lady Qi. Once he knew who the "human swine" was, he became sick and abandoned his authority to his mother.[12]

Zhao Tuo took the opportunity to give bribes, gifts of money and goods to Min-yue, Western Ou and Luo to submit to him, allowing him to rule a kingdom for over ten thousand *li* (over 4,000 kilometres) from east to west, by 181 BCE. His self-declared position lasted a few years until he voluntarily gave it up during the visit of Lu Jia, now representing the newly ascended Emperor Wen of Former Han, and agreed for Nan-yue to become a vassal, sending envoys to the court at Luoyang in the spring and fall. In 137 BCE he died and his grandson, Zhao Hu, became King of Nan-yue. Zhao Tuo lived a long time. Already active in 221 BCE, he would have been over 100 years old if the actual year of his death was, indeed, 137 BCE.

Figure 55 – Jade burial suit of Zhao Mo at the Museum of the Mausoleum of the Nan-yue King in Guangdong, China.[18]

During the excavation of the construction site in Guangdong in 1983, workers found the entrance to the tomb of the second king of Nan-yue, Zhao Mo (or Zhao Hu), a grandson of Zhao Tuo who ruled from 137 BCE to 122 BCE.[13] The tomb is now open to the public as the Museum of the Mausoleum of the Nan-yue King. The tomb is 20m below ground and divided into seven rooms with thousands of relics that remained undisturbed for over two thousand years.[14] Among them is the burial suit of the king constructed from 2,291 pieces of jade with silk thread (see Fig. 55) and nine seals made from gold and jade. One bears the inscription *"Administrative Seal of Emperor Wen"* on it, one has *"Seal of the Emperor"*, one *"Zhao Mo"*, and another is inscribed with *"The Crown Prince"*, found on the king's body. There is also one seal with the inscription *"Madam of the Right"* which refers to the first concubine.[15] There are also many weapons: body armour, bronze daggers, axes, crossbows, iron arrowheads, spears, and halberds. One of the iron swords is 1.46 metres long, believed to be the longest sword during the Han period. There are also musical instruments. Many of these objects are closely related to the Qin/Han objects from the north, reflecting the fact that Zhao Tuo came from Hebei province, north of the Yangtze river. There are also artefacts made of ivory, amber, and rhinoceros horn, materials likely to have come from Southeast Asia.[16] In fact, there is a bronze jar that resembles a Đông Sơn period artefact with an image of *"The triumphant return of a fleet. The cabins were full of the spoils of war. There was also a scene of soldiers killing the captured"*, the soldiers were wearing skirts and feathered headgear, which resemble those found on the Đông Sơn drums.[17]

The artefact from the tomb reveals that Zhao Mo considered himself an Emperor, not a King, but, as historian Diana Lary notes:

> *"The Nan-yue discoveries were thrilling in the South but in the North, the journal of record, Kaogu, did not announce the finding of the king's tomb for almost a year and then did so only as a fairly minor item."* [19,20]

The tomb provided uncomfortable evidence to the north that,

> *"There was a society in Lingnan* [the land south of Nanling mountain range] *that was not Han, that had a free and expressive culture quite distinct from the Han culture, that had survived over time in the spoken languages of the region and in ethnic memory."* [21]

Perhaps this is why the museum uses the term "King" and not "Emperor" despite the original inscription on the seals.

While his grandson was buried with grandeur in a substantial tomb accompanied by 15 others and numerous treasures, no one has ever found where Zhao Tuo was interred.

11.11.2 – A squatting old man

HE ASKED: *"Who is more capable, me or the Emperor?"*

THE ENVOY REPLIED: *"The people of the Middle Kingdom numbered one hundred million, land measured in ten thousand of miles, lived in the wealthiest place .... Your people are in the ten thousand, all barbarians, living in remote land among the mountains and seas. Your realm is no more than a district of Han, so how can you compare yourself with Han?"*

ZHAO TUO LAUGHED HEARTILY: *"I did not rise in the Middle Kingdom, so I only became a king here but if I were, then what would stop me from becoming like the Han (Emperor)?"* [22]

The above is a portion of dialogue between Zhao Tuo and Lu Jia, the envoy of the Former Han Emperor Gaozu (202-195 BCE) in 196 BCE when the latter came to Nan-yue to confer the title upon the King of Nan-yue. Zhao Tuo greeted Lu Jia not seated upon the throne as one might presume, but by squatting (like a Yue). In any event, the meeting went smoothly and Lu Jia returned to Han's court with a pearl handbag worth thousands of gold pieces.

Some 15 years later, after Zhao Tuo claimed himself as Emperor Wu, Lu Jia returned in 181 BCE to convince him to become a vassal of the Han empire and drop his title, to which Zhao Tuo complied. Han Emperor Wen (180-157 BCE) wrote to Zhao Tuo to say he had withdrawn his two generals from Changsha, had contact with Zhao Tuo's brothers, and had repaired his ances-tor's graves. He too suggested Zhao Tuo should drop the title "Emperor" and continue to be a vassal of the Han. In return, he allowed Zhao Tuo to rule the land south of Nanling without interference: [23]

> *"... My officials advised "taking the king's land is not enough to make ours larger, taking the king's wealth is not enough to make us richer, so from Nanling to the south, you can govern yourself"*

Emperor Wen also sent Zhao Tuo 50 thick, 30 moderately thick, and 20 thinly padded jackets (presumably to cater for each changing season).

Zhao Tuo was notably submissive in his reply:

> *"On the risk of death, kowtowing twice to submit my letter",*

and defended himself by stating that he only attacked Changsha because he was forced by Empress Lu Zhi's decree to stop exporting bronze, iron agricultural tools, female horses, oxen and goats to Nan-yue. He also explained that he claimed "Emperor" for fun, because the heads of his small neighbouring states, all barbarians, called themselves kings. [24]

> "Besides, the southern regions are low-lying and wet, among the barbarians, to the west is the Western Ou, half of the population is weak but they face south and claim a king, to the east, there is Min-yue with a thousand people also declare a king, to the north west, there is Changsha, half are barbarians also claim a king." [25]

This passage in Shiji is similar, but includes the land of the Lo (Lạc):

> "Moreover, the southern regions are low-lying and wet and lie among the barbarians; to the east, Min-yue with a population of a thousand people has claimed a king; to the west is Western Ou and the Lo Lo (Naked Lo), also declared themselves kings." [26]

Zhao Tuo said further that he was an old man, having lived in the land of the Yue for 49 years, but always looked toward the north to worship the Han, despite the fact he ruled over a land of thousands of *li* long in all directions, and an army of over one million soldiers with body armour. But now that Emperor Wen had restored his "King" title, he would drop "Emperor."[27]

Zhao Tuo sent the Emperor a pair of round white pearls, one thousand sets of bird feathers, ten rhinoceros' horns, five hundred valuables, one box of Lethocerus Indicus, forty pairs of live kingfishers (Halcyon) and two pairs of peacocks. The material in the box is translated by a writer, Châu Hải Đường, as *"Quế đố"*, which translates as 'an insect that eats cinnamon'. He suggests that it is Cà Cuống or Lethocerus Indicus, a giant water bug, which is a prized food. It can be eaten (boiled or fried) or used as essence in cooking; a delicacy in the Red River Delta region.[28]

It is interesting to compare the difference between the two types of gifts: manufactured products from the north and natural commodities from the south. Also note the defiance in Zhao Tuo's letter despite its heavily submissive tone. In fact, according to Shiji, he continued to use the "Emperor" title within Nan-yue but his envoy would change it to "King" when he appeared at Han's court.[29]

11.11.3 – The end of a dream

"In the evening .... Tower Ships attacked and burned the enemy [positions], [instead] *drove them to the camp of the Wave-calming* [General]. *In the early morning, the city was subdued. Lu Jia,* [Zhao] *Jiande, and several hundred of their followers escaped to the sea; they went west by boat."* [30]

The paragraph above describes the final scene of the battle for Panyu, the capital of Nan-yue. Both Chancellor Lu Jia and Nan-yue's last king, Zhao Jiande, were finally caught and the kingdom of Nan-yue came to an end. Zhao Tuo ruled Nan-yue for seventy years, his reign was passed on to his grandson and great grandsons but his dynasty came to an end in 111 BCE, a total of five generations over 93 years from his ordination as king. Following this dynastic rule Nan-yue, including north and upper central Vietnam, was absorbed into the Han empire. It would be a thousand years before the people of the Red River Delta would rule themselves again.

Nan-yue under Zhao Tuo and Zhao Mo was a vassal of the Former Han empire but neither king attended court in the capital at Luoyang. Zhao Mo sent his son Zhao Yingqi to court as an imperial guard, claiming ill health at the request of his own presence. Ten years on, Zhao Mo did become ill. His son was allowed to return, and became the next king of Nan-yue. Unlike his forebears, he promptly hid the imperial seal Wudi of Zhao Tuo and Wendi of his father. While away, he married Jiu Shi, a Han woman from Handan, Hebei, the same birth province as Zhao Tuo. After Zhao Yingqi's death in 113 BCE his young son, Zhao Xing, ascended the throne; his wife became the Queen Dowager. Jiu Shi brought about the end of Nan-yue's existence as an independent kingdom, albeit as a vassal.

Prior to his death, the Former Han Emperor had requested Zhao Mo's presence at court several times but he, like his father before him, claimed to be ill and did not attend. Once he died, Emperor Wu sent a new envoy by the name of Anguo Shaoji to Nan-yue to instruct the new king and his mother to come to Luoyang to pay respects, like other feudal lords, something the previous three kings of Nan yue had refused to do. And who was this person? None other than Jiu Shi's former lover! The Nan-yue populace was enraged as the sexual liaison continued. Jiu Shi, a native of Han, was worried about the threat of rebellion and wanted Nan-yue to come under the internal jurisdiction of the Han as other feudal lords of the interior. At a reception for the Han envoys, she told Chancellor Lu Jia:

"If Nan-yue belongs to [internally dependent on the Han empire], *it will benefit the state, but why does* [the Chancellor] *find this inconvenient?"* [31]

Lu Jia refused, and Jiu Shi wanted him removed. Emperor Wu caught wind of this and decided to send 2000 men with Jiu Shi's younger brother down to Panyu to assist her. While this envoy travelled south, Lu Jia decided to act. He and his brother, a commander of the troops outside the imperial palace, entered the palace, killed Jiu Shi, her son (the king), the Han's envoy and his entourage, and installed the older son of Zhao Yingqi, named Zhao Jiande, who married a Yue woman, as the next king.

As to the fate of the 2,000 Han men, the Yue lured them further into Nan-yue land and annihilated them in an ambush some forty *li* (about 16 kilometres) from the capital Panyu (near Guangzhou). The stage was set for outright war but this time, in the autumn of 112 BCE, Former Han Emperor Wu took no chance; he issued an amnesty and ordered the convicts and an army of 100,000 with the tower ships to suppress the rebellion at Nan-yue in a multi-pronged attack converging in Panyu.[32]

The first was a force under the Commandant of the Guards, Lu Bode, who was already camped at Guiyang, Chenzhou, across the border from Nan-yue in Henan province, about four hundred kilometres north of Panyu. He and his men had travelled with the envoy Anguo Shaoji a year earlier. Lu Bode was appointed by Emperor Wu as the Water Calming General (Fubo Jiangjun), the same title bestowed upon Ma Yuan, another Han general who was sent down from the north to suppress the rebellion of the Trưng sister in Northern Vietnam 154 years later in 42 CE.

The second army was commanded by the Chief Commandant of the Nobility, Yang Pu, who was appointed as the General of Tower Ships: Lou Chuan Jiangjun. There were two other commanders, both Yue natives who had surrendered to the Han previously. Both commanded different types of ships from the tower ships.[33] One was made the General of the Pole-ax Ships: Ge Jiangjun.[34] The other became General Who Brings Down Severity, or General for Descending the Rapids: Xia Lai Jiangjun. The fifth commander was made the Marquis Who Gallops To Duty (Chi-yi Hou) officer, who was to bring convicts from Ba Shu country as additional reinforcement.

From the information given in Shiji, SKTT, and Google Maps, I have reconstructed the attack routes as follows, (see Fig. 56):

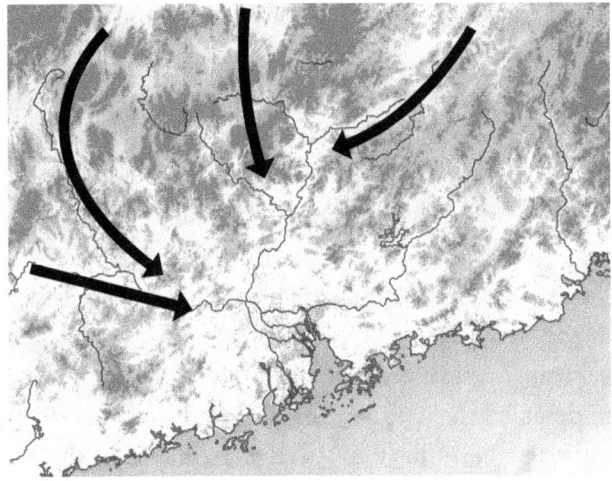

Figure 56 – Former Han's invasion of Nan-yue.

1. Lu Bode took the central route and set out from Guiyang. His troops travelled south to the Lianjiang river, possibly from Yangshan county (one of the passes to Nan-yue from Hunan) or via the Xingzi river to Lianzhouzhen. Once his ships were on the Lianjiang, it was relatively straightforward to travel all the way to the Bei river, which possibly connected at Lianjiangkouzhen; from there they could sail down to Panyu via a number of different waterways connected to the Xi river.

2. Yang Pu was on the Lu Bode eastern flank. He started out from Yuzhang, in Nanchang, near Poyang lake, descending on the Heng P'u pass, possibly travelling down Ganjiang to Ganzhou, Zhangsui and Zhenjiang rivers to Shaoguan.

3. Two Yue generals took the western flank of Lu Bode.[35] They began at Lingling, in Youngzhou, Hunan. They travelled south by the Xiangjiang river to Xing'an, took the Lingqu canal the Qin troops dug many years earlier and continued on the Lijiang river, as quoted in Shiji. From Lijiang river they connected with the Guijuang river to Wuzhou. From there, the Guigiang flows into the bigger Xunjiang and continues until it meets the Beijiang river where it connects with the rest of the Han armies.

4. Further to the west of the Yue general locations, the convicts of Ba Shu country (now Sichuan) were collected at Ye Lang in Guizhou province, west of Hunan. They could come to Guangzhou along many tributaries connected to the Xunjiang river flow by Wuzhou.

The invasion was arranged into four separate columns, marked by different arrows, converging on Panyu in modern Guangzhou. The battle was over even before the two western columns arrived.

Commandant Yang Pu was first to arrive in the vicinity of Panyu in the winter of 111 BCE, over a year later. By Shiji account, the fighting was swift and there was none of the prolonged guerrilla warfare the Qin had faced when they invaded Bai-yue one hundred years earlier. The terrain around Panyu was relatively flat given its location near the river mouth, and Nan-yue forces were no match for the Han armies once they broke through the defensive positions at the mountain passes. Yang Pu selected his best troops and defeated the Yue at a site believed to be Lianjiangkouzhen (where the Lianjiang river joins the Bei river). They broke through at Shihmen (north-west of Guangzhou), destroyed the stone wall built across the river at the entrance to Panyu, took the supply ships of the Yue, and with several tens of thousands of his troops, waited for Lu Bode. Lu Jia and Zhao Jiande retreated to the citadel at Panyu.[36]

Lu Bode arrived, and together with Yang Pu proceeded to lay siege to the city; Yang Pu came from the south-east, and Lu Bode took the north-west position. At nightfall, Yang Pu attacked and set fire to the city wall, set up camp and sent in an emissary to persuade the Yue to surrender. Those who did were given papers with official seals and allowed to go back to entice the others.[37] Yang Pu pressed on and drove the Yue troops towards Lu Bode camp, and in the early morning the city surrendered, Lu Jia, the king, and a few hundred others fled to the sea. They were eventually captured; the fighting was over, even before the two other western wings of the Han army arrived.[38]

After a period of forced rest, Yang Pu and other generals continued to attack Eastern Yue (a territory combining Min-yue and Eastern Ou), which they occupied some time in 111-110 BCE.[39]

11.11.4 — Just one of the many commanderies in the empire.

On the news of the arrival of Han troops, Shiji tells us, the King of Cangwu and the Prefect of Jiejang decided to submit. The Inspector of Guilin[40] convinced the Western Ou and the Lo (Lạc) to surrender to the Han.[41] All three were granted the title of Marquises.

TKCS describes the event as follows: when Lu Bode arrived at Hepu, the king of Yue sent envoys with one hundred cows, one thousand jars of rice wine, and the household records (returns of the population) of the two prefectures: Giao Chỉ and Cửu Chân as an offering to Lu Bode. Lu Bode appointed the two envoys (or legates) as governors (*taishou*) of these commanderies, but the Lạc Tướng (Lạc general) still governed the people.[42,43] SKTT tells the story slightly differently again:

> "Our country sent three envoys with 300 water buffaloes ... and the household records of three districts Giao Chỉ, Cửu Chân and Nhật Nam to surrender to Lu Bode. He appointed all three to be the governors of these districts."[44]

In any case, the region was then divided into nine commanderies.[45] Four are in China: Nanhai (Guangzhou), Yulin (Guilin), Cangwu (near Wuzhou) and Hepu (near Beihai). Three are in Vietnam: Jiaozhi (Giao Chỉ), Jiuzhen (Cửu Chân) and Rinan (Nhật Nam). Hainan island also became part of the Han empire and was divided into two counties: Zhuya and Dan'er. (see Fig. 58).

The Han emperor's central government controlled commanderies, which in turn were subdivided into prefectures; some of these prefecture-level areas were granted to the marquises, and called marquisates. There were also kingdoms with their own administration system; their fealty to the emperor was to pay homage annually, submit the returns of the population and a proportion of their taxes collected to the central government. They were responsible for raising and training their armed forces but were not allowed to mobilise them without an express order from the central government. The empire of 108 BCE had two metropolitan areas, 84 commanderies, and 18 kingdoms.

Of the commanderies that are in Vietnam territory, Giao Chỉ included the Red River Delta, Cửu Chân covered three provinces north of Ngang pass: Thanh Hóa, Nghệ An, and Hà Tĩnh, and Nhật Nam, south of the pass. There is a mountain range that runs at approximately forty-five degrees from the northeast to the sea through Cúc Phương National Park, which forms the boundary between Thanh Hóa and Ninh Bình provinces. Therefore it seems reasonable to assume that this mountain range would form the ancient northern boundary between Cửu Chân and Giao Chỉ.

Nhật Nam means "south of the sun", and it includes six present-day provinces: Quảng Bình, Quảng Trị, Thừa Thiên-Huế and Quảng Nam, Quảng Ngãi, Bình Định provinces to Cả pass, Mũi Đại Lãnh (or Cap Varella) in Phú Yên province. However, other sources limit the southernmost border of the Former Han empire to Hải Vân pass excluding three provinces south of it, i.e., Quảng Nam, Quảng Ngãi, and Bình Định.

By Shiji's account, Han's policy was to leave the locals to manage their affairs according to their traditions and not force them to pay different types of taxes;

"However, the newly formed prefectures always rebelled and killed the ruling officials." [46]

In fact, such a rebellion in 192 in Tượng Lâm (Xianglin) prefecture (the southernmost prefecture of Nhật Nam province) created a new kingdom, Linyi which lasted for nearly six hundred years before it became Champa. Both kingdoms were independent of the Chinese dynasties until Champa was absorbed into Vietnam in the 19th century CE.

11.11.5 - *A timeline of Nan-yue history*

214 BCE	The Qin emperor appointed Zhao Tuo as one of his generals during the conquest of Bai-yue. Qin occupied the land south of the Nanling mountain range and set up three commanderies: Guilin, Xiang, and Nan-hai. Death of Qin Shi Huang, First Emperor of China
210 BCE	
209 BCE	First rebellion against the Qin by Chen Sheng: the Dazexiang uprising
208 BCE	At Nan-hai, Zhao Tuo's superior, Ren Xiao appointed him the new Commandant. Ren Xiao died shortly after.
207 BCE	The Qin dynasty ended.
207 BCE	Zhao Tuo annexes the commanderies of Guilin and Xiang, declared himself king of Nan-yue, and established the capital at Panyu.[47]
202 BCE	Civil war in northern China ended, Emperor Gaozu established the Han dynasty.
196 BCE	Envoy Lu Jia, representing Emperor Gaozu, conferred Zhao Tuo as the King of Nan-yue.
195 BCE	Emperor Gaozu died.
184 BCE	Empress Lu Zhi sent Chou Tsao to invade Nan-yue.
180 BCE	Empress Lu Zhi died.
180-179 BCE	Zhao Tuo bribed/offered gifts to Min-yue, Western Ou, and Lo to submit to him, proclaimed as Emperor Wu.
179-178 BCE	Envoy Lu Jia, representing Han Emperor Wen, visited Nan-yue and persuaded Zhao Tuo to replace the emperor title with king.
137 BCE	Zhao Tuo died.
113 BCE	Nan-yue's dowager wanted the kingdom to become a vassal of the Han. Lu Jia refused, and killed her and the envoy from Han's court.
112 BCE	Han sent an expedition of 200,000 in four columns to invade Nan-yue.
111 BCE	Han generals burned Panyu, divided Nan-yue into seven commanderies, with three in Vietnam. One thousand years of Northern rule began.

CHAPTER 12

HISTORY REVISITED

Thus far, the stories seem to flow nicely from one historical character to the next. But over the centuries, as historians have undertaken more research, supported by archaeological, linguistic, and genetic evidence, these stories have begun to change. Nationalistic pride casts its shadow over such stories, which shifts emphasis and perspective, and we find ourselves seeing these in a different and more complex light.

Zhao Tuo was a hero in the eyes of one historian and a villain in another, and the current view of Zhao Tuo is that he was a foreign invader.[1,2] The Qin armies at one point invaded Vietnam and went as far south as Cà pass. The common view holds that they were driven out and stopped at the current border with Vietnam (see 12.12.2). Some authors even doubt the existence of An Dương Vương himself.[3]

12.12.1 – Hero or villain

I grew up learning that Zhao Tuo was one of the Vietnamese kings, following Hùng kings and An Dương Vương. He was one of our heroes, and Lê Văn Hưu, a 13th century historian, makes it clear:

> *"Zhao Tuo Wudi founded our Việt nation, proclaimed himself as an Emperor, equal to the Han's"* and all *"the kings following him should imitate Wudi to protect the realm by establishing the military... and ruled with humanity so that the northerners would not be able to look furtively at us* [threatening us].*"* [4]

There are several temples dedicated to him and according to VSTA, Zhao Tuo married a Lac woman, Trình Thị, from Đường Xâm village who gave birth to Trọng Thủy. [5,6] There is now a temple dedicated to Zhao Tuo and his wife, Trình Thị Lan Nương, at Đồng Xâm temple, Kiến Giương district, Thái Bình province. [7]

Zhao Tuo is said to *"have married a Yue woman, adopted Yue customs, encouraged Han men to do the same"*, whether the Yue woman is the woman above person we will never know. [8]

Nan-yue's Chancellor Lu Jia is also a Vietnamese hero and there are a number of temples and street names dedicated to him. [9] In fact, there is a grave at Đặng Lễ, Ân Thi District in Hưng Yên province, about 46 kilometres southeast of Hanoi, where his headless body was thought to be taken by his soldiers for burial after his decapitation by the Han in 111 BCE. However, not everyone agrees. Ngô Thời Sỹ, an 18th-century historian, thought:

> *"*[Zhao Tuo].. *was a great man at his time... But for our country, he did not contribute anything but was our first threat. If he did not cause a military conflict* [with the Han] *then even if the Han emperor Wudi* [141-87 BCE] *wanted to expand* [his] *country... at most, he would only destroy the Zhao family and retook the old commanderies of the Qin but not swallowed up Giao Chỉ. Our country became a vassal* [of the northern rulers] *from the* [Former] *Han to the Tang* [618-907], [and we can] *trace the original disaster to Zhao Tuo, who else?"* [10]

Another historian, Đào, did not mince words:

> *"Zhao Tuo was a foreign invader, the history of the Zhao dynasty at Nan-yue cannot be within the history of Vietnam."* [11,12]

For me, a man who became a king and an emperor of a kingdom about the size of France, 1,900 kilometres from his birthplace, Zhao Tuo was a remarkable man. He succeeded through a combination of military prowess and cunning. If his grandson's tomb is anything to go by, Nan-yue became a wealthy and civilised kingdom under his rule. But we can agree that he should not be considered one of the Vietnamese kings, because modern Vietnam has not evolved from Nan-yue in terms of territory, culture, and language.

12.12.2 – Crossing over Cả pass – The commandery of Xiang

In 221 BCE, Qin armies marched over the mountain passes of Nanling into Bai-yue land. When the war ended in 214 BCE, the Qin occupied most of Bai-yue land and divided it into three commanderies: Nan-hai, Guilin, and Xiang (See Fig. 57). Historians agree that the first two were in Guangxi and Guangdong provinces of China. What they disagree upon is the location of Xiang and its southernmost border. Some believe Xiang was inside southern China, whereas others suggest it extended as far south as Cả pass in central Vietnam.[13]

Having undertaken the research, I support the "inside China camp", because Cả pass is too far south of the Nanling mountains. The main transport mode of Qin armies was by ship on river routes and there is no obvious river route all the way down to Cả pass.[14] From Guilin in the Nanling mountain range to the border near Lạng Sơn, the favourite invasion route to the Red River Delta is about 600 kilometres; from there down to Cả pass is over 1,300 kilometres. In fact, most rivers on the march would act as barriers, as they flow to the sea more generally in the west-to-east direction. A further deterrence is a mountainous terrain around Lạng Sơn by the Vietnam-China border; the hot and wet climate of the region with its proximity to the Tropic of Cancer, the formidable fortification at Cổ Loa citadel, and, not least, the likely fierce resistance by the local people. It is unlikely that Zhao Tuo pushed on with an army that suffered terribly over several years, struggling to get where they were. He was more likely to consolidate his gains around Nan-hai and nearby regions to the west, which became the commandery of Guilin and Xiang.

I have mapped these three commanderies, as shown on Fig. 57 based on the work of historian Michael Loewe.[15] One should also remember a note in SKTT which explains that Xiang was *"West of Guangxi and south of Guizhou"*[16] which matches the position as shown on the map, and which is also confirmed by historian Phan Huy Lê.[17] My position is in line with Đào who makes a similar argument:

> *"Based on the military and geography considerations, Qin army, who fought on land, it would have been impossible to march from Guangxi to the south of central Vietnam."* [18]

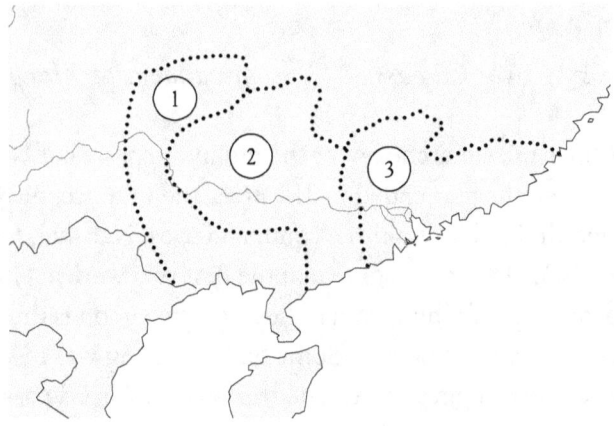

Figure 57 – Three commanderies established by the Qin in 214 BCE.
Key: 1. Xiang 2. Guilin 3. Nan-hai

Xiang had its seat (or administration centre) at Chongzuo; Guilin's seat was at Guiping, and Nan-hai seat was at Panyu.[19] Chongzuo is by the Zuo river, it is about 90 kilometres from Lạng Sơn. Guiping is northeast of Guigang where the Xunjiang river is divided into two branches, the Qian and Yu rivers.

Nan-yue in 207 BCE included all three commanderies but in 179 BCE it was expanded (see Fig. 58).

The northern border of the commanderies is the Nanling mountain range; the starting line of the invasion, which has remained much the same as it is now, over 2,000 years later, between the provinces of Guangxi, Guang-dong and Hunan, Jiangxi, and Fujian. The southern border is up against the wild, mountainous region around Cao Bằng and Lạng Sơn, which would have been a reasonable choice for a front line if Zhao Tuo had decided to stop and consolidate. The location of the commandery seat at Chongzuo lends support to the proposition that Xiang did not extend to the Red River Delta; if it did, the commandery seat would be there as the Han had created later at Luy Lâu, near Hanoi.

12.12.3 – A shifting land

Some 15 years after annexing both Guilin and Xiang in 179 BCE, Zhao Tuo intimidated and bribed Min-yue, Western Ou (Âu) and Luo (Lạc) states into submission to him (see 11.11.1). Historians agree Min-yue is now modern Fujian; Western Ou, as discussed previously was the region around the Zuo and Youjiang rivers, Luo was north and upper central Vietnam (see 8.8.3). These then became vassals of Nan-yue. Zhao Tuo defeated An Dương Vương at the battle of Cổ Loa (see 9.9.1) and not by intimidation or bribery. Given the size and location of Cổ Loa and the weapons found there it would be surprising if the ruler of Cổ Loa and surrounding areas had simply submitted to Zhao Tuo without a fight. In any case, having conquered Âu Lạc, Zhao Tuo left behind two representatives (legates) to oversee the two counties, Giao Chỉ and Cửu Chân, with the southernmost border of Cửu Chân most likely at Ngang pass.

I have redrawn the map of the commanderies under the Han dynasty in 108 BCE as shown in Fig. 58. This shows the extent of Guilin commandery, which absorbed Xiang commandery, and also extended further to the west possibly to include some eastern part of Yunnan.

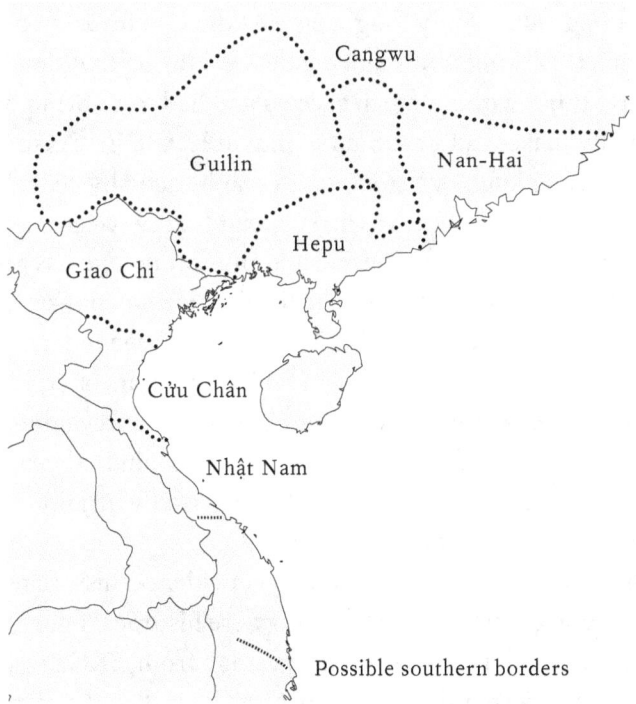

Figure 58 – Commanderies (Zhuya and Dan'er, not shown) under Former Han (108 BCE) (after Loewe).[20]

The southern border of Nhật Nam could be as far as Cả pass according to one source, or Hải Vân pass according to another (see 12.12.2), thus the dotted line.

Nan-yue in 111 BCE may have included all seven commanderies above. However, it may not have included Nhật Nam, which may have been occupied later by the Han.

12.12.4 – The 28-year gap

Main historical works such as SKTT mark the end of the Hùng kings in 257 BCE with the new ruler, An Dương Vương, beginning his reign from then until 208 BCE, when he was defeated by Zhao Tuo, and the kingdom Âu Lạc (Ou and Lo) became part of Nan-yue. However, as Shiji shows, Zhao Tuo did not absorb other Yue states including the land of Western Ou (Âu) and Lo (Lạc) until after Han empress Lu Zhi died in 180 BCE (see 11.11.5). In fact, at that time, he was referring to Western Ou and Lo as independent kingdoms. After much research and debate, most Vietnamese historians agree 180 or 179 BCE was the year the historical kingdom of Âu Lạc came to an end, and not 208 BCE.[21]

What happened to Âu Lạc during the twenty-eight years from 208 to 180 BCE? According to Phan, after uniting the tribes from Western Ou and Lo, An Dương Vương successfully fought against the Qin invasion of 221-214 BCE and retained the kingdom's independence. During that time, Zhao Tuo invaded several times without much success and had to resort to bribery and trickery to finally make Âu Lạc submit to him in 179 BCE.[22] As for fighting against the last Hùng king, one story states that he actually ceded his throne to An Dương Vương, and there was no such fighting between them.[23]

Zhao Tuo lived through this period and thus far no one has provided a satisfactory answer about how long he lived. It is known that when Han envoy Lu Jia visited him in 179 or 178 BCE, he had been in Nan-yue for 49 years.[24] If he died in 137 BCE as cited in Shiji or 41 years later, it would then amount to ninety years of his time in Nan-yue. One source quotes that he lived until a ripe old age of 121 years,[25] or over one hundred years according to another.[26] In any case, he lived through the period when northern and central Vietnam became part of his domain.

Based on ancient texts and archaeological evidence, historians agree that both An Dương Vương and Zhao Tuo were historical figures. From the timeline shown in Shiji, Han shu and the passage from TKCS (see 9.9.1), historians generally accept that the battle of Cổ Loa did take place, and Zhao Tuo was involved in the fighting.

Given the size and location of Cổ Loa, and the weapons found there, it would be surprising to find the ruler of Cổ Loa and surrounding areas would simply submit to Zhao Tuo without a fight. Whether the final defeat of An Dương Vương was by all-out warfare or subsequent bribery by Zhao Tuo, or the betrayal of Mỵ Nương, one will never know.

Interestingly, neither Shiji nor Han shu mentions An Dương Vương, and the addition of Nhật Nam commandery to the Han dynasty is not mentioned in Shiji, only cited in Han shu. According to a 19th century Vietnamese work, "The Imperially Ordered Annotated Text Completely Reflecting the History of Viet" (*Khâm Định Việt Sử Thông Giám Cương Mục* [CM]), Nhật Nam was already part of Cửu Chân under Nan-yue, but Phan believed Nhật Nam was additional territory taken by the Han.[27,28]

CHAPTER 13

A TIME TO TRADE

A pass, a pass yet a pass,
Praise to whoever cleverly sculpted the craggy scene,
Red lipstick doors and dense roofs,
Green boulders scattered with moss.

"The pass of Ba Dội" by Hồ Xuân Hương (Vietnamese poet 1772-1822).[1,2]

To travel along the coast from Ngang pass to the southernmost provinces of Central Vietnam, Bình Thuận provinces where the popular beach resort of Mũi Né, Phan Thiết is located, one has to cross at least 15 mountain passes (see Fig. 59). Some of these passes have become historical landmarks which separated different settlements, regions and kingdoms over the centuries up to the present time.

The land of these passes has witnessed many great historical events, but unfortunately we do not have much to tell; not least in the period before 111 BCE. This is because there is little historical record of the people living in this region, unlike the stories told thus far which all relate to events at locations north of Ngang pass. The oldest inscription about stories in this region was written on a stone stele in the 3rd or 4th century in Sanskrit and old Cham, which is a much later period than that which this book covers.[3]

So unfortunately, I am unable to provide interesting historical tales for those people south of Ngang pass. However, the archaeological story of the region is fascinating and it is to archaeology I will turn. Archaeologists have excavated many burial sites along the coast of Central Vietnam and they name a civilisation after the first site was found at the village of Sa Huỳnh. This civilisation thrived from 500 BCE to 100 CE and evolved into the kingdom of Linyi (2nd to 8th centuries) followed by Champa (9th to 19th centuries) before it was absorbed into Vietnam. The Sa Huỳnh people manufactured thousands of beads, many earrings and other ornaments (Figures 64 to 67) and traded these to other Southeast Asian countries. They had elaborate burials and were seagoing people. The Chams, who followed them, adopted Indian culture and written language from around the 4th century to the 15th when many converted to Islam. They lived in a mandala (federation) of small kingdoms spread along the coast with settlements by the large river mouths.

The Chams left behind the ruins of beautiful towers and temples all along these settlements including Mỹ Sơn sanctuary in Hội An, Po Nagar Cham Tower in Nha Trang (see Fig. 60), and Po Shanu Cham Towers in Mũi Né.

Further south from the land of the Chams one enters a region east and south of Trị An lake, from where Đồng Nai river flows, once part of the Funan empire and Óc Eo civilisation.[4] The Funan empire (1st to 7th centuries) at one time extended to include most of southern Vietnam, Cambodia, and Thailand as far as the northern Malay Peninsula. Óc Eo civilisation was characterized by gold artefacts and Indian cultural practices.[5]

From 111 BCE, the history of Vietnam continued along two different paths: the people north of Ngang pass were under Northern rule for a thousand years until the 10th century; south of it, the Sa Huỳnh and the Chams/Funanese were free to rule themselves, at least from the 3rd century. However, from the 10th century, after the northern rulers were forced to return to the north, the people from both regions had many interactions, mainly through wars. The physical border between the north and the south shifted down from one mountain pass to another until it reached the final destination at Đất Mũi by Cape Cà Mau National Park in the 19th century.

South of Ngang pass, one continues to travel along three provinces: Quảng Bình, Quảng Trị, and Thừa Thiên-Huế for about 320 kilometres until one reaches Hải Vân (ocean cloud) pass.

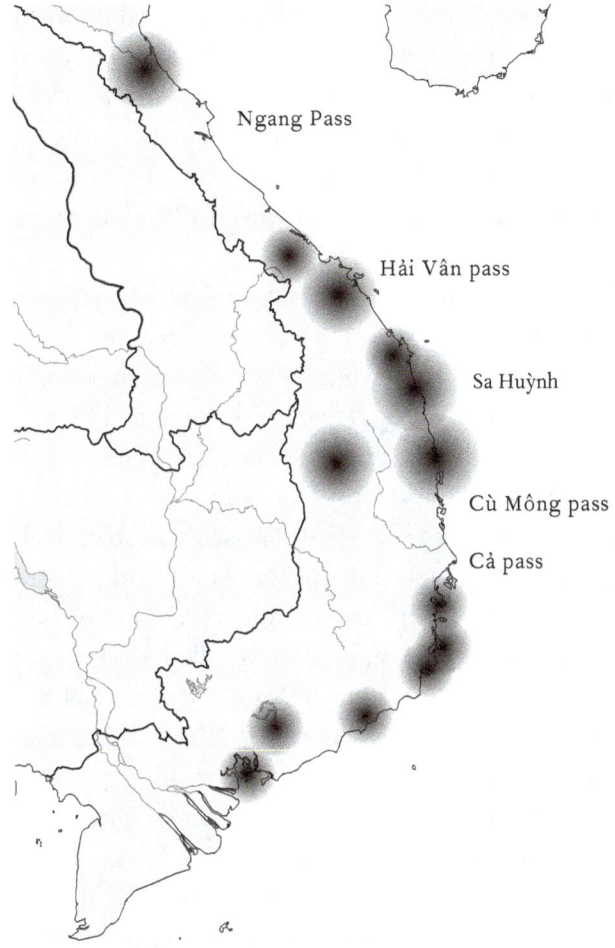

Figure 59 – Indicative clusters of Sa Huỳnh sites.[6]

Figure 60 – Po Nagar Champa Tower at Nha Trang.[7]

The provinces share a narrow strip of flat land squeezed between the Trường Sơn mountain range to the west and the sea to the east. For centuries, this sandy, hot region was the frontier, a no-man's land which witnessed numerous battles between competing armies of northern dynasties and Linyi; Đại Việt and Champa; Trịnh and Nguyễn lords; North and US-South Vietnam and provided the north-south divide in 17th, 18th and 20th centuries at the two rivers of Gianh and Bến Hải.

Until 2005, when a tunnel was built, the only way to get from Nguyễn's capital of Huế to the seaside city of Đà Nẵng was to climb to the top of Hải Vân pass, where the view is spectacular, then down to the other side over 21 kilometres length of winding road. King Minh Mạng had a gate built at the top of the pass similar to the one at Ngang pass, and the gate is still there.

Immediately south of Hải Vân pass the land flattens out and one arrives at Đà Nẵng, where the French ships first released a salvo of shells ashore in 1858. South of Đà Nẵng is the famous tourist town of Hội An situated by the Thu Bồn river mouth. Further south, one travels across the Trà Khúc river and from there one reaches another pass called Sa Huỳnh. Between this and Hải Vân are the provinces of Quảng Nam and Quảng Ngãi.

During Han times, this region was part of Nhật Nam (Rinan) commandery (see 11.11.4). While historians generally agree that the northern border of Nhật Nam is at Ngang pass, its southern frontier, which is also the southernmost border of the Han empire, has been subjected to different interpretations.[8] My view is that the southern border of Nhật Nam, which was also the southernmost border of the Han empire, was at Hải Vân pass and possibly extended to the Thu Bồn river. I base this conclusion on the record that this was where the first successful rebellion against the Han started in the 2nd century.

It was from Thu Bồn and Trà Khúc and other river valleys along the north central coast of Vietnam, that a civilisation, Linyi (the name is Chinese in origin, 192 to 758) and its successor, Huanwang (Hoàn Vương, 758 to 856) and Champa (the name is Indian in origin, 866 to 1832) sprang up in the 2nd century, lasting until it was finally absorbed into Vietnam.[9,10]

Of beads and earrings

Of the 15 or so passes mentioned above, there is a pass called Sa Huỳnh which is about 310 kilometres north of Nha Trang. At about 15 kilometres north of this pass is the village Sa Huỳnh (translated as golden sand) and in 1909 a French customer officer M. Vinet came across a number of jars containing human remains at Phú Khương by this village.[11] This discovery initiated a chain of archaeological excavations, which gave rise to the name of a bronze/iron age culture called Sa Huỳnh culture as distinct from Đông Sơn culture discussed earlier.

Serious excavations of Sa Huỳnh followed, notably by French archaeologists including Madeleine Colani in 1934, the scientist who discovered the first Hoabinhian sites, as previously mentioned. Following in her steps, a large number of Sa Huỳnh-culture sites have been excavated by a number of Vietnamese and international archaeologists.[12] In 1978, two Vietnamese archaeologists: Chử Văn Tần and Đào Linh Côn excavated a site near Sa Huỳnh where Colani and her colleagues worked 44 years earlier. There is now a museum at Long Thạnh hamlet at Phổ Thạnh commune with exhibits from the Sa Huỳnh sites. This is a far cry from the time of Colani and her colleagues where

> "Colani excavated 55 jars in 1934 and remarked that the interval between her excavations and those of Mme Labarre, the natives had dug up a number of jars and sold the cornelian beads they had found inside them to the Chinese ... Parmentier mentioned the site was constantly disturbed purposefully for the beads, 'and the children have found thousands of baubles with which they amuse themselves'... broken jars left about." [13]

Along Central Vietnam, archaeologist Lâm Thị Mỹ Dung shows the northernmost of Sa Huỳnh sites at Bãi Cọi in Hà Tĩnh.[14,15] The southernmost sites are at Giồng Cá Võ[16] near Hồ Chí Minh City and Giòng Lớn[17] at Bà Rịa Vũng Tàu. However, a large number of Sa Huỳnh sites are located in the Thu Bồn river valley in Quảng Nam province. Of the 18 sites that archaeologist Nguyễn Kim Dung[18] used to study the ornaments found, eight are around Thu Bồn river valley in Quảng Nam province. A large number of sites and archaeological findings indicates that the Linyi kingdom was established in this province.[19] In fact, the capital of Linyi is believed to be at Trà Kiệu on the bank of this river, at least in the later years of the kingdom.[20]

The sites are often found on dunes along the coasts or rivers. Typical burial vessels consist of cylindrical or egg-shapes with hat-shaped lids buried vertically in the ground with grave goods. In addition, there are a variety of objects related to daily life and ritual, including bronze and iron implements, pottery jars, deep jars, shallow bowls, and thousands of ornaments either placed with the human remains inside the jars or adjacent to them.[21,22] Compared with the Đông Sơn sites, north of Ngang pass, where many bronze instruments of war were found, the bronze and iron objects found at Sa Huỳnh sites appear to be for daily use.[23] Similarly, while the evidence of local ironwork was spare under Đông Sơn civilisation, it was already introduced to Sa Huỳnh tradition.[24] Interestingly, not many human remains were found in these burial jars. Archaeologists are still not certain if the remains were cremated or disposed of at sea.[25]

Ninety per cent of the ornaments found at Sa Huỳnh sites are beads made from glass, jade carnelian, agate, amethyst, crystal and gold.[26] At a site in Lai Nghi in Quảng Nam province, archaeologists found more than 7,000 gold, glass, carnelian and agate beads.[27] Many of these items appear to have been imported into Vietnam from elsewhere, such as trade beads from India.[28] There are also earrings, bracelets, gold marks and Former Han mirrors.

The ear ornaments, especially those made from nephrite jade (one of the two types of jade minerals, the other is jadeite) stand out. Two specific forms are: a) Lingling-o penannular earring with three-pointed circumferential projections, and b) the double animal-headed (bicephalous) ear pendant.[29] Lingling-o is adapted from the name of such ornaments by the southern Ifugaos, a Philippine tribe living near Luzon, north of Manila.[30]

Many of the recovered earrings and pendants from sites in Taiwan, the Philippines, Central and Southern Vietnam, East Malaysia and peninsular Thailand are virtually identical in size and shape. Chemical analyses have indicated that the raw material used in their production was sourced from Fengtien, Hualien County, in Eastern Taiwan; however, many were made from local nephrite.[31,32]

In Reinecke's detailed study of bicephalous ear pendants, he notes that Sa Huỳnh was almost certainly the centre of their production and utilisa-tion, where far more have been recovered than anywhere else in South East Asia.[33] From the studies of Sa Huỳnh ornaments, Nguyễn concluded that Sa Huỳnh inhabitants of Central Vietnam were well-connected to trans-regional trading networks; they imported raw materials, and manufactured and exported their ornaments throughout South East Asia.[34]

Jade has been used in Vietnam for centuries. Trang Kênh in Hải Phòng is one of the largest and oldest jade workshops in Northern Vietnam, as old as 1500 BCE.[35] However, most jade artefacts in northern Vietnam are either white or pale orange in colour.[36]

Figure 61 – Burial jar, Sa Huỳnh culture, An Bằng site, Quảng Nam province, c. 2500-2000 years BP, National Museum of Vietnamese History, Hanoi.[49]

Figure 62 – Cooking pots, Sa Huỳnh culture, National Museum of Vietnamese History, Hanoi.[50]

Land of the golden sand

"Sa Huỳnh culture is regarded as an Iron Age phenomenon dating from ca. 500 BC through AD 100, mostly along the central coast of Vietnam... Sa Huỳnh and related cultures in central Vietnam can be divided into three major phases: Pre-Sa Huỳnh (prior to 500 BC), Typical Sa Huỳnh (500 BC- AD 100) and Early Cham (AD 100-500)... Jar burials are among the most notable characteristics of Sa Huỳnh assemblages." [37]

Archaeological sites of Sa Huỳnh culture have been found all along the central coast of Vietnam from Quảng Bình province south of Ngang pass, to east of Ho Chi Minh city and the highland around Pleiku.[38,39] The bulk of these sites was found at Quảng Nam and Quảng Ngãi provinces from Hải Vân to Sa Huỳnh passes. According to Bellwood,

> "The Sa Huynh culture can circumstantially be associated with the Austronesian-speaking settlement of Vietnam from Borneo"

and the early speakers of the Chamic languages in Central Vietnam, a Malayo-Polynesian subgroup of the Austronesian language family and closely related to the Malaysic language of western Borneo, Sumatra and Peninsular Malaysia.[40,41] Bellwood suggests that,

> "The ancestor of the Chamic languages was introduced into Vietnam from Island Southeast Asia about two thousand years ago, or slightly before from western Borneo, and probably with knowledge of ironworking."[42]

By contrast, Bellwood believes it was with the speakers of Mường (including ancestral Vietnamese within the Austroasiatic language family) in the Red River Delta that

> "the invading Chinese came into most contact during the Qin and Han times."

Island Southeast Asia comprises the tropical islands lying between mainland East Asia and Taiwan to the northwest and Australia, and New Guinea to the southeast.[43]

Anthropologist Wilhelm Solheim offers an alternative to Bellwood and suggests the Sa Huỳnh culture shares more affinities with the Central Philippines. Studies of pottery at the Hòa Diêm site by archaeologist Mariko Yamagata suggest:

> "*The closer affinity of later jar-burial people (Hoa Diem 1) to the insular Southeast Asian group suggests an Iron Age colonization from the Philippines across the South China Sea.*" [44,45]

While I do not have enough knowledge of the subject to offer a view, it would be an interesting task to compare the two sea routes, one from the Philippines and one from western Borneo, to assess which route would be easier for travel. On a simplistic level, the predominant monsoon winds across the East Sea in the northeast and southwest direction tend to make it easier to sail to central Vietnam from western Borneo and southern Malaysia along the coast than from the Philippines in the east-west direction.[46,47]

Compared with what is known about the Lạc people in the north there is less knowledge of the Sa Huỳnh settlers. We know they manufactured many beads, earrings, and other ornaments and traded these. They were likely to be seagoing people and had elaborate burials. We know much more about the people south of Ngang pass from when the kingdoms of Linyi/Champa came into existence, but the continuity from Sa Hùynh civilization to these kingdoms is not a view accepted by all researchers. Some suggest it was the Lạc people from the north fleeing the Han who established Linyi.[48] While it is agreed that there was intermixing between the two groups, I tend to support the view that the original settlers of the Sa Hùynh civilisation went on to establish Linyi/Champa. Historical events demonstrate that during Linyi times, the movement of people was northward with repeated raids across Ngang pass by the kings of Linyi, not southward by the inhabitants of contemporary Hà Tĩnh or Nghệ An provinces.

Figure 63 – Tools and weapons. The dagger on the right is most likely a Đông Sơn weapon.[51]

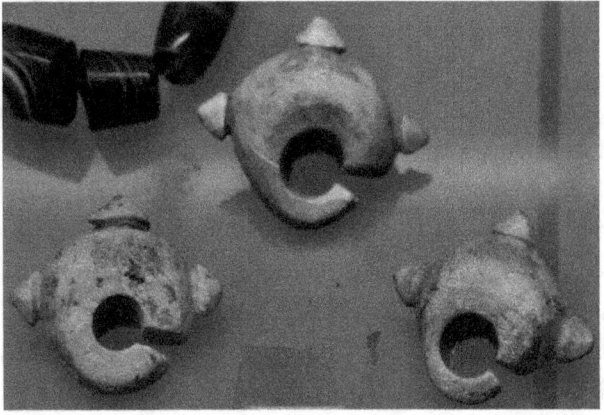

Figure 64 – Lingling-o penannular earring (Three node pendant), artefacts of Phú Hòa site (Đồng Nai province).[52]

Figure 65 – Bicephalous agate earrings, 2,500-2,000 BP found at Giồng Cá Võ site, Cần Giờ district, Ho Chi Minh City.[53]

A TIME TO TRADE

Figure 66 – Earrings on a skull (bicephalous ear ornament), History Museum, Ho Chi Minh City.[54]

Figure 67 – Beads (Agate), 2,500-2,000 BP found at Giồng Cá Võ site, Cần Giờ district, Ho Chi Minh City.[55]

CHAPTER 14

CONCLUSIONS

Over the years, historians have tried to identify the locations cited in old texts or records to match the names of places in their time to help them understand historical events. In the past, however, maps were difficult to come by and historians such as Ngô or Đào or Aurousseau must have struggled to obtain the information they needed. Today, people like myself have a far smoother time with easily accessible information through the internet and Google Maps.

With such maps, I now have a better geographical understanding of historical sites, the establishment of kingdoms, and the trade routes, as well as plans of battles that changed the course of history. Most of all, it helps me remember historical events: I can visualise in my mind where each location is and what took place there.

In simplistic terms, on the basis of archaeological records, geography and historical texts, Vietnam evolved from four major settlements. The first is the region where three main rivers of Đà, Hồng (Red) and Lô meet before flowing into the Red river and continuing to the sea, where the legendary Hùng kings fir st started.[1] The second region covers Bắc Ninh and Bắc Giang provinces, just north of the Đuống river, where An Dương Vương built his capital around Cổ Loa citadel (see Fig. 8). The third is by the Mã river delta of Thanh Hóa, where the founder of the Nguyễn dynasty started. The fourth is the birthplace of Linyi/Champa, located around Quảng Nam and Thừa Thiên-Huế provinces in Central Vietnam (see Fig. 68). There are other ancient settlements, such as those which gave rise to the Óc Eo civilisation and those of the Central Highlands. I have not included them here since, while they became part of the history of Vietnam, they did not play as significant a role in its development as the other four.

At the beginning of northern rule in 111 BCE the land north of Ngang pass, including the first three regions, had many more people than to the south of it; several magnitudes more by the year 2 CE.[2] Those in the north were technologically more advanced and more familiar with warfare than those in the south, as evidenced in their manufacture of the bronze drums, weapons, and the construction of Cổ Loa citadel.

However, maps are not enough: historical events may be interpreted, remembered, and recited varyingly at different times. Historians will long continue to debate over some of these contentious events: were Hùng and Lạc kings the same? Did they exist? Did Zhao Tuo travel to northern Vietnam? Where was the capital of Linyi? And so on. I will leave these to the professional historians, but for me having written this book, through the maps, I am far more enlightened and I can now relate the places I visited in Vietnam with the historical events with which they are associated.

For the most part, I have met the objectives of what I set out to do; to answer the questions of what, where, when, why and how a historical event occurred. I am fairly confident of the what and the where; as to the other questions, I have tried my best to answer these but I am sure, as new archaeological evidence arises and changes occur in the politics of the day, past events may be interpreted differently, but, hopefully, the geographical knowledge will remain. One interesting observation is that at the break up of Tang China in the 10th century, the southern kingdoms appeared to revert to the natural borders formed by the mountain ranges that separated them over one thousand years earlier.

As to the true nature of legends and myths, I do not disagree with scholarly works but I will say that there is credence in what people believed at the time. So, what if the Ân invaders in the story of Saint Gióng are fictional, and Âu Cơ did not come from Dongting lake? Knowing the stories, understanding them and visiting the places within them, has been an enjoyable experience for me and that is enough.

As to relaying them, I appreciate the approach taken by the 15th-century historian Ngô Sĩ Liên who, writing about First Immortal at Mt Tản Viên story, puts it like this:

> *"As for the Sơn Tinh (the mountain spirit) and Thủy Tinh (the water spirit), it is bizarre, but believing in books is better than having no books, so let's retell the old stories even if only to convey the doubt."* [3]

And he did tell them.[4] I look forward to completing my journey with the books yet to be written and share my findings with other travellers through Vietnam's past.

Tan Pham, April 2021

Figure 68 – Four main settlements that have expanded into Vietnam

APPENDIX I

KEY SOURCES OF EARLY VIETNAMESE HISTORY IN CHINESE LANGUAGE

The end of Nan-yue was the beginning of Northern rule, when Vietnam became a province of the Former Han empire. From then until the 10th century, when Vietnam became independent, all writings of its history are Chinese sourced.[1] The key texts for this book are Shiji [2],[3] Han shu[4] and Thủy Kinh Chú Sớ[5] (Additional explanation of Commentary of the water classic or Shui jing zhu).[6] Some have been translated into English and Vietnamese. The Chinese Text Project (https://ctext.org) and Chinese Notes (https://chinesenotes.com) also provide an excellent sources of references, in Chinese, and here Google Translate has been instrumental in aiding my undertaking.

Among these works the name of Văn Lang is mentioned but not of Hùng kings directly even though most historians agree Hùng kings are the same as Lạc kings.[7] An Dương Vương is also briefly included, and Âu Lạc is cited many times, but Zhao Tuo and Nan-yue feature most prominently. Beyond these sources there are some excellent books, both in Vietnamese and English, that cover this period. I have also used these to make cross references where needed.[8,9]

Similarly, I have checked some of the references against later Vietnamese works such as VSL, SKTT and CM (see below). Details of these references are described in Appendix 2.

For references on archaeological artefacts, I relied upon articles published in Vietnam Archaeology Journals and other relevant conference proceedings.[10]

Abbreviations

CM   Khâm Định[11] Việt Sử[12] Thông Giám Cương Mục[13] (CM) – *"The Imperially Ordered Annotated Text Completely Reflecting the History of Viet"*.[14]

LNCQ Lĩnh Nam Chích Quái (LNCQ), *"A Collection of Strange Stories from Linh Nam"*.[15]

Shiji (53) Memoir 53 or Chapter 113 of "The Grand Scribe's Records, Volume X: Volume X: The Memoirs of Han China, Part III".

SKTT Đại Việt Sử Ký Toàn Thư– or *"Complete Book of the Historical Records of Great Viet"*[16], a 15th-century Vietnamese work.[17]

TKCS Thủy Kinh Chú Sớ (*Additional Explanation of Commentary of the Water Classic or Shui jing zhu*).[18]

VSL   Việt Sử Lược (VSL), *"Abridged History of Viet"*.[19]

VSTA Việt Sử Tiêu Án. *"A Brief History of Viet"*.[20]

Below are further details of these sources in chronological order; the first four were compiled in the time period from 239 BCE to about 92 CE, which envelopes the period of An Dương Vương and Zhao Tuo (180 to 111 BCE) relevant to this book.

1. LÜSHI CHUNQIU or *"Master Lü's Spring and Autumn Annals"* is an encyclopaedic and classic Chinese text compiled around 239 BCE under the patronage of the Qin Dynasty Chancellor Lü Buwei.[21] The relevant reference is Chapter 117.[22]

2. HUAINANZI is an ancient Chinese text, a collection of essays that resulted from a series of scholarly debates held at the court of Liu An, Prince of Huainan, sometime before 139 BCE.[23] The relevant reference is Chapter 18.[24]

3. SHIJI or *"The Records of the Grand Historian"* or *"The Grand Scribe's Records"*, is a monumental history of ancient China, completed around 94

BC by the Han dynasty official Sima Qian, after having been initiated by his father, Sima Tan, Grand Astrologer to the imperial court.[25] The work covers the period from the legendary Yellow Emperor (2711-2598 BCE) to the reign of Emperor Wu of Han (141-87 BCE). There are several English translations of Shiji, the most recent and comprehensive volumes are eight volumes edited by William H. Nienhauser, Jr.; Volumes I, II, V, VII, VIII, IX, X (Memoirs 53 to 61), XI (Memoirs 45 to 52). For stories related to Vietnam, the relevant chapters are Memoirs 52[26] (or 112[27]), 53 (or 113)[28], 54 (or 114)[29] and 58 (or 118)[30], also Chapter 30[31], Chapter 41[32], Chapter 43[33], Chapter 97[34].

4. HAN SHU or *"Book of Former Han"* or *"History of the Han"* is a history of China, covering the Former, or Western Han dynasty from the first Emperor in 206 BCE to the fall of Wang Mang in 23 CE.[35] The work was composed by Ban Gu (32-92 CE), a Later Han court official. For stories related to Vietnam, the relevant volumes are 7[36], 28[37], 64[38] and 95 (or 65).[39]

5. HOU HAN SHU or *"Book of the Later Han"*, is one of the Twenty-Four Histories and covers the history of the Han dynasty from 6 to 189 CE, a period known as the Later or Later Han.[40] The book was compiled by Fan Ye and others in the 5th century. For stories related to Vietnam, the relevant volumes are Volume 14 (or 24).[41]

6. SHUI JING ZHU SHU (THỦY KINH CHÚ SỚ) is a additional explanation of the Shui Jing Zhu (*Commentary on the Water Classic*) compiled by Li Daoyuan during the Northern Wei Dynasty (386-534 CE).[42] Shui Jing Zhu is a work on the ancient geography of China, describing its waterways and ancient canals and is expanded from the source text, the older (and now lost) Shui Jing (*Water Classic*) written during the Three Kingdoms period (220-280). I use the Vietnamese translation of the 19th-century work, published in 1955.[43] It is a thick book (nearly one thousand pages) and the relevant volumes are Volumes 36 and 37.

APPENDIX 2

SOURCES OF VIETNAMESE HISTORY BY VIETNAMESE AUTHORS WRITTEN PRE-19TH CENTURY

Searching for books

Without history books, these tales could not be recounted. But for Vietnamese historians, finding old books is a tale in itself, sadly not a happy one. Reading the words Lê Quý Đôn (1726-1784) wrote in his book – what appears to be the first bibliography of Vietnamese literature (*Nghệ Văn Chí*) – is rather depressing for those of us who love and seek out books.[1] Lê Quý Đôn, a child prodigy, poet, historian, encyclopaedist, envoy to China, and prolific writer in the 18th century writes:

> "Our nation is called a civilised country (meaning a country with culture and books), from the king above, the mandarins below, together with the people, all write books. But now, gathering them together, there are barely one hundred copies."[2,3]

Further, he listed a total of 116 titles, of which ten were no longer in existence.[4] By contrast, in England at about the same time, one of the private collections had some 6,000 books.⁵ Of the 116 titles, only 19 were histories. He went on to lament the lack of libraries, agencies, or officials to collect and look after books and papers. He further commented on the sad fact that the scholars who studied for examinations would obtain what they needed for the tests and ignore any old books unrelated to the exam subjects. Those who were interested in old books would keep them for themselves and not share these around. *"Therefore, the business of finding books is very difficult."* ⁶ Lê Quý Đôn blamed the burning of the capital of Thăng Long (Hanoi) by the Chams in 1371, the pillage of books by the Chinese Ming dynasty in 1406, the rebellion of Trần Cảo in 1516, and the fires during the Lê and Trịnh times for the destruction and loss of books and official documents.⁷ In his time, books and other written forms were inscribed and copied by hand on papers. A few were printed from woodcuts, a technology the Vietnamese had used since the 12th century, but they were mostly Buddhist scriptures. It was not until 1697 that the first history work, SKTT, was produced by woodcut printing.⁸ These books were written in classical Chinese characters (*Chữ Nho* or *Chữ Hán*) that the northern rulers brought with them to Vietnam, or in *Chữ Nôm*, a logographic writing system the Vietnamese used, based on these characters to fit the Vietnamese language. Thus, the term Hán Nôm is used to represent the entire body of written materials produced in Vietnam prior to the adoption of *Chữ Quốc Ngữ* (National Language Script) as the current language of Vietnam. My grandfather (b. 1891) was educated in Hán Nôm (both *Chữ Nho and Chữ Nôm)*, my father (b. 1914) was educated in French and *Quốc Ngữ*; I was educated in just *Quốc Ngữ*.⁹

Fig. 69 shows a comparison and a timeline of three languages:

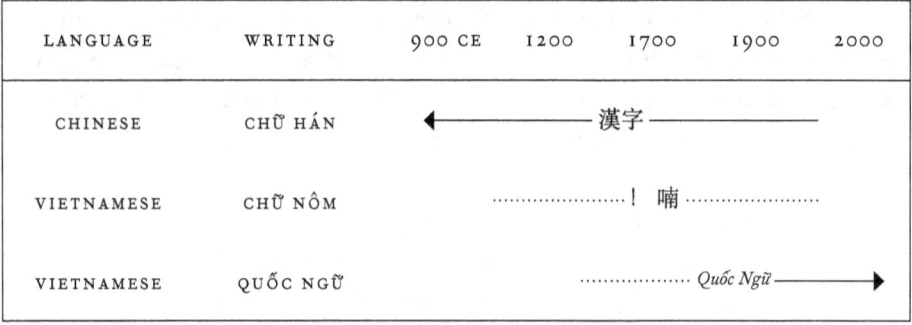

Figure 69 – Hán, Nôm and Quốc Ngữ (Vietnamese language) ¹⁰

The number of Hán Nôm books as recorded by scholar and historian Phan Huy Chú (1782-1840), about sixty years later, nearly doubled to 207.[11,12] In 1990, Trần reported a total of 429 books, of which 166 were history-related.[13] The sad state of affairs is vividly described by two French researchers, L. Cadière and P. Pelliot, during the French colonial time in their 1904 paper: *"Nowhere have we seen the intellectual heritage of a people dissolved with such rapidity."*[14] They attribute the causes to climate, wars, and less use of the printing press in Vietnam than in China, Japan, and Korea.

Fortunately, since the early 20th century, a great deal of effort has been made by local and foreign scholars to collect, restore, translate and maintain the surviving Hán Nôm works. In the 1960s, there was The Committee for the Translation of Vietnamese Historical Documents of Huế University in Huế.[15,16] In Ho Chi Minh City, there was the Hán Nôm Department of the Faculty of Literature established around the same time.[17] At the Vietnam National University, Hanoi, there is a Bachelor program in Hán Nôm. The main research, archival, and reference library of Hán Nôm documents is at the Institute of Hán Nôm Studies in Hanoi, established in 1979 through the Department of Hán Nôm Studies.[18].

As of 2004, its library had 20,000 Hán Nôm books[19], 20,000 Hán Nôm woodcuts and more than 48,000 Hán Nôm inscriptions on steles, headstones, bronze bells, chime stones[20] and wooden signs. The Institute acquired these items from state and private collections by donation and exchange, and also the transfer of resources from the l'Ecole française d'Extrême-Orient in 1980, notably the Catalogue Des Livres en Han Nom.[21] There is also a Catalogue of Vietnamese Inscriptions.[22] However, according to Chu, the documents of Nôm script at the Institute are very modest, totalling 1,559 titles including those written in Nôm script, in a mixture of Hán and Nôm and those in Hán but written in Nôm.

The state of the Sanskrit and old-Cham inscriptions on steles is just as sad, where around two hundred steles were discovered and catalogued, with less than one hundred translated.[23]

History books by Vietnamese authors before the 19th century

The primary sources for early Vietnamese history were compiled by Chinese authors. Vietnamese historical works first appeared in the 12th century CE (by Đỗ Thiện), over a thousand years later, and the writers of these texts refer to the same Chinese sources for the earlier period of Vietnamese history.

However, they do include records from local temples and pagodas that were not included in Chinese sources, offer explanations, make notes and express their views. I have found these helpful in collecting material for this book. The lists below are key documents in chronological order.

1. *Đại Việt Sử Ký* (History of the Great Việt)

    This book is now lost. It is considered by some to be the first history book by a Vietnamese historian, written by Lê Văn Hưu (1230-1322) in 1272. Lê Văn Hưu is a foremost Vietnamese historian with many streets in the country named after him. In 1964, a team from the local and central museums preservation bureau found his tomb and a record of his family genealogy.[24] He was born in 1230 in Đông Sơn district, Thanh Hóa province. By coincidence, this is also the same district where the first Đông Sơn bronze drum was found. In 1247, at the age of seventeen, he sat the national examination and took the second title of the three top positions: Trạng Nguyên, Bảng Nhãn and Thám Hoa. He completed the Đại Việt Sử Ký twenty-five years later in 1272. His original work no longer exists but is considered by historians to be absorbed into SKTT.

    There were also contemporary history works but most were lost. Historians have since been debating the relationships between them. There were *Sử ký* (History) by Đỗ Thiện in about 1127, *Việt Chí* (Annals of Viet) by Trần Tấn (or Trần Phổ or Trần Chu Phổ) about 1233 and *Đại Việt Sử Lược* (Abridged history of Dai Viet) or *Việt Sử Lược* (VSL) by an unknown author (s) in 1377-1388. There is some speculation that the author of VSL is Hồ Tông Thốc, an official during the reign of King Trần Nghệ Tông (1370-1372), the author of *Việt Sử Cương Mục* (An Outline of the Viet History) and *Việt Nam Thế Chí*. Both works were lost at the time Ngô Sỹ Liên compiled SKTT in 1479.

2. *An Nam Chí Lược* (ANCL) (Abridged Annals of An Nam).[25]

    There was another book no Vietnamese historian wanted to mention until the 20th century, even though it was available in China with copies in the British Museum (1750), Japan (1884), and France (1896).[26] The reason is simply that it was written by a figure who surrendered to the Mongols (under their rule of China as the Yuan dynasty) during their second invasion of northern Vietnam in 1285. He escaped to China when the Mongols retreated, but returned with them in their third invasion in 1287. When the Mongols were defeated a third time, Lê Tắc (1263-1342), the author of the book in question, barely escaped with his life en route back to China, and lived there until his final days. As late as 1939, writer Trần Thanh Mại wrote in Tao Đàn, a literature, culture, and art magazine published in Hanoi in 1939, of Lê Tắc and An Nam Chí Lược as *"A history writer who sold out his country, an infamous book."* [27]

There were 20 different introductions to his book, with the one dated 1307 the earliest and the one dated 1884 the latest. He also wrote his own introduction in 1333. Therefore, it appears that Lê Tắc wrote his book soon after he escaped from Đại Việt (Vietnam was called Đại Việt at the time) and settled in China in 1292. His book covers the period from Zhao Tuo of Nan-yue to the time he fled Đại Việt, at the end of the 13th century.

Lê Tắc's family came from Ái Châu (Thanh Hóa, Nghệ An provinces) and was, by his own account, a child prodigy *"Taught to study, sat the exam for child prodigies at the age of nine."* [28]

3. *Việt Điện U Linh* (VDUL) (Compilation of the Departed Spirits in the Realm of Viet). [29]

VDUL was written by Lý Tế Xuyên, an official (possibly a librarian) during the reign of King Trần Hiến Tông (1329-1341). The preface of the book as written by him is dated 1329.[30] Lý Tế Xuyên made a number of references to two books[31] now lost, *Giao Châu Ký* [32] *(Records of Jiaozhou)* written by Zhao Chang (Triệu Vương or Triệu Xương)[33] and *Giao Chỉ Ký (Records of Jiaozhi)*[34] written by Zeng Gun (Tăng Công or Tăng Cổn).[35] It is a little confusing as SKTT refers to this book written by Zeng Gun as *Giao Châu Ký* but made no reference to any book written by Triệu Vương.[36]

Zhao Chang was the Protector General (*duhu*) of An Nam (previously Giao Chỉ) twice in 791-802 and 804-806; Zeng Gun was the Military Governor (*jiedushi*) of An Nam in 878-880 under the Tang dynasty.

The title of *Giao Châu Ký* appeared under different authors, Diêu Văn Thức of the Later Han (25-220), Đặng Trung Phẩu, Lưu Hân Kỳ of the Jin (265-420), Lưu Trường Chi of the Liu Song (420-479) and Zeng Gun of Tang (618-906). All were lost except for a few pages by Lưu Hân Kỳ that was found.[37] VDUL did not mention other authors except Zeng Gun for *Giao Chỉ Ký*.

4. *Việt Sử Lược* (VSL) (An Abridged History of Viet). [38]

The original book is titled Đại Việt Sử Lược (An Abridged History of Great Viet) and was written by an unknown author(s) in around 1377. This was lost until a copy was found in the collection of Siku Quanshu[39] or the Chinese "Complete Library of the Four Treasures"[40], during the Qianlong Emperor of the Qing dynasty (1736-1795), over 350 years later. It was printed in China under the name of Việt Sử Lược (An Abridged History of Viet) (VSL) with the word Đại (or Great) removed.
VSL covers the period from the Hùng kings to the final king of the Lý dynasty in 1225 with a list of the kings in the Trần dynasty until 1377.

While Vũ Quỳnh (1452-1516), a scholar-official during the Lê dynasty, was contributing to SKTT, he and Kiều Phú also restored and edited:

5. *Lĩnh Nam Chích Quái* (LNCQ) (A Collection of Strange Stories from Lingnan)[41]

Attributed to Trần Thế Pháp, a book of a similar genre to VDUL. Of its publication in 1492 he wrote in a preface:

"Not far from ancient times, the customs of the southern country were simple, there was no national history book (Bureau of History) *to record so many stories were lost. Fortunately, there were others not lost as they were told and retold by the common people."*

Vũ Quỳnh suggests the original author was in the Lý (1009-1225) and Trần dynasties (1225-1400).[42] However, in terms of history books, the most important document is:

6. *Đại Việt Sử Ký Toàn Thư* (SKTT)[43] (Complete Book of the Historical Records of Great Viet).

This book was originally written in Han characters and compiled by Ngô Sỹ Liên in 1479, as an effort by the scholars at the time to replace the books lost during the Ming occupation. In 1981[44] the oldest version of the book was found by Phan Huy Lê, a Vietnamese historian and a descendant of Phan Huy Chú, at the library of the Société Asiatique in Paris, France. This version, termed Chính Hòa, was printed from woodcuts in 1697.[45] At that time, there were seven other versions in

Vietnam but none was as old.⁴⁶ The find prompted such excitement among the Vietnamese historians that they immediately formed a committee to translate it into Vietnamese. The first volume of SKTT was published in 1983; Vol. II followed in 1985, and it was reprinted in 1992 together with Vol. III and IV.⁴⁷

SKTT covers the history of Vietnam from the time of Hùng kings to 1675. Phan considers SKTT the *"mother book"* embodied in other *"children"* history volumes produced previously; from Đại Việt Sử Ký to the final complete works by Lê Hy in 1697, a period that span 425 years.

Other historians worked on SKTT over this period, including Ngô Sĩ Liên, who initiated the compilation in 1479, based on the work by Lê Văn Hưu, Phan Phu Tiên (1455). Vũ Quỳnh and Lê Tung made their contributions in 1509 and 1554. Phạm Công Trứ followed in 1665 and Lê Hy and his team of twelve contributors complete the work in 1697. Other than Lê Văn Hưu's, the *"children"* books also include Ngô Sỹ Liên's first version of *Đại Việt Sử Ký Toàn Thư* and *Tam Triều bản Kỷ* (Records of the Three Reigns), Phan Phu Tiên's *Sử ký Tục Biên* (or *Đại Việt Sử Ký Tục Biên*) (Continuation of the History of Great Viet) or *Quốc sử biên lục* (1455), Vũ Quỳnh's (1452-1516) *Đại Việt Thông Giám Thông Khảo* (or *Việt Giám Thông Khảo*) (Complete Study of the History of Viet)(1511), *Tứ Triều Bản Kỷ* (Records of the Four Reigns), Phạm Công Trứ 's *Bản Kỷ Tục Biên (or Việt Sử Toàn Thư Bản Kỷ Tục Biên)* (1655) Lê Tung's *Đại Việt Thông Giám Tổng Luận* and Lê Hy's *Bản Kỷ Tục Biên (or Sử ký tục biên) (1697)*.

7. *Việt Sử Tiêu Án* (VSTA) (1775) (A Brief History of Việt).⁴⁸

VSTA covers the period from the Hùng kings to 1428.

8. Khâm Định Việt Sử Thông Giám Cương Mục (CM) (The Imperially Ordered Annotated Text Completely Reflecting the History of Viet).⁴⁹

This book was edited by Grand Chancellor Phan Thanh Giản (1796-1867) and first printed by the Bureau of History of the Nguyen Dynasty (*Quốc Sử Quán Triều Nguyễn*) in 1884, covering the period from the Hùng kings to the last king of the Lê dynasty in 1789. This Bureau produced many books in classical Chinese language from 1821 until 1945.

APPENDIX 3

NAMES IN VIETNAMESE, PINYIN CHINESE AND ENGLISH

APPENDIX 3

VIETNAMESE	PINYIN CHINESE	ENGLISH
1. ADMINISTRATIVE UNITS (UNDER QIN AND HAN)		
Bộ	Zhōu	Circuit (or Province)
Quận	Jùn	Commandery
Huyện	Hien, Xiàn	Prefecture (or District, County)
2. DYNASTIES		
Ân	Shang or Yin	
Chu	Zhou	
Đông Hán		Eastern Han
Đường	Tang	
Hạ	Xia	
Lương	Liang	
Minh	Ming	
Ngô	Wu	
Nguyên	Yuan	
Nguy	Wei	
Sở	Chu	
Tần	Qin	
Tấn	Jin	
Tây Hán		Western Han
Tề	Qi	
Thanh	Qing	
Thương	Shang or Yin	
Tống	Song	
Triệu	Zhao	
Tùy	Sui	
Yên	Yan	
3. HISTORICAL WORKS / DESCRIPTIONS		
Chí		Annals
Chính Biên		Principal
Cương		Sketch, general, summary[1]
Ký		Records
Hán Thư	Han shu	
Hậu Hán Thư	Hou Han shu	
Hoài Nam Tử	Huainanzi	

VIETNAMESE	PINYIN CHINESE	ENGLISH
Lã Thị Xuân Thu	Lüshi Chunqiu	
Lược		Summary, abridged, annotated
Lục		Records, copies
Mục		Details expanded from "Cương"
Sử Ký	Shiji	
Thông		Complete
Thực (Thật) lục		Veritable records
Thủy Kinh Chú Sớ	Shuijing zhu shi	
Tiền Biên		Prequel
Tục Biên		Sequel

4. LOCATIONS

VIETNAMESE	PINYIN CHINESE
An Huy	Anhui
Ba Thục	Ba Shu
Chân Định	Zhengding
Châu Nhai	Zhuya
Chiết Giang	Zhejiang
Cửu Chân	Jiuzhen
Đam Nhĩ	Dan'er
Dạ Lang	Yelang
Dự Chương	Yuzhang
Dương Sơn	Yang-san
Giang Tây	Jiangxi
Giao Châu	Jiaozhou
Giao Chỉ	Jiaozhi
Hà Nam	Henan
Hồ Bắc	Hubei
Hồ Nam	Hunan
Hợp Phố	Hepu
Hoành Phố	Heng-pu
Hoàng Khê	Huang-hsi
Lạc Dương	Luoyang, capital of Latter Han
Lâm Lư	Lung-lu
Lĩnh Nam	Lingnan
Linh Cừ	Lingqu
Linh Lăng	Lingling
Lục Lương	Luliang

APPENDIX 3

VIETNAMESE	PINYIN CHINESE	ENGLISH
Luy Lâu	Leilou	
Nam Hải	Nanhai	
Nam Ninh	Nanning	
Nhật Nam	Rinan	
Phiên Ngung	Panyu	
Phủ Châu	Fuzhou	
Phúc Kiến	Fujian	
Quảng Châu	Guangzhou	
Quảng Đông	Guangdong	
Quảng Tây	Guangxi	
Quế Dương	Guiyang	
Quế Lâm (under Qin) and Uất Lâm (under Han)[2]	Guilin	
Quý Châu	Guizhou	
Tây An	Xi'an	
Thạc Môn	Shih-men	
Thành Đô	Chengdu	
Thương Ngô	Cangwu	
Thiệu Hưng	Shaoxing	
Thượng Hải	Shanghai	
Trường An	Chang'an, capital of Former Han	
Trường Sa	Changsa	
Tứ Xuyên	Sichuan	
Tượng Quận	Xiang	
Vân Nam	Yunnan	
Vũ Hán	Wuhan	
Yết Dương	Jiejang	

5. OFFICIAL TITLES

Đô Úy	Duwei	Commandant
Hạ Lại Tướng Quân	Xia Lai Jiangjun	General Who Brings Down Severity/General for Descending the Rapids
Hầu	Hou	Marquis
Lâu Thuyền Tướng Quân	Lou Chuan Jiangjun	General of Tower Ships
Phục Ba Tướng Quân	Fubo Jiangjun	Water Calming General
Qua Thuyền Tướng Quân	Ge Jiangjun	General of the Pole-ax ships

VIETNAMESE	PINYIN CHINESE	ENGLISH
Thái Thú	Taishou	Governor
Thứ Sử	Cishi	Inspector or Regional Inspector
Trì Nghĩa Hầu	Zhi (Ch'ih-yi) Hou	Marquis Who Gallops To Duty

6. PEOPLE

VIETNAMESE	PINYIN CHINESE
An Quốc Thiếu Quý	Anguo Shaoji
Cù Thị (Cù Hậu)	Jiu Shi
Chu Táo	Zhou Zao (Chou Tsao)
Dịch Hu Tống	Yi Song (I Hsi Sung)
Đô Khê	Du Ji (or Tu Chi) or Sun Tu or Sun Du
Đồ Thư	Tu Sui
Dương Bộc	Yang Pu
(Hán) Cao Hoàng Đế	Emperor Gaozu of Han
(Hán) Văn Hoàng Đế	Emperor Wen of Han
Hạng Vũ	Xiang Yu
Hoàng Đồng	Huang Tong
Lộ Bá Đức	Lu Bode
Lữ Hậu (Hán Cao Hậu)	Lu Zhi
Lữ Gia	Lu Jia
Lưu Bang	Liu Bang
Mã Viện	Ma Yuan
Nhâm Hưu (Nhâm Ngao)	Ren Xiao
Tần Thủy Hoàng	Qin Shi Huang
Tô Hoằng	Su Hung (or Su Hong)
Triệu Anh Tề (Minh Vương)	Zhao Yingqi
Triệu Đà	Zhao Tuo
Triệu Hưng (Ai Vương)	Zhao Xing
Triệu Hồ (Văn Vương)	Zhao Hu (or Zhao Mo)
Triệu Kiến Đức (Thuật Dương Vương)	Zhao Jiande
Trần Thắng	Chen Sheng
Tư Mã Thiên	Sima Qian
Việt Câu Tiễn	Goujian
Viêm Đế Thần Nông	Shen Nung
Vũ Đế	Wudi

VIETNAMESE	PINYIN CHINESE	ENGLISH
7. RIVERS MOUNTAINS AND LAKES		
Bá Dương (hồ)	Poyang lake	
Cô Tô (núi)	Mt. Gusu	
Cối Khê (núi)	Mt. Kuaiji	
Đại Dữu (or Đại Dũ) (núi)	Mt. Dayu	
Đỗ Bang (núi)	Mt. Dupang	
Động Đình (hồ)	Dongting lake	
Dương Tử (sông)	Yangtze or Yangzi	
Hoàng Hà (sông)	Huang He	Yellow river
Hữu Giang (sông)	Youjiang	
Kỳ Điền (núi)	Mt. Qitian	
Minh (or Manh) Chử or Cửu Nghi) (núi)	Mt. Mengzhu	
Ngũ Lĩnh (núi)	Wuling or Nanling mountains	
Tả Giang (sông)	Zuo Jiang	
Tín Giang (or Dư Can or Dư Hãn) (sông)	Xinjiang – Yugan is a county	
Việt Thành (or Đàm Thành) (núi)[3]	Mt. Yuechengling	
Vũ Di (núi)	Mt. Wuyi	
8. STATES, KINGDOMS		
Âu Lạc	Ou Luo	
Bách Việt	Bai-yue	A hundred Viet
Chiêm Thành	Zhancheng	Champa
Dạ Lang	Yelang	
Điền	Dian	
Đông Âu	Dong-ou	
Lạc Việt	Luo-yue	
Lâm Ấp	Linyi	
Mân Việt	Min-yue	
Nam Việt	Nan-yue	
Tây Âu	Xi-ou	
Việt	Yue	

APPENDIX 4

VIETNAMESE URBAN AND RURAL DISTRICTS (QUẬN AND HUYỆN)

In administrative terms, Vietnam is divided into provinces (*Tỉnh*), and each with a city (*Thành Phố*) as an administration centre. Generally speaking, the borders between the provinces are the rivers or mountain ranges. The province is further divided into a number of districts (*Quận, Thị Xã, Huyện*); below the district level is the lowest official administration unit, called commune or ward (*Phường, Xã, Thị Trấn*), below this is another level entitled hamlet (*Làng, Thôn, Ấp, Xóm, Bản, Buôn, Sóc*).

The five cities of Hanoi, Hải Phòng in the north, Đà Nẵng in the central, Hồ Chí Minh City and Cần Thơ in the south are administratively equivalent to provinces; they report directly to the central government. The names of the province and the administration city are generally different but not always, thus Quy Nhơn is the administrative centre of Bình Định province but Thanh Hóa city and its province have the same name. *Quận* under the Northern rule period has different meanings (see Appendix 3). For example, Vietnamese historians translate Commandery *Cửu Chân* as *Quận Cửu Chân*; in modern terms there is no equivalent administrative unit to a commandery, *Cửu Chân* would include three provinces of Thanh Hóa, Nghệ An and Hà Tĩnh. There also is no equivalent of a circuit (or *Châu*).

APPENDIX 4

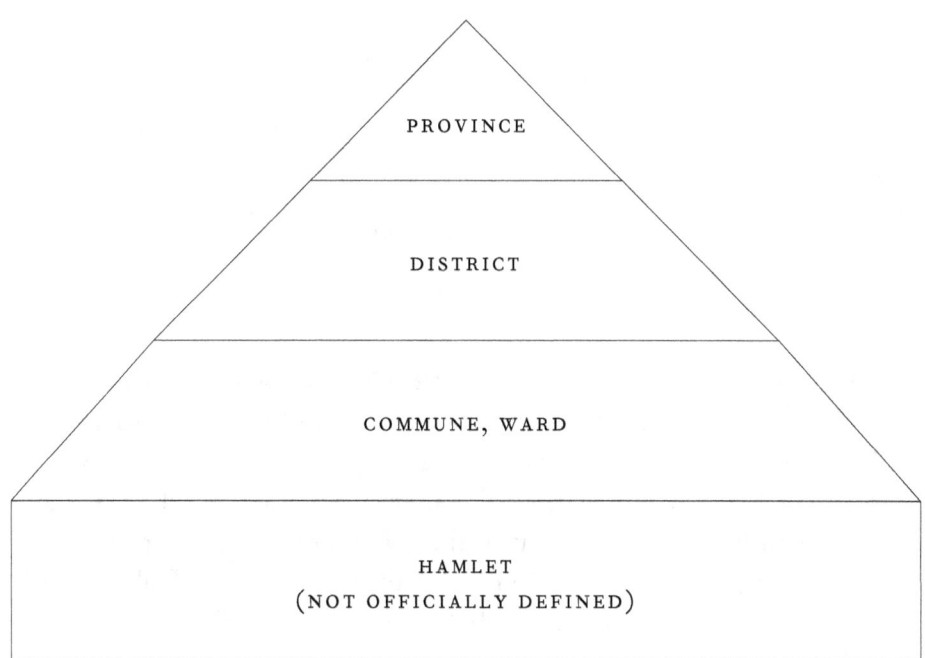

Figure 70 – Administration units in modern Vietnam

APPENDIX 5

THE KINGDOM OF VĂN LANG

The Hùng kings ruled over a kingdom called Văn Lang with 15 counties entitled by slightly different names by different historical works, as listed below.

It is interesting to note that while VSL, compiled in the 14th century, listed two prefectures located in contemporary southern China, by the time CM was published in the 19th century, there were none. VSL refers to these as tribes (*bộ lạc*) not prefectures. In LNCQ, they are called *"bộ"*, also *"quận"*. SKTT and CM also refer to them as *"bộ"*. Unless these works meant *bộ* as a short description of *bộ lạc*, *"bộ"* normally means "circuit" which suggests a very large region and is thus incorrect. *"Quận"* means county or prefecture would be a more accurate description. Note also the boundary description does not match the counties in all four works.

Some of the names in VSL were from the Han times (202 BCE-220 CE) but others were from the Jin (266-420), and a few from the Tang dynasty (618-907) periods. For a more detailed discussion of these names, refer to Đào.[5] For example, Gia Ninh was renamed under the Tang dynasty and located at the southwest of Vĩnh Phú (Vĩnh Phúc) province, including Việt Trì.[6]

Reference was also made to the ancient kingdom of Ye-lang in Guizhou province of China, in relation to Văn Lang, but the subject has attracted little scholarly interest.[7] The main reason being that Ye-lang was in a remote mountainous region in southern China (see Fig. 13), too far north of Vietnam to play any significant role in its history in the years following the Hùng kings.

VSL (14th century)	LNCQ (15th century)	SKTT (17th century)	CM (19th century)
BOUNDARY DESCRIPTION			
	East to of Nam Hải, West to Ba Shu, South to Hồ Tôn, North to Dongting lake.[1]	East to the sea of Nam Hải, West to Ba Shu, South to Hồ Tôn, North to Dongting lake.[2]	East to the sea of Nam Hải, West to Ba Shu, South to Hồ Tôn, North to Dongting lake.[3]
PREFECTURE			
Giao Chỉ	Giao Chỉ	Giao Chỉ	Giao Chỉ
Việt Thường thị	Việt Thường	Việt Thường	Việt Thường
Vũ Ninh	Vũ Ninh	Vũ Ninh	Vũ Ninh
Quận Ninh			
Gia Ninh			
Ninh Hải	Ninh Hải	Ninh Hải	Ninh Hải
Lục Hải	Lục Hải	Lục Hải	Lục Hải
Dương Tuyền	Dương Tuyền	Dương Tuyền	Dương Tuyền
Tân Xương			
Bình Văn		Bình Văn	Bình Văn
Văn Lang	Văn Lang		Văn Lang
Cửu Chân	Cửu Chân	Cửu Chân	Cửu Chân
Nhật Nam	Nhật Nam	Nhật Nam	
Hoài Hoan	Hoài Hoan	Hoài Hoan	Hoài Hoan
Cửu Đức		Cửu Đức	Cửu Đức
	Chân Định	Vũ Định	Vũ Định
	Quế Lâm	Tân Hưng	Tân Hưng
	Tượng Quận		
	Chu Diên	Chu Diên	Chu Diên
	Phúc Lộc	Phúc Lộc	Phúc Lộc
COUNTIES IN SOUTHERN CHINA FROM THE ABOVE LIST			
Ninh Hải (today Qinzhou) and Dương Tuyền (or Thang Tuyền is a place near Nanning).[4]	Quế Lâm (today Guilin, but translators also included Cangwu county and Liujiang district of Liuzhou, all are in Guangxi province) Tượng Quận was the Xiang commandery under the Qin.	None	None, Ninh Hải is Quảng Ninh and Dương Tuyền is Hải Dương.

Figure 71 – List of prefectures under the kingdom of Văn Lang by different sources

APPENDIX 6

OTHER VIEWS OF VIỆT AND YUE

Đào suggests that the Yue people came to northern Vietnam by sea from a port somewhere along the Chinese coast, south of the Yangtze river.[1] These people called themselves Luo-yue with "Lạc" (Lo or Luo) is the name of a migratory bird they saw on their way south. They then created the image of the same bird on the bronze drums. The Luo-yue people settled in the Red River Delta, intermingled with the local tribes and became the ancestors of the Vietnamese.

I do not necessarily agree with this view; the bird image is more likely to be the local "*con cò* or little egret" (see 7.7.3) as it best matches the real and living little egret, and not birds of legend.[2] Furthermore, the fact that the indigenous people who lived in the Red River Delta were referred to as "*Lạc Việt*", or Luo-yue in ancient texts, does not suggest that their ancestors came from the Yue state in Zhejiang province, some 2,300 kilometres north. Kiều is also of the same view. After a detailed analysis, he concludes.

> "*In terms of ethnicity, the Lạc Việt people are not descendants of the Xian or migrants from King Goujian's times … But the Lạc Việt race was formed by the ancestors of the indigenous people.*"[3,4]

APPENDIX 6

This view, and not that of Đào, whose findings above formed my education at school, is now the accepted view of Vietnamese historians.

Are the Yue the ancestors of the modern Vietnamese? Taylor does not think so:

> *"The current population of Vietnam is more likely to have stemmed from the regions around modern-day Vietnam itself than from the old Yue regions of China."* [5]

Brindley holds that,

> *"The ancient Yue were also likely to have played a significant role in the shape of early Vietnamese history. This is especially the case since the very concept of the Viet peoples and cultures was eventually absorbed by the people of the Red river region and so, at the very least, the Yue played a significant role in the imagined creation of Vietnamese identity."* [6]

Historian Nguyễn Khắc Viện is more definite in his view, and more aligned with Taylor;

> *"The well-established and crucial fact is that towards the end of the 1st millennium BC, there appeared a unique and vigorous civilization, especially in the deltas and surroundings areas, which was soon to be confronted by a decisive challenge: confrontation with Chinese feudal expansion."* [7]

Historian Liam Kelly's view is that,

> *"The stories in LNCQ are not accounts that were passed orally and then recorded by a member, or members, of the elite in the fifteenth century. Instead, it is more likely that these tales were largely created in the fifteenth century."* [8]

I do not necessarily agree with Kelly, I would suggest that the author of LNCQ combined local oral folklore with stories copied or modified from Chinese texts and other stories passed down from the northern newcomers who settled in the Red River Delta as part of the Qin expedition forces in the 3rd century BCE.[9] After all, they made it clear that their book told the stories south of the Nanling mountains, not only tales from northern Vietnam.

APPENDIX 7

OF STONE AXES AND POTTERY JARS

Archaeologists use a number of methods to divide history into several periods, one of the more commonly applied is the three-age system: Stone Age, Bronze Age, and Iron Age in chronological order. The Stone Age is further divided into Paleolithic (Old Stone Age), Mesolithic, and Neolithic (New Stone Age). Tools were made from pebbles or stones during the entirety of the stone age but pottery generally did not appear until the Neolithic period. Some Vietnamese archaeologists only use the terms Paleolithic and Neolithic. The table below shows a summary of the different sites excavated in Vietnam, classified at different ages, and commonly displayed in Vietnamese museums.[1]

a. BP = before present, where present is AD 1950. To convert BCE to BP, simply add 1950, e.g. 700 BCE is 2,650 BP. Similarly, 4,500 BP is 2,650 BCE.
b. Dates taken from Nguyễn.[3]
c. Dates taken from Nguyễn et al.[4]
d. Dates taken from Moser, in another reference, the dates are given as 18,000 – 7,500 BP (see notes b).[5]
e. Dates taken from Nguyễn.[6]
f. Dates taken from Hung.[7]
g. Dates taken from Hà.[8]
h. Dates taken from Đặng.[9]

APPENDIX 7

SITES	LOCATION	PERIOD
PALEOLITHIC AGE		
Thẩm Khuyên cave [b]	Tô Hiệu, Bình Gia, Lạng Sơn	534,000 ± 87,000 BP [a] – 401,000 ± 51,000 BP
Núi Đọ (Mount Đọ) [c]	Dinh Xá, Thiệu Khánh, Thanh Hóa	40,000 – 30,000 BCE
Ngườm rock arch (or shelter) [2,b]	Kim Sơn, Võ Nhai, Thái Nguyên,	23,000 – 18,000 BP
Sơn Vi [b]	Lâm Thao, Phú Thọ	30,000 – 10,000 BP
NEOLITHIC AGE		
Hòa Bình [d]	Hòa Bình	30,000 – 6,000 BP
Bắc Sơn [e]	Bắc Sơn, Lạng Sơn	10,000 – 7,000 BP
Quỳnh Văn [b]	Quỳnh Lưu, Nghệ An	6,000 – 3,500 BP
Đa Bút [b]	Vĩnh Lộc, Thanh Hóa	6,500 – 4,500 BP
BRONZE AGE		
Phùng Nguyên [f]	Phùng Nguyên, Lâm Thao, Phú Thọ	2,000 – 1,500 BCE
Đồng Đậu [f]	Yên Lạc, Vĩnh Phúc	1,500 – 1,100 BCE
Gò Mun [f]	Phong Châu, Phú Thọ	1,100 – 700 BCE
Đông Sơn [f]	Đông Sơn, Hàm Rồng, Thanh Hóa	700 BCE to 200 CE
IRON AGE		
Sa Huỳnh [f]	Đức Phổ, Quảng Ngãi	500 BCE to 100 CE
Óc Eo [g]	Thoại Sơn, An Giang	2nd century BCE – 12th century CE

APPENDIX 8

THE PREFECTURE OF TÂY VU

It should be noted that Western Ou and Luo appear as two different kingdoms in Shiji (53), (see 11.11.4); the translator of Shiji suggests Luo is the same as An Dương Vương's Âu Lạc and located in the Red River Delta.[1] In Han shu, Western Ou is mentioned (see 11.11.2) but not Luo. Ou Luo appears in another passage in Han shu related to the beheading of the king of Tây Vu.[2] Other historians believe Western Ou is Âu in Âu Lạc.[3,4]

Tây Vu was a prefecture under Han times, which included the provinces of Bắc Ninh, Bắc Giang, Thái Nguyên and Vĩnh Yên, north of Đuống and Red river.[5] The historical event surrounding the beheading of its king by the Left-General Hoàng Đồng of Âu Lạc, as mentioned in Han shu, has been given special status as the first rebellion against the northern rulers.[6] This event is described by historian Henri Maspero as a local lord, king of Tây Vu, taking advantage of the final days of Nan-yue in 110/111 BCE (see 11.11.3) to declare independence; however he was beheaded by Hoàng Đồng.[7] My checking of the original references of Shiji and Han shu indicate this event may have happened elsewhere and at a different time.
In Shiji, it is included in Table 20, *"Yearly table of the officials who became*

Marquises since the Jianyuan period", where Jianyuan was the reign period of Emperor Wu of Han from 140-135 BCE, or over 25 years before it was supposed to happen.[8] The record in Han shu, Chronological table 17, *"Table of meritorious officials during the reigns of (Emperors) Jing, Wu, Zhao, Xuan, Yuan and Cheng"* also mentions Hoàng Đồng was given the title of Marquis for 700 households, which would be very small for an area as large as Tây Vu.[9] In 43, Han general Ma Yuan reported Tây Vu had 32,000 hearths and he sought to divide it into two sub-prefectures.[10]

Kiều is even more definite. Based on the similar pronunciation of Ou (Vietnamese Âu) and Vietnamese Vu, the author believed Western Ou to be the same as Western Vu (Tây Vu). If true, this is where the Lord of Western Ou was killed by Qin forces, as noted in Shiji (see 10.10.1), an early event in the war. But in my view, this event could not have happened at Tây Vu given it would require Qin forces to progress another 350 kilometres (the approximate distance from Nanning) all the way to Cổ Loa, the seat of Tây Vu. To advance that distance against fierce opposition by the Yue, this event, if it happened at all, would have taken place later in the war. Furthermore, it is already established that Qin soldiers were unlikely to advance into north Vietnam (see 12.12.2).

ENDNOTES

ENDNOTES

PREFACE

1. Ngô Sĩ Liên. (1998). *Đại Việt Sử Ký Toàn Thư* Khoa Học Xã Hội (Social Science) (1998). (Chính Hòa version (1697).)
2. Vũ, D. M., Trần, T. V., Tạ, N. L., Trương, T. Y., Võ, K. C., Tạ, T. T., Đinh, T. T. C., Nguyễn, V. N., Trần, Đ. C., Nguyễn, N. M., & Viện Sử Học. (2017). *Lịch sử Việt Nam* (Vũ Duy Miên, Ed.). NXB Khoa Học Xã Hội.
3. Trần, T. K. (1999). *Việt Nam Sử Lược*. Văn Hóa Thông Tin. (1921)
4. Phan, H. L. (2018). *Di sản văn hóa Việt Nam dưới góc nhìn lịch sử*. NXB Đại Học Quốc Gia Hà Nội.
5. Phan, H. L. (2018). *Lịch sử và văn hóa Việt Nam tiếp cận bộ phận* (P. T. Phan, Ed. 4th ed.). NXB Đại Học Quốc Gia Hà Nội.
6. Tana, L. (2002). *Nguyễn Cochinchina: southern Vietnam in the seventeenth and eighteenth centuries* (Second ed.). Southeast Asia Program Publications.
7. Hà, V. T. (2018). *The making of Việt Nam*. Thế Giới.
8. Taylor, K. W. (1983). *The Birth of Vietnam*. Berkeley : University of California Press.
9. Taylor, K. W. (2014). *A History of the Vietnamese*. Cambridge University Press.
10. Vu, H. L., & Sharrock, P. D. (2014). *Descending dragon, rising tiger: a history of Vietnam*.
11. While the Linyi rebellion started at the end of the 2nd century, the Jin dynasty did not move the border north of Ngang pass, albeit temporarily, until around the 3rd century. See Đào, D. A. (2006). *Lịch sử Việt Nam - Từ nguồn gốc đến thế kỷ XIX*. NXB Văn Hóa Thông Tin. (1957), p. 116, p. 122.
12. Taylor, K. W. (1983). *The Birth of Vietnam*. Berkeley : University of California Press. , p. 117. Đào, D. A. (2005). *Đất nước Việt Nam qua các đời - Nghiên cứu địa lý học lịch sử Việt Nam*. NXB Văn Hóa Thông Tin. , p. 106.

CHAPTER I

1. Sometime in the early 19th century, Nguyễn Thị Hinh, better known as Bà Huyện Thanh Quan, or "Lady of the Chief of Thanh Quan District" in Thái Bình province, south-east of Hanoi, arrived at Đèo Ngang on her way to Huế, the imperial capital of Vietnam at that time. She had been invited by King Minh Mạng to come south to teach the princesses and the king's concubines. She was a well-known poet among the northern literati and certainly well-educated, which would have been very unusual during a time when women were discouraged from studying. Stopping by Ngang pass, she composed this poem, Traversing Ngang pass (*Qua Đèo Ngang*) as translated above.

Bước tới Đèo Ngang, bóng xế tà,
Cỏ cây chen đá, lá chen hoa.
Lom khom dưới núi, tiều vài chú
Lác đác bên sông, chợ mấy nhà.
Nhớ nước đau lòng, con quốc quốc,
Thương nhà mỏi miệng, cái gia gia.
Dừng chân đứng lại trời, non, nước,
Một mảnh tình riêng, ta với ta.

The "Old country" was northern Vietnam under the Lê dynasty. The water hens make the sound "*Quốc quốc*", while "*Gia gia*" is "Chim đa đa", a Chinese francolin. Bà Huyện Thanh Quan returned to the north after her husband died in the mid-19th century, and died in her early forties in her hometown of Nghi Tàm, near the West Lake of Hanoi. Sadly, she only left about eight wonderful poems and her grave is now lost. Refer to Vũ, V. L. (2008). *Tìm về nơi an nghỉ cuối cùng của các nữ sĩ Đoàn Thị Điểm, Hồ Xuân Hương và Bà Huyện Thanh Quan*. http://antg.cand.com.vn/Tu-lieu-antg/Tim-ve-noi-an-nghi-cuoi-cung-cua-cac-nu-si-Doan-Thi-Diem-Ho-Xuan-Huong-va-Ba-Huyen-Thanh-Quan-292394/.

2. General Statistics Office of Viet Nam. (2018). *Land use (As of 31 February 2017) by Type of land and Use - Number of administrative units as of 31 December by provinces by Cities, provinces, Years and Administrative units (2018)*. https://www.gso.gov.vn/default_en.aspx?tabid=773

3. FAO. (2011). *AQUASTAT Country Profile – Viet Nam*. http://www.fao.org/3/ca0412en/CA0412EN.pdf, p. 4.

4. Map edited by author based on map created by Sadalmelik - Public domain. (2007). *Topographic map of Vietnam. Created with GMT from publicly released GLOBE data*. https://commons.wikimedia.org/wiki/File:Vietnam_Topography.png

5. Reinecke, A. (2012). *Insights into the archaeological research of Vietnam - Những góc nhìn về nghiên cứu khảo cổ học Việt Nam*. Perspectives on the Archaeology of Vietnam, International Colloquium, Hanoi 29th February - 2nd March 2012 = Toàncảnhkhả o cổ họ c Việ t Nam, Hanoi, Vietnam. , p. 21. For clarity, some individual sites are not shown.

6. Cropped photo taken by Linhcandng (thảo luận) CC BY-SA 3.0. (2016). *Hoành Sơn Quan*. https://commons.wikimedia.org/wiki/File:Ho%C3%A0nh_S%C6%A1n_quan_5.jpeg

7. Map edited by author from map created by and used with permission from Ebrey, P. B. *A Visual Sourcebook of Chinese Civilization, China proper*. https://depts.washington.edu/chinaciv/geo/proper.htm.

8. Dongting is a very large lake of fresh water. Normally its area is 2,820 square kilometres and may increase to 20,000 square kilometres in flood season.

9. Peak Advisor. *Nanling Mountains*. https://peakvisor.com/range/nanling-mountains.html

10. Approximate coordinates from Google Maps:
    Yuechengling (25°52'38.1"N 110°25'16.9"E, 25.877252, 110.421369),
    Dupang (25°19'09.6"N 111°09'06.2"E, 25.319320, 111.151709),
    Mengzhu Ling (24°52'59.6"N 111°41'59.3"E, 24.883225, 111.699802),
    Qitian mountain (24°52'59.6"N 111°41'59.3"E, 24.883225, 111.699802),
    Dayu Ling (25°20'01.0"N 114°27'59.8"E, 25.333610, 114.466610),
    Mount Wuyi (Wuyishan) (25°20'01.0"N 114°27'59.8"E, 25.333610, 114.466610).

CHAPTER 2

1. A collection of terracotta statues of warriors and horses was found in 1974. It is now the Mausoleum of the First Qin Emperor in Xi'an, on the southern bank of Wei river, a tributary of the Yellow river, Shaanxi province, China.

2. Champa is a common name for five different small kingdoms: Amaravati (from south of Đèo Ngang to Đà nẵng), Vijaya (Quảng Ngãi, Bình Định), Kauthara (Nha Trang, Khánh Hòa) and Panduranga (Phan Rang-Phan Thiết). Kiều, T. H. (2016). *Góp phần nghiên cứu lịch sử văn hóa Việt Nam - Thời kỳ thiên niên kỷ đầu công nguyên*. NXB Thế Giới. , p. 647.

3. Five dynasties: Liang, Later Tang, Jin, Han, Zhou – Ten kingdoms: Chu, Eastern Han, Former Shu, Later Shu, Min, Southern Han, Southern Tang, Wu and Wu/yue. See Xiu, O., & Davis, R. L. (2004). *Historical Records of the Five Dynasties*. Columbia University Press. , pp. XXV-XXVIII. Interestingly, the break-up generally followed very similar boundary lines that existed during the Qin and Han times for the kingdoms south of the Yangtze. Wu/yue was Eastern Ou or today Zhejiang, Min was Min-yue or today Fujian, Southern Han was Nan-hai or today Guangdong, Guangxi provinces and Chu was north of Nanling or today Hunan.

4. There are actually three different names in this period of independence, Đại Cồ Việt (Great, Great Viet) (968 to 1054), Đại Việt (Great Viet) (1054-1400) and Đại Ngu (Happy and Peaceful Viet) (1400-1407). Between 1407-1414 and 1414-1427, the country was under the rule of the Ming dynasty from China and its name reverted to Giao Chỉ, its title under the Former Han dynasty five hundred years earlier. Once the Ming was driven out, the name returned to Đại Việt (Great Viet) (1428-1804). I adopted Đại Việt for this period as it was used for the longest period of time. From 1804, Emperor Gia Long named his kingdom Vietnam, but in 1839 King Minh Mạng changed it to Đại Nam until 1945 when it reverted to Vietnam to the present time. See Trần, T. K. (1999). *Việt Nam Sử Lược*. Văn Hóa Thông Tin. (1921), p. 15.

5. The name Đại Việt was coined 137 years earlier by the founder of Southern Han kingdom, Liu Yan in 917. See Mote, F. W. (2003). *Imperial China, 900-1800*. Harvard University Press. , p. 15 and Trần, T. K. (1999). *Việt Nam Sử Lược*. Văn Hóa Thông Tin. (1921), p. 75 and Châu, H. Đ. (2018). *An Nam Truyện - Ghi chép về Việt Nam trong chính sử Trung Quốc xưa*. Hội Nhà Văn. , p. 233.

6. Even though Nguyễn Hoàng, a general under the Lê king, went south in 1558, he returned in 1592 to help the king fight the Mạc rebellion and did not go south again until 1600. In 1620, his son stopped paying taxes to the Lê king and founded Đàng Trong as a separate polity from Đàng Ngoài.

7. Trần, T. K. (1999). *Việt Nam Sử Lược*. Văn Hóa Thông Tin. (1921), p. 410.

8. Viện Sử Học, & Quốc Sử Quán Triều Nguyễn. (2002). *Đại Nam Thực Lục* (T. Á. Ngô, D. T. Vũ, Đ. C. Trần, & Đ. H. Lê, Eds. Vol. 1 to 9). NXB Giáo Dục. , Volume 1, p. 473, pp. 531-533.

9. Đỗ, B. (2005). *Những khám phá về Hoàng Đế Quang Trung* (IV ed.). NXB Thuận Hóa. , p. 174. The armoury was called Võ Khố, previously nhà Đồ Ngoại, now at Huế University of Agriculture and Forestry at 102 Phùng Hưng, Thuận Thành ward, Huế. The prison was between An Hoà and Chánh Tây gates.

10. Viện Sử Học, & Quốc Sử Quán Triều Nguyễn. (2002). *Đại Nam Thực Lục* (T. Á. Ngô, D. T. Vũ, Đ. C. Trần, & Đ. H. Lê, Eds. Vol. 1 to 9). NXB Giáo Dục. , Volume 1, p. 466.

11. Vietnamese *cõng rắn cắn gà nhà*.

12. At an international conference in Thanh Hóa, the ancestral land of the Nguyễn, on 18-19 October 2008, the participants agreed that the *"Previous criticism and condemnation to the point of almost negating all the accomplishment of the Nguyễn lords and dynasty was unjust and lacked objectivity, especially when included in textbooks for young people and society at large"*. See Phan, H. L. (2018). *Di sản văn hóa Việt Nam dưới góc nhìn lịch sử*. NXB Đại Học Quốc Gia Hà Nội. , p. 576.

13. Dutton, G. E. (2006). *The Tây Sơn uprising: society and rebellion in eighteenth-century Vietnam.* University of Hawai'i Press. , p. 230.

14. There are citadels in Phú Thọ, Bắc Ninh, Quảng Trị and Thanh Hóa provinces.

15. One example is Vĩnh Tế canal of 87 kilometres in An Giang and Kiên Giang provinces in southern Vietnam.

16. Lê, T. K. (2018). *Lịch sử Việt Nam từ nguồn gốc đến giữa thế kỷ XX* (N. Nguyễn & T. H. Nguyễn, Trans.; Vol. Nhã Nam, NXB Thế Giới). (1955, 1982), (1955, 1982), map 15, near back cover.

17. Annam was a French Protectorate nominally under the rule of a Nguyễn king from Huế, it included the central provinces from Thanh Hóa in the north to Bình Thuận in the south. Tonkin included Hanoi and the northern provinces. It was also a French Protectorate, by contrast, Cochinchina was a French colony that included Saigon and the southern provinces. See *French Indochina c. 1930.* (2013). https://commons.wikimedia.org/wiki/File:French_Indochina_c._1930.jpg.

18. Kutschke, B., & Norton, B. (2014). *Music and Protest in 1968.* Cambridge University Press. https://books.google.co.nz/books?id=NXj_oQEACAAJ . The original Vietnamese version is:

    Một ngàn năm nô lệ giặc Tàu
    Một trăm năm đô hộ giặc Tây
    Hai mươi năm nội chiến từng ngày
    Gia tài của mẹ để lại cho con
    Gia tài của mẹ là nước Việt buồn
    Gia tài của mẹ một rừng xương khô
    Gia tài của mẹ một núi đầy mồ

19. The Black Flag army.

20. Battle for Saigon citadel in 1859.

21. e.g., The Treaty of Peace and Friendship in 1862.

22. e.g., Battle of Thuận An, Huế in 1883.

23. e.g., Harmand Convention 1883.

24. For examples: uprisings by Trương Định (1860-1864) in the south to Phan Đình Phùng in the central (1885-1896) and Hoàng Hoa Thám in the north (1887-1913).

25. Nguyễn, K. V. (2015). *Viet Nam: a long history.* Thế Giới. , p. 149.

26. e.g., Đội Cấn revolt in Thái Nguyên (1917).

27. e.g., Mass protests in Nghệ An, Hà Tĩnh (1930).

28. Gunn, G. C. (2011). The Great Vietnamese Famine of 1944-45 Revisited.

29. Vietnamese boat people from 1975-1995 are estimated at 796,310. During the same period, 42,918 Vietnamese refugees fled overland via Thailand. UNHCR, T. U. R. A. (2000). *The State of The World's Refugees 2000 - Chapter 4.* https://www.unhcr.org/3ebf9bad0.html, p.98.

30. According to the 2019 World Happiness Ranking report, Vietnam's happiness ranking was 94 out of 156, just below China and in the same order as Indonesia's, but a long way below Thailand (52th). Helliwell, J., Layard, R., & Sachs, J. (2019). *World Happiness Report 2019.* New York: Sustainable Development Solutions Network. . It was however ranked 5th out of 140 on the Happy Planet Index published in 2016, New Economics Foundation. (2016). *Happy Planet Index Score.* http://happyplanetindex.org/countries/vietnam.

31. Many remains have been found, collected and buried by their relatives; others were buried in national cemeteries spread around Vietnam. Estimates by Rummel, R. J. (1998). *Statistics of democide : genocide and mass murder since 1900.* LIT ; Distributed in North America by Transaction Publishers, Rutgers University. https://www.hawaii.edu/powerkills/SOD.TAB6.1B.GIF . https://www.hawaii.edu/powerkills/SOD.TAB6.1B.GIF of the war deaths in Vietnam (1954-1975) shows a low of 1,156,000 and a high of 3,206,000. Line 816.

CHAPTER 3

1. Not all historians agree with this version. Some believe An Dương Vương was a local chieftain, (see 8.8.2).
2. Some historical texts indicate Zhao Tuo bribed the Ou and Lou kingdoms to submit to him but others say an attack took place.
3. Current historians agree the year of 208 BCE which had been accepted for many years is incorrect. They now use a later date of 179-180 BCE (see 11.11.5).

CHAPTER 4

1. Trần, T. P. (2011). *Lĩnh nam chích quái* (restored and edited by Vũ Quỳnh and Kiều Phú, Đinh Gia Khánh, Nguyễn Ngọc San, Trans.). NXB Trẻ; Hồng Bàng. (1492), p.38. The translator explained that '*chích*' (collection) is a correct translation and not '*trích*' (excerpt) as previously used, p. 8.
2. Unknown, translated by Trần Quốc Vượng (1959), & compared and corrected by Đinh Khắc Thuân. (2005). *Việt Sử Lược*. Thuận Hóa. (1377), p. 18.
3. SKTT, Vol. 1, p. 135.
4. LNCQ, p. 38.
5. Nguyễn, T. P. C. (2019). *Nghiên cứu về thời đại Hùng Vương của các tác giả ở miền nam Việt Nam trước 1975* Thời đại Hùng Vương trong tiến trình lịch sử Việt Nam - Kỷ yếu hội thảo khoa học quốc gia, Hanoi, 9-2019. , p. 43.
6. Historians divide the Han dynasty into two periods: Former (or Western) Han (202 BCE-9 CE) and Later (or Eastern) Han (25-220). In the period this book covers, I am dealing mainly with the Former Han. I have adopted the terms "Former" and "Later" rather than "Western" and "Eastern" to avoid any confusion that may arise from the perception that the two dynasties may exist at the same time where a geographical term is used.
7. King Zhuang of Zhou is the 15th king of the Chinese Zhou Dynasty (1056-256 BCE). The dynasty ended in 256 BCE, after thirty-seven kings. It is interesting to note the Hùng line also ended around the same time.
8. Tying knots to record events was common in a number of cultures. In South America it is called Quipu. In ancient China, complicated knots were used to record big events, simple knots for small events. See Chen, L. (2018). *Complete book of Chinese knotting: a compendium of techniques and variations.* TUTTLE Publishing. Chen, L. (2018), p. 9.
9. The text in Vietnamese is "*chính sự*" which could be translated as "politics".
10. The word "Lạc" means 'a black horse', in written form, it becomes "Hùng" means 'strong'. Refer to

TKCS, Vol. 37, page 427.

11. Đào, D. A. (2005a). *Đất nước Việt Nam qua các đời - Nghiên cứu địa lý học lịch sử Việt Nam*. Văn Hóa Thông Tin. , p. 19.

12. Hà, V. T. (2018). *The making of Việt Nam*. Thế Giới. , p. 14.

13. Photo by Johnlemon (Flickr) / CC BY-SA (https://creativecommons.org/licenses/by-sa/2.0). (2008). https://upload.wikimedia.org/wikipedia/commons/1/1a/%C4%90%E1%BB%81n_H%C3%B9ng%2C_Ph%C3%BA_Th%E1%BB%8D_%281%29.jpg

14. Interestingly, the expression *"4,000 years of civilization"* in the Vietnamese Constitution, which appeared in the 1980 version, was replaced by *"several thousand years of civilization"* in 1992 and also in the latest version of 2013. See Quốc Hội. *Hiến Pháp nước Cộng Hoà Xã Hội Chủ Nghĩa Việt Nam năm 1980*. https://thuvienphapluat.vn/van-ban/bo-may-hanh-chinh/Hien-phap-1980-Cong-hoa-Xa-hoi-Chu-Nghia-Viet-Nam-36948.aspx and Quốc Hội. (2013). *Hiến Pháp nước Cộng Hoà Xã Hội Chủ Nghĩa Việt Nam*. https://m.thuvienphapluat.vn/van-ban/bo-may-hanh-chinh/Hien-phap-nam-2013-215627.aspx.

15. Ngô, V. H. H. (2019). *Quan điểm của các nhà nghiên cứu sử học miền Bắc về thời đại Hùng Vương từ năm 1967 đến nay* Thời đại Hùng Vương trong tiến trình lịch sử Việt Nam - Kỷ yếu hội thảo khoa học quốc gia, Hanoi, 9-2019. , p. 34.

16. Trần, T. K. (1999). *Việt Nam Sử Lược*. Văn Hóa Thông Tin. (1921), p. 25, raised doubt about the 2,879 BC date. His argument is that each ruling period of the 18 Hùng Kings ruling amounts to around 145 years on average (the last Hùng king reign ended in 257 BCE), therefore the conventionally accepted figure is doubtful.

17. LNCQ, p. 41.

18. While Shen Nung (*Viêm Đế Thần Nông*), the ancestor of Lạc Long Quân, appeared in Chinese ancient text, there was no mention of Lạc Long Quân and Âu Cơ legend in Chinese works.

19. Quốc sử quán triều Nguyễn, & Viện sử học. (1998). *Khâm định Việt sử thông giám cương mục* (Hoa Bằng, Phạm Trọng Điềm,,Trần Văn Giáp (1957), Trans.). Giáo dục. , Vol. 1, p. 73

20. Lê, V. S. (2003). *Việt Nam văn minh sử: lược khảo, tập thượng, từ nguồn gốc đến thế kỷ thứ X*. Lao Động., p 27.

21. Grossin, P. (1926). *La Province Muong de Hoa-Binh. 2e édition*. Impr. d'Extrême-Orient. In Grossin's book, it was written as Tho Dan not Thổ Trắng. In another legend, a square egg went to the first man "Lang-Cuu-Can". This produced him many sons and girls divided in two peoples. The ones skilful in all the arts lived on the plains and were called "Hoa-Dân" in the Kinh-Ky (*kinh kỳ*, Hanoi), the others, simpler, came to the mountains and became "Tho-Dan" among the Mường.

22. Reproduced with permission from Jack. (2013). *Lac Long Quan and Au Co – The Vietnam's ancient legend*. http://vietnamsurprise.com/2013/02/lac-long-quan-and-au-co-the-vietnams-ancient-legend.html

23. Lịch Đạo Nguyên, (Li Daoyuan), Dương Thủ Kính, (Yang, Shoujing), Hùng Hội Trinh, (Xiong, Huizhen), Đoàn Huy Trọng, (Duan, Xizhong), Trần Kiều Dịch, (Chen, Qiaoyi), & Nguyễn Bá Mão. (2005). *Thủy kinh chú sở* (Nguyễn Bá Mão, Trans.). NXB Thuận Hóa ; Trung tâm văn hóa ngôn ngữ Đông Tây. (Giang Tô, China 1999), Vol. 37, p. 427.

24. Nguyễn, D. H. (2013). *Văn minh Lạc Việt*. NXB Văn Hóa Thông Tin., p. 68.

25. Brindley, E. (2018). *Ancient China and the Yue : perceptions and identities on the southern frontier, c.400 BCE - 50 CE.* , p. 34, Lac is "luo" or "Luo" in Chinese which sounds the same as "Lok" meaning bird in Zhuang language. Zhuang people or Zhuangzu, are a Tai-speaking ethnic group who mostly lived in Guangxi province.

26. Nguyễn, K. T., & Vương, L. (1974). Thử tìm nguồn gốc ngữ nghĩa của từ tố "Lạc". Hùng Vương dựng nước - Kỷ yếu của hội nghị nghiên cứu thời kỳ Hùng Vương lần thứ 4, tháng 4 năm 1974, Hanoi., p. 141. The authors noted that Min in Min-yue comes from a river called Minjiang in Fujian province flowing through Fuzhou its capital.

27. Taylor, K. W. (1983). *The Birth of Vietnam*. Berkeley : University of California Press. , p. 12.

28. Đinh, V. N. (1980). Đất Mê Linh - Trung tâm chính trị, quân sự và kinh tế của huyện Mê Linh thời Hai Bà Trưng. *Nghiên Cứu Lịch Sử - Viện Sử Học, 1*, 35-53. , p. 37

29. Taylor, K. W. (1983). *The Birth of Vietnam*. Berkeley : University of California Press. , p. 307

30. SKTT, Vol. 1, p. 133.

31. Nguyễn, K. V. (2015). *Viet Nam: a long history*. Thế Giới. , p. 20

32. Ngô, V. H. H. (2019). *Quan điểm của các nhà nghiên cứu sử học miền Bắc về thời đại Hùng Vương từ năm 1967 đến nay* Thời đại Hùng Vương trong tiến trình lịch sử Việt Nam - Kỷ yếu hội thảo khoa học quốc gia, Hanoi, 9-2019. , p. 40.

33. Kelley, L. C. (2015). Inventing traditions in fifteenth-century Vietnam. *Imperial China and Its Southern Neighbours*. (edited by Victor H. Mair and Liam C. Kelley (Singapore - Institute of Southeast Asian Studies, 2015).) , p. 172.

34. Taylor, K. W. (1983). *The Birth of Vietnam*. Berkeley : University of California Press. , p. 307.

35. Pham, H. (2008). *Do You Know How Vietnamese People Cultivate Wet Rice?* http://thingsasian.com/story/do-you-know-how-vietnamese-people-cultivate-wet-rice

36. LNCQ, p. 38

37. SKTT also mentioned Quảng Nam province; in that case the southern border would be at Hải Vân pass. SKTT, Vol. 1, p. 133.

38. CM, Vol. 1, p. 74.

39. Nguyễn, M. L. (1974). Cương vực nước Văn Lang. Hùng Vương dựng nước - Kỷ yếu của hội nghị nghiên cứu thời kỳ Hùng Vương lần thứ 4, tháng 4 năm 1974, Hanoi., p. 111.

40. Ngô, V. H. H. (2019). *Quan điểm của các nhà nghiên cứu sử học miền Bắc về thời đại Hùng Vương từ năm 1967 đến nay* Thời đại Hùng Vương trong tiến trình lịch sử Việt Nam - Kỷ yếu hội thảo khoa học quốc gia, Hanoi, 9-2019. , p. 35.

41. Đào, D. A. (2005). *Đất nước Việt Nam qua các đời - Nghiên cứu địa lý học lịch sử Việt Nam*. NXB Văn Hóa Thông Tin. , p. 19.

42. TKCS, Vol. 36, pp. 373-374.

43. Nguyễn, H. T. (2019). *Thư tịch cổ Trung quốc viết về Văn Lang, Âu Lạc, An Dương Vương, thành Cổ Loa*. Thời đại Hùng Vương trong tiến trình lịch sử Việt Nam - Kỷ yếu hội thảo khoa học quốc gia., Hanoi, 9-2019. , p. 73.

44. Kiều, T. H. (2016). *Góp phần nghiên cứu lịch sử văn hóa Việt Nam - Thời kỳ thiên niên kỷ đầu công nguyên*. NXB Thế Giới. , p. 251.

45. Nguyễn, H. T. (2019). *Thư tịch cổ Trung quốc viết về Văn Lang, Âu Lạc, An Dương Vương, thành Cổ Loa*. Thời đại Hùng Vương trong tiến trình lịch sử Việt Nam - Kỷ yếu hội thảo khoa học quốc gia., Hanoi, 9-2019. , p. 74. See also Zhao Ying, Liu Xu, Zhang Zhao, Jia Wei, & Zhao Xi. (941-945). *Old Book of Tang* https://ctext.org/wiki.pl?if=gb&res=456206, Volume 41 Treatises 21: Geography 4.

46. Nguyễn, H. T. (2019). *Thư tịch cổ Trung quốc viết về Văn Lang, Âu Lạc, An Dương Vương, thành Cổ Loa*. Thời đại Hùng Vương trong tiến trình lịch sử Việt Nam - Kỷ yếu hội thảo khoa học quốc gia., Hanoi, 9-2019. , p. 73.

47. Kiều, T. H. (2016). *Góp phần nghiên cứu lịch sử văn hóa Việt Nam - Thời kỳ thiên niên kỷ đầu công nguyên*. NXB Thế Giới. , p. 240.

48. Figure based on map by TUBS / CC BY-SA (https://creativecommons.org/licenses/by-sa/3.0). (2011). https://upload.wikimedia.org/wikipedia/commons/3/31/Jiangsu_in_China_%28%2Ball_claims_hatched%29.svg.

49. Đào, D. A. (2005). *Đất nước Việt Nam qua các đời - Nghiên cứu địa lý học lịch sử Việt Nam*. NXB Văn Hóa Thông Tin. , p. 19.

50. LNCQ translators, p. 8, suggest that while the Chinese authors would use the term Lĩnh Nam, in a wider sense, to cover the land south of Nanling mountains, they believe Lĩnh Nam, in the narrow sense, would only cover Vietnam, at about seven hundred kilometres south of Nanling mountains. Now that I have studied the map, one can interpret Lĩnh Nam as the land south of Nanling mountains. See also the map of Lingnan in p. 310 of Allard, F. (1994). Interaction and Social Complexity in Lingnan during the First Millennium B.C. *Asian Perspectives, 33*(2), 309-326. http://www.jstor.org/stable/42928324 . Other authors define Lĩnh Nam as including Guangdong, Guangxi, Hainan island in China, north and central Vietnam down to Ngang pass, see Nguyễn, N. T. (2011). *Văn hóa Bách Việt vùng Lĩnh Nam trong quan hệ với văn hóa truyền thống ở Việt Nam - Luận án tiến sĩ văn hóa học* Đại Học Quốc Gia Tp. Hồ Chí Minh, Trường Đại Học Khoa Học Xã Hội và Nhân Văn,. goo.gl/5G33JN, p. 53.

51. "Vụ Tiên" is a southern constellation according to Taylor, K. W. (1983). *The Birth of Vietnam*. Berkeley : University of California Press. , p. 304. But "Vũ Tiên" is Vietnamese for the constellation of Hercules.

52. By inventing the cart and plow, taming the ox and yoking the horse, and by teaching his people to clear the land with fire, Shennong reputedly established a stable agricultural society in China. His catalogue of 365 species of medicinal plants became the basis of later herbological studies. See Washington State University College of Pharmacy. (2006). *Shen Nung 2696 BCE*. https://www.asmalldoseoftoxicology.org/shen-nung.

53. Translation by Hà, V. T. (2018). *The making of Việt Nam*. Thế Giới.

54. Yellow Emperor or Huangdi (2698-2598 BCE) – is one of the Five Emperors following Three Sovereigns (Shen nung is one of three) who are the mythological rulers of ancient China. Sima Qian, & translated by Phan Ngọc. (2018). *Sử ký Tư Mã Thiên : (trọn bộ hai tập)* (Vol. 1, 2). Văn học. , Vol. 1, p. 37.

55. In Vietnam, it is not uncommon for husband and wife to address each other as father and mother.

56. LNCQ, p. 37.

57. Hubei province, see LNCQ, p. 38. This position does not make sense to us as it is a long way north of Dongting lake. One possible location is a place near Xiang Jiang (Sông Tương) in Hunan province, perhaps in Changsha, south of Dongting lake.

58. LNCQ, p. 38.

59. Brindley, E. (2018). *Ancient China and the Yue : perceptions and identities on the southern frontier, c.400 BCE - 50 CE*. , p. 21.

60. Ibid. p. 22.

61. Kiều, T. H. (2016). *Góp phần nghiên cứu lịch sử văn hóa Việt Nam - Thời kỳ thiên niên kỷ đầu công nguyên*. NXB Thế Giới. , p. 503.

62. Shiji (53), p.23.

63. Southworth, W. A. (2004). The coastal states of Champa. In B. P. IGlover I (Ed.), *Southeast Asia: from prehistory to history*. (pp. 209-233). Routledge Curzon. , p. 213.

64. Brindley, E. (2018). *Ancient China and the Yue : perceptions and identities on the southern frontier, c.400 BCE - 50 CE*. , p. 22.

ENDNOTES

65. Ibid. p. 31 – the original reference can be found in Chapter 117 (Yanjun Lan, Yanjun), Lu Bu-wei. (247-239 BCE). *Lü Shi Chun Qiu*. https://ctext.org/lv-shi-chun-qiu/ens, Paragraph 3.

66. Trương, T. D. (2018). *Khảo chứng tiền sử Việt Nam - Researching of Vietnam prehistory*. NXB Tổng Hợp Thành Phố Hồ Chí Minh. , p. 170.

67. Brindley, E. (2018). *Ancient China and the Yue : perceptions and identities on the southern frontier, c.400 BCE - 50 CE*. , p. 24.

68. Ibid. p. 30.

69. Sima Qian, & translated by Phan Ngọc. (2018). *Sử ký Tư Mã Thiên : (trọn bộ hai tập)* (Vol. 1, 2). Văn học. , Vol. 1, p. 195.

70. Chinese Text Project. (2006-2020). *Shiji-Historical Records- [Western Han] 109 BC-91 BC Sima Qian*. https://ctext.org/shiji, Chapter 41, Yue Wang Ju Jian Family or House of King Goujian of Yue, paragraph 1. https://ctext.org/shiji/yue-wang-ju-jian-shi-jia.

71. Li Jinhui. (2003). *Stunning Capital of Xia Dynasty Unearthed*. http://www.china.org.cn/english/2003/Nov/79635.htm.

72. Twenty generations seem a little short as King Goujian period, at 496–465 BCE, is around 1,100 years later than the last year of the Xia dynasty. Twenty generations work out as 55 years per generation which would be too long, 30 years per generation is more likely. At this rate, King Goujian would be around 40 generations removed.

73. Brindley, E. (2018). *Ancient China and the Yue: perceptions and identities on the southern frontier, c.400 BCE - 50 CE*. , p. 91.

74. Ibid., p. 92.

75. Ibid. p.30. Some of the terms are Yu-yue, Gan-yue, Min-yue, Dong-ou [Eastern Ou], Dong-yue [Eastern Yue], Nan-yue, Xi-ou [Western Ou], Luo-yue [Lạc Việt], Yang-yue, Dian-yue, Teng-yue and Yue-xi.

76. Sima, Q., Farmer, J. M., & Nienhauser, W. H. (2010). *The Grand Scribe's Records, Volume IX : The Memoirs of Han China, Part II* [Book]. Indiana University Press. , Memoir 54, The Eastern Yueh. p. 29.

77. Hubei Provincial Museum. *The sword of Goujian*. http://www.hbww.org/Views/E_ArtGoodsDetail.aspx?PNo=e_Collection&No=e_GZZQ&Guid=ebc8eff0-8a90-4d27-a0ef-5915247ba857&Type=Detail

78. LNCQ, p.40.

79. Brindley, E. (2018). *Ancient China and the Yue : perceptions and identities on the southern frontier, c.400 BCE - 50 CE*. , p. 167.

80. Chinese Text Project. (2006-2020). *Shiji-Historical Records- [Western Han] 109 BC-91 BC Sima Qian*. https://ctext.org/shiji. Chapter 43, Family, Zhao Shijia, paragraph 67.

81. Văn, T. (2007). *Thời đại Hùng Vương: lịch sử, kinh tế, văn hóa, xã hội*. NXB Văn Học. , pp. 177-183.

82. Siyuwj. (2019). *Sword of Goujian*, / *CC BY-SA (https://creativecommons.org/licenses/by-sa/4.0)* https://commons.wikimedia.org/wiki/File:Sword_of_Goujian,_2019-06-15_07.jpg.

83. Discott, CC BY-SA (https://creativecommons.org/licenses/by-sa/3.0),. (2011). *A statue of a man, dating from the State of Yue, located in the State Museum of Zhejiang province, Hangzhou, Zhejiang, China*. https://commons.wikimedia.org/wiki/File:Yue_statue.jpg.

84. There is another similar statue at the bottom of a bronze cane found in Shaoxing City. See Shi Jia. (2018). *Exhibition of unearthed artifacts reveal life and times of Zhejiang's historical past*. https://www.shine.cn/feature/art-culture/1806180236/

85. Based on a map obtained from Yu, N. (2005). *CC BY-SA 3.0, https://commons.wikimedia.org/w/index.php?curid=305427*. https://commons.wikimedia.org/wiki/File:Qin_empire_210_BCE.jpg.

CHAPTER 5

1. Lý, T. X. (2012). *Việt điện u linh* (Đ. R. Trịnh & G. K. Đinh, Trans.). NXB Hồng Bàng. (1329)Lý, T. X. (2012), "*23. Tản viên hựu thánh khuông quốc hiển ứng vương*", p. 107.

2. See VDUL, p. 6. Subsequently, there are several versions of this story but I recite only this version as it is the earliest, in the version of LNCQ, p. 93, the king was the 18th (and last) Hùng king. SKTT also cites this story (p. 135) and added that the king of Shu never forgave the Hùng king for the refusal of his marriage proposal; he finally had his revenge when his grandson defeated the last Hùng king (see Chapter 8). The local story at the temples is different again whereby Sơn Tinh was Nguyễn Tuấn, he and his two brothers helped the people to develop the land, protect the village against floods, they also helped the Hùng king to fight against Shu invaders. The upper temple is believed to be built during the time of An Dương Vương (3rd century BCE) and there was no mention of Thủy Tinh in this local version.

3. *Climate in Hanoi (Ha Noi Municipality), Vietnam.* (2020). https://weather-and-climate.com/average-monthly-Rainfall-Temperature-Sunshine,hanoi,Vietnam.

4. Photo by author, 28 January 2020.

5. One such statue is at Ngã sáu Phù Đổng, Bến Thành, Quận 1, Ho Chi Minh City but it shows him carrying what looks like a bamboo staff, not an iron whip.

6. I am unsure when this would be, as other versions do not mention any Hùng king. Riding an iron horse and cracking an iron would indicate an iron age which for northern Vietnam could be after the arrival of the Former Han in the 2nd century BCE.

7. At the time of LNCQ, 1 *thước* = 1/3 m but is only 0.23 m during Qin and Han times.

8. LNCQ, "*Truyện Đổng Thiên Vương*", p. 46.

9. Photo by author, 17 December 2019.

10. LNCQ, "*Truyện nhất dạ trạch*", p. 49.

11. Not the same My Nương under the golden turtle story in Chapter 9.

12. Today Chử xá is about 16 kilometres north of the Chử Đồng Tử - Tiên Dung temple. Both are in Hưng Yên province.

13. Văn Giang market, near Ecopark township, about 5 kilometres east of the village of Chử xá. About 40 kilometres south of this market is Phố Hiến, the biggest trading port in the north in the 17th and 18th centuries, where the Dutch, British, Chinese and Japanese all had trading posts. Sadly, unlike Hội An, the equivalent port in the south, there is not much to see in Phố Hiến, apart from a few temples.

14. Ngưỡng Quang is a Vietnamese translation of Yangon, the capital of Myanmar. In other texts, it is Phật Quang (or the aurora of Buddha). The monk is believed to be Indian, see Hoàng, T. T., & Nguyen, T. T. (2008). *The history of Buddhism in Vietnam.* Institute of Philosophy, Vietnamese Academy of Social Sciences. , p. 18. Apparently, Indian merchants not only bought and sold gold, but also spread the teaching of Buddha. See Lê, V. S. (2003). *Việt Nam văn minh sử: lược khảo, tập thượng, từ nguồn gốc đến thế kỷ thứ X.* Lao Động. , p. 249.

15. The text cited "*canh ba*" which is between 11 pm to 1 am.

16. Photo by author, 20 January 2020 at Đền Chử Đồng Tử.

17. Dror, O. (2007). *Cult, Culture, and Authority : Princess Lieu Hanh in Vietnamese History.* University of Hawaii Press. , p. 71.

18. Vụ Bản district, Nam Định province.

19. Dror, O. (2007). *Cult, Culture, and Authority : Princess Lieu Hanh in Vietnamese History*. University of Hawaii Press. , p. 83

20. Vân Cát is today at Kim Thái, Vụ Bản district, Nam Định province where Phủ Dầy temple is.

21. A part of a book called Truyền kỳ tân phả (New collection of marvellous stories) – translation by Dror, O. (2007). *Cult, Culture, and Authority : Princess Lieu Hanh in Vietnamese History*. University of Hawaii Press. , p. 84.

22. Đoàn, T. Đ. (2013). *Truyền kỳ tân phả* (L. C. Ngô & V. G. Trần, Trans.). NXB Trẻ, NXB Hồng Bàng. (1811).

23. Dror, O. (2007). *Cult, Culture, and Authority : Princess Lieu Hanh in Vietnamese History*. University of Hawaii Press. , p. 83.

24. The reign of King Lê Thiên Hựu (1556-1557).

25. Or also Heavenly Grandfather, or *Ngọc Hoàng Thượng Đế* in Vietnamese, a god in Taoism.

26. Đoàn, T. Đ. (2013). *Truyền kỳ tân phả* (L. C. Ngô & V. G. Trần, Trans.). NXB Trẻ, NXB Hồng Bàng. (1811), p. 138.

27. Compiled by World Heritage Encyclopedia™ licensed under CC BY-SA 3.0. *Đạo Mẫu*. http://community.worldheritage.org/articles/Religion_in_Vietnam: "*The term "Đạo Mẫu" refers to the worship of mother goddesses in Vietnam. These include the worship of goddesses such as Thiên Y A Na, The Lady of the Realm (Bà Chúa Xứ), The Lady of the Storehouse (Bà Chúa Kho) and Princess Liễu Hạnh, legendary figures like Âu Cơ, the Trung Sisters (Hai Bà Trưng), and Lady Trieu (Bà Triệu), as well as the cult of the Four Palaces. Đạo Mẫu is commonly associated with spirit mediumship rituals—known in Vietnam as lên đồng—much as practiced in other parts of Asia, such as Taiwan, Singapore and Hong Kong*".

28. The festival is held annually at Phủ Dầy, Vụ Bản district, Nam Định province. Photo by Vũ Tiến Lâm / CC BY-SA (https://creativecommons.org/licenses/by-sa/4.0). (2017). *Lễ hội Phủ Dầy*. https://upload.wikimedia.org/wikipedia/commons/a/af/L%E1%BB%85_h%E1%BB%99i_Ph%E1%BB%A7_D%E1%BA%A7y.jpg.

29. Lê, T. (2002). *An Nam Chí Lược* (Ủy ban phiên dịch sử liệu Việt Nam của Viện Đại Học Huế (1961), Trans.). Thuận Hóa. (1285), p. 67.

30. SKTT, Vol. 1, p. 134.

31. Trần, T. K. (1999). *Việt Nam Sử Lược*. Văn Hóa Thông Tin. (1921), p. 26.

32. LNCQ, "Truyện Bánh Chưng", p. 60 and "Truyện Giếng Việt", p. 70.

33. VDUL, p. 129, in the same story, Mt. Vệ Linh is the same as Mt Sóc Sơn, p. 131.

34. VDUL, "*22. Xung thiên dung liệt chiêu ứng uy tín đại vương*", p. 103.

35. Trần, Q. V. (1995). The legend of Ông Dóng from the text to the field. *Essays into Vietnamese Pasts*, 13-41. , p. 17.

CHAPTER 6

1. A typical example is Alves, M. J. (2001). *What's so Chinese about Vietnamese?* Ninth Annual Meeting of the Southeast Asian Linguistics Society, Arizona State University, Program for Southeast Asian Studies.

2. A typical example is Macholdt, E., Arias, L., Duong, N. T., Ton, N. D., Van Phong, N., Schröder, R., Pakendorf, B., Van Hai, N., & Stoneking, M. (2020, 2020/05/01). The paternal and maternal genetic history of Vietnamese populations. *European Journal of Human Genetics, 28*(5), 636-645. https://doi.org/10.1038/s41431-019-0557-4.

3. GSI evolved from the Mission Archeologique de I'Indochine established by the French colonial government in 1898, not long after the last battle of the Sino-French war in 1885 which ended when the French formally created Indochina in October 1887. The first archaeological excavation began in 1906 by Henri Mansuy, Colani's superior. In 1908, GSI was formally created from its predecessor, the Department of Natural Resources. GSI mapped the geology of Indochina and neighbouring areas. GSI is now at the Geology Museum in Hanoi at 6 Phạm Ngũ Lão, Hanoi.

4. Moser, J. (2012). The Hoabinhian Definition In the Past and Today: A Short Historical Review of Defining the Hoabinhian. 3-12., p. 11.

5. Notably Trần Quốc Vượng, Nguyễn Khắc Sử and Lại Văn Tới.

6. Notably Andreas Reinecke, Nam C Kim. Many excavation teams have come from Germany, Sweden, Poland, Italy, Korea and Japan.

7. Tống, T. T. (2012). *A general outline on the history of archeology in Vietnam - Vài nét về lịch sử khảo cổ học Việt Nam*. Perspectives on the archaeology of Vietnam International Colloquium, Hanoi 29th February - 2nd March 2012 = Toàn cảnh khảo cổ học Việt Nam, Hanoi, Vietnam., p. 29.

8. *Bronze Age,*. (2020). https://en.wikipedia.org/wiki/Bronze_Age#cite_note-35. The Bronze Age did not occur at the same time everywhere; different groups of people began to use bronze at varying times. In Western Europe, the Bronze Age thrived from about 3200 BCE until 600 BCE. In China, the earliest bronze artefacts have been found in the Majiayao culture site (between 3100 and 2700 BC). In Ban Chiang, Thailand, (Southeast Asia) bronze artefacts have been discovered dating to 2000 BCE.

9. Charles, F. W. H., Katerina, D., & Thomas, F. G. H. (2015). A New Chronology for the Bronze Age of Northeastern Thailand and Its Implications for Southeast Asian Prehistory [article]. *PLoS ONE*(9), e0137542. https://doi.org/10.1371/journal.pone.0137542.

10. Reinecke, A. (2012). *Insights into the archaeological research of Vietnam - Những góc nhìn về nghiên cứu khảo cổ học Việt Nam*. Perspectives on the Archaeology of Vietnam, International Colloquium, Hanoi 29th February - 2nd March 2012 = Toàn cảnh khảo cổ học Việt Nam, Hanoi, Vietnam.

11. Bellwood, P. (2012). *Vietnam and the Prehistory of Eastern Asia – A multidisciplinary perspective on the Neolithic - Việt Nam và tiền sử Đông Á - một hướng tiếp cận đa ngành về thời kỳ đồ đá mới* Perspectives on the archaeology of Vietnam International Colloquium, Hanoi 29th February - 2nd March 2012 = Toàn cảnh khảo cổ học Việt Nam, Hanoi, Vietnam., (pages 48, 53, 55)

12. Nguyễn, L. C. (2019). Những nghiên cứu cổ nhân học quan trọng của Việt Nam (1906-2018). *Tạp chí khoa học Đại học Đà Lạt, 9, số 3*, 17-55., p.48.

13. There are 28 Stone Age sites north of Ngang pass, 8 in the central and 8 further in the south, totalling 44.

14. Reinecke, A. (2012). *Insights into the archaeological research of Vietnam - Những góc nhìn về nghiên cứu khảo cổ học Việt Nam*. Perspectives on the Archaeology of Vietnam, International Colloquium, Hanoi 29th February - 2nd March 2012 = Toàn cảnh khảo cổ học Việt Nam, Hanoi, Vietnam., p. 22, for clarity, some individual sites are not shown.

CHAPTER 7

1. Imamura, K. (2010, 01/01). The Distribution of Bronze Drums of the Heger I and Pre-I Types: Temporal Changes and Historical Background.
2. Phạm, Đ. M. (2014). Đông Sơn Signs in Southern Vietnam *Vietnam Archeology No. 9/2014.*, p. 34.
3. Heger, an Austrian archaeologist, first classified the bronze drums in 1902 into 4 types (I, II, III and IV). Type I is the oldest and also called Dong Son drum. See Heger, F. (1902). *Alte Metalltrommeln aus Sudost-Asien.* Leipzig. .
4. Nguyễn, D. H. (2013). *Văn minh Lạc Việt.* NXB Văn Hóa Thông Tin. , pp. 334-339.
5. Nguyễn, G. H., & Trịnh, N. C. (2014). Đông Sơn culture – 90 years of discovery and research *Vietnam Archeology No. 9/2014*, 2-17. , p. 7.
6. Đào, D. A. (2006). *Lịch sử Việt Nam - Từ nguồn gốc đến thế kỷ XIX.* NXB Văn Hóa Thông Tin. (1957), p. 59.
7. Hoàng, X. C. (2012). *Đồ đồng văn hóa Đông Sơn - The bronze artifacts of Dong Son culture.* NXB Văn hóa thông tin.
8. Located at 216 Trần Quang Khải St. Tràng Tiền, Hoàn Kiếm, Hanoi
9. It was found in 1937 at Nội hamlet, Văn Hoàng commune, Phú Xuyên district, forty kilometres south of Hanoi. There is a commune called Hoàng Hạ in Hà Nam province but according to the National Museum information, this is not where the drum was found. See Ministry of Culture-Sport and Tourism. (2018). *Bảo Tàng Lịch Sử Quốc Gia, Vietnam National Museum of History.* http://baotanglichsu.vn/en.
10. Found in 1893 at Ngọc Lũ commune, Hà Nam province, about forty-five kilometres south of where the Hoàng Hạ drum was found. Both sites are on the western side of the Red river.
11. Found in 1982 at Mả Tre site, Xóm Chợ (Chợ commune), Cổ Loa, Đông Anh district, Hanoi.
12. Located at 2 Nguyễn Bỉnh Khiêm St. Bến Nghé Ward, Ho chi Minh City.
13. Located at 206 Trường Thu, Lam Sơn, Thanh Hóa City.
14. Nguyễn, D. H. (2013). *Văn minh Lạc Việt.* NXB Văn Hóa Thông Tin. , p. 339.
15. Such as Lạng Sơn and Hải Phòng.
16. Musée Guimet. *Tambour du Sông Dà dit «tambour Moulié».* https://www.guimet.fr/collections/asie-du-sud-est/tambour-du-song-da-dit-tambour-moulie/
17. Mattet, L., Barbier, J. P., Menz, C., Amiet, P., Chamay, J., Studio Ferrazzini, B., Musée d'art et, d. h., Musée, B.-M., & Museo Barbier-Mueller de Arte, P. (2008). *Le profane et le divin : arts de l'Antiquité de l'Europe au Sud-est asiatique : fleurons du Musée Barbier-Mueller.* Hazan ; Musées d'art et d'histoire: Musée Barbier-Mueller.
18. Hà, V. T. (2019). *Chữ trên đá, chữ trên đồng, minh văn và lịch sử.* NXB Trí Thức. , p. 23.
19. Musée Guimet. *Tambour du Sông Dà dit «tambour Moulié».* https://www.guimet.fr/collections/asie-du-sud-est/tambour-du-song-da-dit-tambour-moulie/
20. Nguyễn, Đ. T. (1998). *Lịch sử tư tưởng Việt Nam* (Vol. 1). NXB TP. Hồ Chí Minh. , p. 66. The author quoted a passage in the work during the Ming (1368-1644) dynasty about the losses of 93 bronze drums by Tây man A Đại, a tribal chief to the Ming. See also History of Ming (Mingshi), Volume 212 Biographies 100: Yu Dayou, Qi Jiguang, Liu Xian, Li Xi, Zhang Yuanxun http://chinesenotes.com/mingshi/mingshi212.html.

21. Higham, C. F. W. (2012). *The Đông Sơn chiefdom - Lãnh địa Đông Sơn*. Perspectives on the archaeology of Vietnam international colloquium, Hanoi 29th February - 2nd March 2012 = Toàn cảnh khảo cổ học Việt Nam, Hanoi, Vietnam. , p. 89.

22. Tạ, Đ. (2017). *Nguồn gốc và sự phát triển của trống đồng Đông Sơn - Sách chuyên khảo*. NXB Trí Thức. , pp. 298-318.

23. Nguyễn, Đ. T. (1998). *Lịch sử tư tưởng Việt Nam* (Vol. 1). NXB TP. Hồ Chí Minh. , p. 70. Located at Đan Nê hamlet, Yên Thọ commune, Yên Định district, Thanh Hóa province, by the western bank of Mã river, at about forty kilometres upstream from Đông Sơn village

24. Photo by MikeHS CC BY-SA 3.0. (2009). *Tambor de la cultura Dong Son, de Vietnam (800 BC) al Museu Guimet, de París*. https://upload.wikimedia.org/wikipedia/commons/b/be/Trong_dong_Dong_Son_Guimet.jpg

25. Hà, V. T. (2018). *The making of Việt Nam*. Thế Giới. , p. 48.

26. Tạ, Đ. (2017). *Nguồn gốc và sự phát triển của trống đồng Đông Sơn - Sách chuyên khảo*. NXB Trí Thức. , p. 416.

27. Photo by the author at the National History Museum in Hanoi, 11 December 2019.

28. Photo by the author at the National History Museum in Hanoi, 11 December 2019.

29. Photo by Daaé Public domain via Wikimedia Commons. (2010). *Co Loa bronze drum at the Hanoi Museum*. https://upload.wikimedia.org/wikipedia/commons/5/50/Co_Loa_drums.JPG

30. A prefecture under Han times that included the provinces of Bắc Ninh, Bắc Giang, Thái Nguyên and Vĩnh Yên, north of Đuống and Red rivers, see Appendix 8.

31. Tạ, Đ. (2017). *Nguồn gốc và sự phát triển của trống đồng Đông Sơn - Sách chuyên khảo*. NXB Trí Thức. , p. 259.

32. Ibid., p. 589.

33. Bellwood, P. (1993). Southeast Asia before History. In N. Tarling (Ed.), *The Cambridge History of Southeast Asia: Volume 1: From Early Times to <I>c.</I>1800* (Vol. 1, pp. 51-136). Cambridge University Press. https://doi.org/DOI: 10.1017/CHOL9780521355056.004 , p. 122.

34. Concentrated in southern and interior Sarawak and Kalimantan.

35. Tạ, Đ. (2017). *Nguồn gốc và sự phát triển của trống đồng Đông Sơn - Sách chuyên khảo*. NXB Trí Thức. , p. 588.

36. Nguyễn, Đ. T. (1998). *Lịch sử tư tưởng Việt Nam* (Vol. 1). NXB TP. Hồ Chí Minh. , pp. 58-62.

37. L'Illustration : journal universel. (1862). L'Illustration : journal universel. *40 no. 1031 - 29 Novembre 1862*. , p. 356. A copy can be downloaded from https://babel.hathitrust.org/cgi/pt?id=mdp.39015010958018&view=1up&seq=352

38. Đào, D. A. (2006). *Lịch sử Việt Nam - Từ nguồn gốc đến thế kỷ XIX*. NXB Văn Hóa Thông Tin. (1957), p. 71

39. Taylor, K. W. (1983). *The Birth of Vietnam*. Berkeley : University of California Press. , p. 313.

40. LNCQ, p. 40, told us that people under Hùng kings *"got salt from ginger roots and cooked rice in bamboo sticks"*. Bamboo-cooked rice (*cơm lam*) is a common dish in the northwest mountainous area of Vietnam, the region where the Hùng king had his capital and where the many ethnic Tai (Thái) live. One can reasonably conclude that the Lạc of Đông Sơn era did not live by the seas where one can easily get salt from evaporating seawater.

41. The length and pattern of the headgear on the drum figures would resemble peacock feathers (or Southeast Asia green peafowl, Pavo muticus) which were widely distributed through northern Myanmar, southern China, Vietnam, Laos, Thailand and Java.

42. Trần, Q. V. (1995). The legend of Ông Dóng from the text to the field. *Essays into Vietnamese Pasts*, 13-41. , p. 37.

43. I am unable to locate the source of this picture. I downloaded it from https://www.flickr.com/photos/doremon360/1413043985/in/album-72157602087357972/ but similar images appear on the website of the Vietnam National Museum of History http://baotanglichsu.vn/vi/Articles/1001/28538/bao-vat-quoc-gia-viet-nam-trong-djong-ngoc-lu.html. The nearest reference is Nguyễn, D. C. (2019). *Hoa Văn Việt Nam - Từ thời tiền sử đến nửa đầu thời kỳ phong kiến*. NXB Hồng Đức. (2003) but the author appeared to copy it from somewhere else.

44. Little egret (Cò trắng, Egretta Garzetta). This type has 2 long plumes on the nape, as can be seen clearly in one of the images.

45. Bồ nông chân xám.

46. Cò thìa.

47. Cò bợ.

48. Công.

49. Vẹt.

50. Gà.

51. Chim xít.

52. Chim bìm bịp.

53. Gà lôi.

54. Tạ, Đ. (2017). *Nguồn gốc và sự phát triển của trống đồng Đông Sơn - Sách chuyên khảo*. NXB Trí Thức. , p. 441.

55. Photo taken by the author at the National History Museum in Hanoi on 11 December 2019.

56. Bò U (zebu).

57. It was found in 1961 at Đào Thịnh commune, Trấn Yên district, Yên Bái province. The jar is believed to be used originally for food storage but became a coffin when found. Ministry of Culture-Sport and Tourism. (2018). *Bảo Tàng Lịch Sử Quốc Gia, Vietnam National Museum of History*. http://baotanglichsu.vn/en

58. Nguyen, V. (2009-2020). *The Center for Southeast Asian Prehistory (CESEAP)*. http://www.drnguyenviet.com/

59. Photo taken by Bình Giang. (2009). *The trigger portion of a Dong Son crossbow dating from 500 BCE-0*. https://commons.wikimedia.org/wiki/File:Dong_Son_crossbow_trigger.JPG

60. Photo downloaded from The Met Fifth Avenue in Gallery 244. *Dagger 500 B.C.–A.D. 100 Vietnam*. https://www.metmuseum.org/art/collection/search/60866. This photo has Open Access status.

61. Photo taken by the author at Thanh Hóa Provincial Museum on 12 December 2019. Its age is estimated at about 2000 BP (or 50 BCE), 46.5 cm long, 5 cm wide and weighs 620 grams. Found at Nưa mountain, Tân Ninh commune, Triệu Sơn district in 1961.

62. Linum usitatissimum – sợi lanh,

63. Trịnh Đình Dương, Trương Thị Lan, Hoàng Thị Vân, Dương Thị Mỹ Dung, Lê Thùy Dung, Trần Thị Nga, & Trương Thị Phương Thảo. (2019). *Sưu tập cổ vật tiêu biểu văn hóa Đông Sơn - Bảo tàng Thanh Hóa - The collection of Dong Son culture typical artifacts - Thanh Hoa Provincial Museum* NXB Thanh Niên - Youth Publishing House. , p. 21.

64. Photo taken by the author at Thanh Hóa Provincial Museum on 12 December 2019.

65. Photo by Gryffindor - CC BY-SA 3.0. (2008). *Lamp base in the shape of a kneeling man*. https://up-

load.wikimedia.org/wikipedia/commons/d/df/National_Museum_Vietnamese_History_28.jpg

66. Dương, H. (2013). *Bronze lamp in the shape of a kneeling man (Lsb.1391)*. http://baotanglichsu.vn/en/Articles/1004/13779/bronze-lamp-in-the-shape-of-a-kneeling-man-lsb-1391.html

67. Đào, D. A. (2005). *Đất nước Việt Nam qua các đời - Nghiên cứu địa lý học lịch sử Việt Nam*. NXB Văn Hóa Thông Tin. , p. 52.

68. Phạm, Q. Q. (2019). *Về những cây đèn đồng hậu Đông Sơn*. http://baotanglichsu.vn/vi/Articles/3101/69641/ve-nhung-cay-djen-djong-hau-djong-son.html

69. Photo taken by Bình Giang - Public domain. (2009). *A bronze dagger, Dong Son Culture*.

70. Gong (*cồng chiêng*).

71. The Mường, Thái and H'mông.

72. Photo by author at the National History Museum in Hanoi on 11 December 2019.

73. Photo by author at the National History Museum in Hanoi on 11 December 2019. This item was found among 108 objects buried in a boat coffin, found in 1961 at Việt Khê construction site, Phủ Ninh commune, Thủy Nguyên district, Hải Phòng city.

74. Hoàng, X. C. (2012). *Đồ đồng văn hóa Đông Sơn - The bronze artifacts of Dong Son culture*. NXB Văn hóa thông tin.

75. Kim, N. C. (2015). *The Origins of Ancient Vietnam*. Oxford University Press. , p. 138.

76. Higham, C. F. W. (2012). The Đông Sơn chiefdom. , p. 89.

77. Wilpers, M. (2018). *The Smithsonian's Biggest Drum*. https://music.si.edu/story/smithsonian%E2%80%99s-biggest-drum.

78. Heger, an Austrian archaeologist, first classified the bronze drums in 1902 into 4 types (I, II, III and IV). Type I is the oldest and also called Dong Son drum. Most Karen bronze drums are Heger Type III. See Heger, F. (1902). *Alte Metalltrommeln aus Sudost-Asien*. Leipzig.

79. Han, X. (1998). The Present Echoes of the Ancient Bronze Drum: Nationalism and Archeology in Modern Vietnam and China. *Explorations in Southeast Asian studies*, *2*(2), 27-46. , p.10.

80. Imamura, K. (2010, 01/01). The Distribution of Bronze Drums of the Heger I and Pre-I Types: Temporal Changes and Historical Background. , p. 31.

81. Perlin, J. (2017). Peak wood and the Bronze Age. *Pacific Standard*, (June 14). . Some 120 pine trees were required to prepare the six tons of charcoal needed to produce one copper ingot shaped roughly like a dried ox hide and weighing between 45 and 65 pounds (20 to 30 kg).

82. Hà, V. T. (2018). *The making of Việt Nam*. Thế Giới. , p. 31.

83. Minh Thư. (2007). *Tuyển chọn ca dao hay nhất*. NXB Văn hóa dân tộc , Vietnamese popular folk poetry: "Con cò mà đi ăn đêm, đậu phải cành mềm lộn cổ xuống ao", p. 335.

84. Chế Lan Viên, & selected by Vũ Tuấn Anh. (2009). *Chế Lan Viên, tác phẩm chọn lọc*. NXB Giáo dục Việt Nam.

85. "Con cò" by singer Tùng Dương.

86. Avibase. (2020). *Avibase - Bird Checklists of the World Vietnam*. https://avibase.bsc-eoc.org/checklist.jsp?region=VN

87. Photo used with permission by Bjarne Nielsen, Egretta garzetta, taken at the Danube-delta in Romania May 16. 2011.

88. Hoàng, X. C. (2012). *Đồ đồng văn hóa Đông Sơn - The bronze artifacts of Dong Son culture*. NXB Văn hóa thông tin. , p.200.

89. Photo by author at the National History Museum in Hanoi on 11 December 2019.

CHAPTER 8

1. SKTT, Vol.1, p. 136.
2. Đào, D. A. (2005). *Đất nước Việt Nam qua các đời - Nghiên cứu địa lý học lịch sử Việt Nam*. NXB Văn Hóa Thông Tin. , p. 44.
3. Lại, V. T. (2012). *Cổ Loa: the capital of the Âu Lạc kingdom in the 3rd and 2nd centuries BCE - Cổ Loa: kinh thành của nhà nước Âu Lạc vào thế kỷ 3-2 tr CN*. Perspectives on the Archaeology of Vietnam International Colloquium, Hanoi 29th February - 2nd March 2012 = Toàn cảnh khảo cổ học Việt Nam, Hanoi, Vietnam. , p.130.
4. I created this map from Google Maps and information obtained from Kim, N. C. (2015). *The Origins of Ancient Vietnam*. Oxford University Press. , p.160; Phan , H. L. (2018). *Lịch sử và văn hóa Việt Nam tiếp cận bộ phận* (P. T. Phan, Ed. 4th ed.). NXB Đại Học Quốc Gia Hà Nội. , pp. 115-116 and Đặng, H. S. (2019). *Nước Âu Lạc thời An Dương Vương* Thời đại Hùng Vương trong tiến trình lịch sử Việt Nam - Kỷ yếu hội thảo khoa học quốc gia, Hanoi, 9-2019. , p. 403. The SW gate (m) shown is more in the western direction and it should be named west gate. Similarly, other satellite photos, see Trịnh, H. H. (ibid.). *Kết quả nghiên cứu thành Cổ Loa (giai đoạn 2007-2014)*. , p. 412 seem to indicate the southern section of the outer wall may have curved around Xóm Mít commune (red dots) and not gone straight through, as is shown.
5. Photo by author on 4 December 2019.
6. Kim, N. C. (2015). *The Origins of Ancient Vietnam*. Oxford University Press. , pp. 144-145.
7. Lại, V. T. (2012). *Cổ Loa: the capital of the Âu Lạc kingdom in the 3rd and 2nd centuries BCE - Cổ Loa: kinh thành của nhà nước Âu Lạc vào thế kỷ 3-2 tr CN*. Perspectives on the Archaeology of Vietnam International Colloquium, Hanoi 29th February - 2nd March 2012 = Toàn cảnh khảo cổ học Việt Nam, Hanoi, Vietnam. , p. 129.
8. Kim, N. C. (2015). *The Origins of Ancient Vietnam*. Oxford University Press. , p. 207.
9. Approximate distance as measured by Google Maps.
10. Lại, V. T. (2012). *Cổ Loa: the capital of the Âu Lạc kingdom in the 3rd and 2nd centuries BCE - Cổ Loa: kinh thành của nhà nước Âu Lạc vào thế kỷ 3-2 tr CN*. Perspectives on the Archaeology of Vietnam International Colloquium, Hanoi 29th February - 2nd March 2012 = Toàn cảnh khảo cổ học Việt Nam, Hanoi, Vietnam. , p.130.
11. Kim, N. C. (2015). *The Origins of Ancient Vietnam*. Oxford University Press. , p. 161.
12. At Gò Đống Dân, Xóm Bãi, xã Cổ Loa, see Trịnh, H. H. (2019). *Kết quả nghiên cứu thành Cổ Loa (giai đoạn 2007-2014)*. Thời đại Hùng Vương trong tiến trình lịch sử Việt Nam - Kỷ yếu hội thảo khoa học quốc gia, Hanoi, 9-2019. , p. 413.
13. Ibid. p. 424. The inner wall excavation location was at 21.11580,105.87532 coordinate of Chợ ward, Cổ Loa commune.
14. Kim, N. C. (2015). *The Origins of Ancient Vietnam*. Oxford University Press. , p. 161.
15. Ibid. p. 172.
16. Ibid. p. 207.
17. Ibid. p. 212.
18. Ibid. p. 185.
19. Trịnh, H. H. (2019). *Kết quả nghiên cứu thành Cổ Loa (giai đoạn 2007-2014)*. Thời đại Hùng Vương trong tiến trình lịch sử Việt Nam - Kỷ yếu hội thảo khoa học quốc gia, Hanoi, 9-2019. , p. 434.

20. Ibid. p. 434.

21. Kim, N. C. (2015). *The Origins of Ancient Vietnam*. Oxford University Press. , p. 168.

22. Trịnh, H. H. (2019). *Kết quả nghiên cứu thành Cổ Loa (giai đoạn 2007-2014)*. Thời đại Hùng Vương trong tiến trình lịch sử Việt Nam - Kỷ yếu hội thảo khoa học quốc gia, Hanoi, 9-2019. , p. 430.

23. Kim, N. C. (2015). *The Origins of Ancient Vietnam*. Oxford University Press. , p. 179.

24. Phan , H. L. (2018). *Lịch sử và văn hóa Việt Nam tiếp cận bộ phận* (P. T. Phan, Ed. 4th ed.). NXB Đại Học Quốc Gia Hà Nội. , p. 118.

25. Ibid. p. 114.

26. Trịnh, H. H. (2019). *Kết quả nghiên cứu thành Cổ Loa (giai đoạn 2007-2014)*. Thời đại Hùng Vương trong tiến trình lịch sử Việt Nam - Kỷ yếu hội thảo khoa học quốc gia, Hanoi, 9-2019. , p. 419.

27. Ibid. p. 436.

28. Ibid. p. 434.

29. TKCS, Book 36, p. 427.

30. CM, Vol. 1, p. 79.

31. SKTT, Vol. 1, p. 134.

32. Lockhart, B. M., & Duiker, W. J. (2006). *Historical dictionary of Vietnam*. Scarecrow Press. , p. 23.

33. Đinh, N. V. (2019). *Vấn đề nhà nước Nam Cương và nguồn gốc của Thục Phán*. Thời đại Hùng Vương trong tiến trình lịch sử Việt Nam - Kỷ yếu hội thảo khoa học quốc gia, Hanoi, 9-2019. , pp.187-195.

34. Ulrich Theobald. (2011). *Ailao*. ChinaKnowledge.de, An Encyclopaedia on Chinese History, Literature and Art. http://www.chinaknowledge.de/History/Altera/ailao.html

35. Backus, C. (1981). *The Nan-chao kingdom and T'ang China's southwestern frontier*. Cambridge University Press. , map on p. 117.

36. Kiều, T. H. (2016). *Góp phần nghiên cứu lịch sử văn hóa Việt Nam - Thời kỳ thiên niên kỷ đầu công nguyên*. NXB Thế Giới. , pp. 82-98.

37. The translator of LNCQ explained that there was a Qui Thành (turtle citadel) built in Chengdu of Sichuan province by a Qin general (Zhang Yi, 328-310 BCE) who invaded Ba Shu in 316 BCE. He tried many times but failed until someone told him to follow the path of a turtle, which followed a circular path, after that he was able to build it. LNCQ, p. 20. I am unable to find any reference to such a citadel in Chengdu.

38. Sima, Q., Farmer, J. M., & Nienhauser, W. H. (2010). *The Grand Scribe's Records, Volume IX : The Memoirs of Han China, Part II* [Book]. Indiana University Press. , Memoir 54, p. 31, footnote 13.

39. Brindley, E. (2018). *Ancient China and the Yue : perceptions and identities on the southern frontier, c.400 BCE - 50 CE*. , p. 35.

40. For example: Taylor, K. W. (1983). *The Birth of Vietnam*. Berkeley : University of California Press. , p. 15, "Western Ou lay in the upper basin of the Hsi [Xi] river in modern Kuang-hsi [Guangxi])"

41. Brindley, E. (2018). *Ancient China and the Yue : perceptions and identities on the southern frontier, c.400 BCE - 50 CE*. , p. 35.

42. In Aurousseau's view, it was the same as Tonkin or north Vietnam, see Aurousseau, L. (1923). La première conquête chinoise des pays annamites (IIIe siècle avant notre ère). http://www.persee.fr/web/revues/home/prescript/article/befeo_0336-1519_1923_num_23_1_5933 , p. 176, p. 234. In fact, he used this as evidence that Qin armies did invade Vietnam in the 3rd century BCE.

43. Nguyễn, K. T., & Vương, L. (1974). Thử tìm nguồn gốc ngữ nghĩa của từ tố "Lạc". Hùng Vương dựng nước - Kỷ yếu của hội nghị nghiên cứu thời kỳ Hùng Vương lần thứ 4, tháng 4 năm 1974, Hanoi., p. 141.

44. Ye, F. (5th century). *Hou Han shu - Book of the Later Han*. https://ctext.org/hou-han-shu , https://ctext.org/hou-han-shu/nan-man-xi-nan-yi-lie-zhuan , paragraph 14 of Volume 86 "Treatise on the Nanman, Southwestern Barbarians". English translation from Vietnamese by Châu, H. Đ. (2018). *An Nam Truyện - Ghi chép về Việt Nam trong chính sử Trung Quốc xưa*. Hội Nhà Văn. , p. 188.

45. Ye, F. (5th century). *Hou Han shu - Book of the Later Han*. https://ctext.org/hou-han-shu , Biography 84, https://ctext.org/hou-han-shu/nan-man-xi-nan-yi-lie-zhuan , paragraph 17 or Volume 86, *Treatise on the Nanman, Southwestern Barbarians*. Also Châu, H. Đ. (2018). *An Nam Truyện - Ghi chép về Việt Nam trong chính sử Trung Quốc xưa*. Hội Nhà Văn. , p. 192.

46. Edmondson, J. A. (1994). Change and Variation in Zhuang. *University of Texas at Arlington*. http://sealang.net/sala/archives/pdf8/edmondson1994change.pdf , p. 149.

CHAPTER 9

1. Vietnamese historians previously used 208 BCE, see 12.12.3.

2. LNCQ, pp. 76-81.

3. Mỵ nương (or Mị nương), the first term is a Tai word for "mother", the second is a Chinese term for "maiden". See Kelly, L. (2013). Tai words and the place of the Tai in the Vietnamese past. *Journal of the Siam Society, 101*, 55-84. , p82. The combination means "princess", see Kelley, L. C. (2015). Inventing traditions in fifteenth-century Vietnam. *Imperial China and Its Southern Neighbours*. (edited by Victor H. Mair and Liam C. Kelley (Singapore - Institute of Southeast Asian Studies, 2015).) , p. 172.

4. LNCQ, p. 81.

5. In SKTT, Vol. 1, p. 139, it was the rhinoceros' horn that parted the sea.

6. Cartwright, M. (2017). *Crossbows in Ancient Chinese Warfare*. https://www.ancient.eu/article/1098/crossbows-in-ancient-chinese-warfare/

7. Photo by author, 4 December 2019.

8. VDUL pp. 52, 53 and SKTT, pp. 184, 185.

9. "is the story of golden turtle believable? .. maybe..". SKTT, Vol. 1, p. 140.

10. Artwork by ViVi2K downloaded from Nguyễn, T. Đ. (2017). *Vua nào nước ta đánh tan 50 vạn quân của Tần Thủy Hoàng?* https://baomoi.com/vua-nao-nuoc-ta-danh-tan-50-van-quan-cua-tan-thuy-hoang/c/22423045.epi

11. Photo by Bình Giang. (2009). *The trigger portion of a Dong Son crossbow dating from 500 BCE-0*. https://commons.wikimedia.org/wiki/File:Dong_Son_crossbow_trigger.JPG

12. The crossbow triggering mechanism normally has at least two levers, one for holding the string and one to release it. It also has two pins to enable the rotation of the levers. Photo by Yprpyqp. (2011). *Han crossbow trigger components*. https://commons.wikimedia.org/wiki/File:Han_crossbow_trigger_components.jpg#/media/File:Han_crossbow_trigger_components.jpg

13. Depts.Washington.Edu. *Crossbows*. https://depts.washington.edu/chinaciv/miltech/crossbow.htm

14. Photo by Yprpyqp - Own work CC BY-SA 4.0. (2014). https://commons.wikimedia.org/w/index.php?curid=67546191

15. Photo by author on 3 December 2019.

16. In VSL, the magic crossbow can shoot *ten arrows at the same time and train ten thousand soldiers*, VSL, p. 18.

17. Later sources referred to Mt Vũ Ninh which is the same as Mt Trâu Sơn. Đào, D. A. (2005). *Đất nước Việt Nam qua các đời - Nghiên cứu địa lý học lịch sử Việt Nam*. NXB Văn Hóa Thông Tin. , p. 74. There is a district called Vũ Ninh, a suburb of Bắc Ninh city, but it is not the same as Mt Vũ Ninh. It is more likely Zhao Tuo withdrew to Mt Vũ Ninh where it would be easier to defend than the flat terrain around district Vũ Ninh. Now, there is now a temple for him at Mt Trâu Sơn.

18. Mt Trâu Sơn, same as Mt Châu Sơn, 21° 8' 17" N 106° 14' 5" E is located at Ngọc Xá, Quế Võ District, Bac Ninh Province, Vietnam. See mindat.org. (2020). *Núi Châu Sơn, Tỉnh Bắc Ninh, Vietnam*. https://www.mindat.org/feature-9871431.html

19. Now the district of Đông Anh where Cổ Loa citadel is located. Đào, D. A. (2005). *Đất nước Việt Nam qua các đời - Nghiên cứu địa lý học lịch sử Việt Nam*. NXB Văn Hóa Thông Tin. , p. 87, p. 97.

20. TKCS, Vol. 36, p. 427.

21. Lê, M. T., & Viện nghiên cứu Phật học Việt Nam. (2005). *Lục độ tập kinh và lịch sử khởi nguyên của dân tộc ta*. NXB Tổng hợp thành phố Hồ Chí Minh. , p. 169.

22. Ngô, T. S. N. P. (2001). *Việt sử tiêu án* (Hội Việt Nam nghiên cứu liên lạc văn hóa Á châu, Trans.). Văn sử (1991), digitised by Công Đệ, Doãn Vượng, Lê Bắc. (1775), p. 9.

23. Aurousseau, L. (1923). La première conquête chinoise des pays annamites (IIIe siècle avant notre ère). http://www.persee.fr/web/revues/home/prescript/article/befeo_0336-1519_1923_num_23_1_5933 , p. 172

24. From southern China, on paper, Qin's ships could have travelled upstream by one or two river routes into North Vietnam. One is by Sông Bằng which flows through the city of Cao Bằng and the other is by Sông Kỳ Cùng which flows by the city of Lạng Sơn. From Lạng Sơn, Qin troops could march all the way to Bắc Giang, (at about 100 km south-west) or three quarters of the way to Don Me and the rest by boat on the Thương river. Flowing to the sea through China territory, Sông Kỳ Cùng becomes Ping'er river. It and Sông Bằng river then flow into Lijiang/ Zuojiang river that flows in the north-east direction through Chongzuo in Guangxi province, the southernmost commandery of the Qin dynasty. From there, the river continues to Nanning, onto Guangzhou and reaches the sea by Hong Kong, a distance of about 900 km.

25. Note that over 2,000 years ago, the river course may have been different from what it is now but it should not alter the designer's plan to use it as a defensive feature.

26. Phan, H. L., Bùi, Đ. D., Doãn, P. Đ., Phạm, T. T., & Trần, B. C. (2019). *Một số trận quyết chiến chiến lược trong lịch sử dân tộc*. NXB Hồng Đức. , p. 17

27. Đào, D. A. (2006). *Lịch sử Việt Nam - Từ nguồn gốc đến thế kỷ XIX*. NXB Văn Hóa Thông Tin. (1957), p. 223

28. VSTA, p. 9.

29. Lê, V. S. (2003). *Việt Nam văn minh sử: lược khảo, tập thượng, từ nguồn gốc đến thế kỷ thứ X*. Lao Động., p. 147. I am unable to locate this river.

30. Made from pieces of leather or metal fixed together by metal studs or leather straps – see Fig. 53.

31. Mt Tiên Du is the same as Mt Lạn Kha where Phật Tích pagoda is. It is about 20 km east of Cổ Loa. See Lê, V. S. (2003). *Việt Nam văn minh sử: lược khảo, tập thượng, từ nguồn gốc đến thế kỷ thứ X*. Lao Động. , p. 147.

32. The translator of VSTA explains Bình Giang as being Đuống river, which would be a reasonable explanation as a demarcation line. However, since both Cổ Loa and Tiên Du (and Vũ Ninh) are

located north of the river, it would make no sense that the king and his enemy would be on the same side of the river. There is one district called Bình Giang, but it is in Hải Dương province and south of Bắc Ninh, a long way from Tiên Du. Besides, Zhao Tuo was unlikely to go through here if he was attacking Cổ Loa. It is not on the most direct route. From the map, it would seem the Cầu river which separates Bắc Ninh and Bắc Giang provinces would be a better fit (see Fig. 49). There is also a mountain range in Bắc Giang province where Núi Non Vua (Mt Non Vua) is located. It is about sixty kilometres northeast of Cổ Loa. Zhao Tuo troops could have camped there instead, as it is a little further from Cổ Loa.

33. SKTT, Vol. 1, p. 139.

34. Both dates, 257 and 208 BCE, are doubtful. Historians now agree this battle should be dated at around 180-179 BCE, if so, An Dương Vương could not have gained power in 257 BCE, 77 years earlier. If he were twenty-five to thirty years of age in 257 BCE, which would seem a reasonable age for a man who took power by force, he would have died at a remote beach far away from his capital as an old man well over one hundred years old.

CHAPTER 10

1. Gu, B. (111). *Han shu - Book of Han*. https://ctext.org/han-shu/zh , Chapter 34 (or 64) – Biography of Yan Zhu, paragraphs 10, 11.

2. Same passage is also in ANCL, p. 129.

3. Aurousseau, L. (1923). La première conquête chinoise des pays annamites (IIIe siècle avant notre ère). http://www.persee.fr/web/revues/home/prescript/article/befeo_0336-1519_1923_num_23_1_5933 , p. 206

4. Unknown (18??–18??) - Public domain. (2007). *Qin Shi Huang's imperial tour across his empire. Depiction in an 18th century album. Source: Portal, Jane (Ed.). The first emperor: China's Terracotta Army. Cambridge, Massachusetts: Harvard University Press, 2007 ISBN 978-0-674-02697-7 Invalid ISBN (p.112)*. https://upload.wikimedia.org/wikipedia/commons/4/47/Qin_Shi_Huang_imperial_tour.jpg

5. Chinese Text Project. (2006-2020). *Huainanzi, Western Han (206 BC-9)* https://ctext.org/huainanzi/ren-xian-xun/ens. Renjian, In the World of Man -Chapter 18, Paragraph 25.

6. Translation from French translation, see, p. 172. A huge army; Loewe expressed doubts about the credibility of such large numbers. See *The Cambridge History of China: Volume 1: The Ch'in and Han Empires, 221 BC–AD 220*. (1986). (D. Twitchett & M. Loewe, Eds. Vol. 1). Cambridge University Press. https://doi.org/DOI: 10.1017/CHOL9780521243278 , p. 99. However, the land of Bai-yue the Qin invaded was large. The combined land area of Guangxi, Guangdong, Fujian and Zhejiang is 639,580 square kilometres, about the size of France and twice as large as Vietnam.

7. Chinese Text Project. (2006-2020). *Shiji-Historical Records- [Western Han] 109 BC-91 BC Sima Qian*. https://ctext.org/shiji. Chapter 6 - Qin Shi Huang Ben Ji, Paragraph 37.

8. Translated from French translation by Aurousseau, L. (1923). La première conquête chinoise des pays annamites (IIIe siècle avant notre ère). http://www.persee.fr/web/revues/home/prescript/article/befeo_0336-1519_1923_num_23_1_5933 , p. 180.

9. Sima, Q., & Chan, C. M. (2016). *The Grand Scribe's Records, Volume X : Volume X: The Memoirs of Han China, Part III* [Book]. Indiana University Press. , Memoir 58, [The Kings of] Huai-nan and Heng-shan, translated by Marc Nürnberger, p. 195.

10. Chinese Text Project. (2006-2020). *Shiji-Historical Records- [Western Han] 109 BC-91 BC Sima Qian.* https://ctext.org/shiji. Chapter 6 - Qin Shi Huang Ben Ji, Paragraph 17.

11. Aurousseau, L. (1923). La première conquête chinoise des pays annamites (IIIe siècle avant notre ère). http://www.persee.fr/web/revues/home/prescript/article/befeo_0336-1519_1923_num_23_1_5933 , p. 140

12. Ibid., p. 179.

13. See map 1, p. 39, Chapter 1 of *The Cambridge History of China: Volume 1: The Ch'in and Han Empires, 221 BC–AD 220.* (1986). (D. Twitchett & M. Loewe, Eds. Vol. 1). Cambridge University Press. https://doi.org/DOI: 10.1017/CHOL9780521243278 .

14. There is also a similar description in Phan , H. L. (2018). *Lịch sử và văn hóa Việt Nam tiếp cận bộ phận* (P. T. Phan, Ed. 4th ed.). NXB Đại Học Quốc Gia Hà Nội. p. 104.

15. The Nan-yue in Huainanzi was not the same as the Nan-yue under Zhao Tuo's rule: the latter included Guangdong, Guangxi provinces in China plus northern Vietnam whereas the former was mostly Guangdong province (see Fig. 5).

16. Aurousseau, L. (1923). La première conquête chinoise des pays annamites (IIIe siècle avant notre ère). http://www.persee.fr/web/revues/home/prescript/article/befeo_0336-1519_1923_num_23_1_5933 , pp. 173-174.

17. Phan , H. L. (2018). *Lịch sử và văn hóa Việt Nam tiếp cận bộ phận* (P. T. Phan, Ed. 4th ed.). NXB Đại Học Quốc Gia Hà Nội. p. 104.

18. Kiều, T. H. (2016). *Góp phần nghiên cứu lịch sử văn hóa Việt Nam - Thời kỳ thiên niên kỷ đầu công nguyên.* NXB Thế Giới. pp. 36-37.

19. Aurousseau, L. (1923). La première conquête chinoise des pays annamites (IIIe siècle avant notre ère). http://www.persee.fr/web/revues/home/prescript/article/befeo_0336-1519_1923_num_23_1_5933 , pp. 177-178.

20. Chinese Text Project. (2006-2020). *Huainanzi, Western Han (206 BC-9)* https://ctext.org/huainanzi/ren-xian-xun/ens, *18, Paragraph 25* Translated from French translation by Aurousseau, L. (1923). La première conquête chinoise des pays annamites (IIIe siècle avant notre ère). http://www.persee.fr/web/revues/home/prescript/article/befeo_0336-1519_1923_num_23_1_5933 , p. 176.

21. Sima, Q., Farmer, J. M., & Nienhauser, W. H. (2010). *The Grand Scribe's Records, Volume IX : The Memoirs of Han China, Part II* [Book]. Indiana University Press. , Chapter 112, pp. 382-383, Marquis of P'ing-chin and Chu-fu [Yen], Memoir 52, translated by Christiane Haupt.

22. Tower ships or a *"louchuan"*, are a type of Chinese naval vessel, primarily a floating fortress. They were used to transport troops and weapons, and were fully arm to attack other ships, even land fortifications. They are the ancient Chinese equivalents of the modern battleship. A picture of such a ship can be found in Zeng Gongliang, Ding Du, & Weide, Y. (1044). *Wujing Zongyao or 'Collection of the Most Important Military Techniques'.*

23. Chinese Text Project. (2006-2020). *Shiji-Historical Records- [Western Han] 109 BC-91 BC Sima Qian.* https://ctext.org/shiji Chapter 48 - Chen Shi Family, Paragraph 24, translated from French translation by Aurousseau, L. (1923). La première conquête chinoise des pays annamites (IIIe siècle avant notre ère). http://www.persee.fr/web/revues/home/prescript/article/befeo_0336-1519_1923_num_23_1_5933 , p. 181.

24. Aurousseau, L. (1923). La première conquête chinoise des pays annamites (IIIe siècle avant notre ère). http://www.persee.fr/web/revues/home/prescript/article/befeo_0336-1519_1923_num_23_1_5933 , p. 236

25. Sima, Q., & Chan, C. M. (2016). *The Grand Scribe's Records, Volume X : Volume X: The Memoirs of Han China, Part III* [Book]. Indiana University Press. , Chapter 53, Memoir 53, p. 2.

26. Arpon, J. (2012). *Warriors formation from backwards. Xi'an, China.* https://commons.wikimedia.org/wiki/File:Terracota_warriors_002.jpg

27. Arpon, J. (June 2012). *Terracota warrior. Archer close-up (inside glass). Xi'an, China.* https://commons.wikimedia.org/wiki/File:Terracota_warrior_close-up.jpg

---

CHAPTER 11

1. There is a Panyu district in Guangzhou. TKCS, Vol. 37, p. 491, mentioned the name Panyu (Phiên Ngu in Vietnamese) after two mountains, "Phiên" mountain, three *li* southeast of Nan-hai district and "Ngu" mountain one *li* south west of the same district. There is a Nanshan mountain between Dafushan and Dishuiyan forest parks in Panyu district. These are the two high grounds in Panyu but I have no information as to whether these are those referred to in the reference.

2. A Chinese *li* at the time of Qin and Han dynasties is 415.8 m. Ren Xiao was not so far out. As an approximation, the distance of Guangdong, from the east (Dacheng Bay) by the East China Sea to the west (Chengdongzhen) by border to Guangxi, is about 700 to 800 kilometres (or less than 2,000 *li*)

3. By this time Panyu was under Qin occupation so Ren Xiao may have meant Zhao Tuo would have the support from other Qin people because what he advised Zhao Tuo to do was effectively an act of treason.

4. Chinese Text Project. (2006-2020). *Shiji-Historical Records- [Western Han] 109 BC-91 BC Sima Qian.* https://ctext.org/shiji, https://ctext.org/shiji/nan-yue-lie-zhuan, Chapter 113, Treatise on the Nanyue , paragraph 1.

5. Shiji (53), p. 3 These rebellions began in 209 BCE so this conversation must have taken place after that.

6. Châu, H. Đ. (2018). *An Nam Truyện - Ghi chép về Việt Nam trong chính sử Trung Quốc xưa.* Hội Nhà Văn. , p. 184.

7. See note 22, p. 4 in Shiji (53), Chapter 113, Memoir 53.

8. From note 22, p. 4 in Shiji (53), , of the above reference, Google Maps indicate two mountain passes located at the northeast of Shaoguan, one is at Zhoutianzhen (about 36 km from Shaoguan) and one further out, about 130 km) at Mt. Dayuling (Dayu County) where the Qin 4th army was in 214 BCE. The other passes are near Yangshan and Yingde.

9. *The Cambridge History of China: Volume 1: The Ch'in and Han Empires, 221 BC–AD 220.* (1986). (D. Twitchett & M. Loewe, Eds. Vol. 1). Cambridge University Press. https://doi.org/DOI: 10.1017/CHOL9780521243278 , p. 85

10. Date given by SKTT, Vol 1, p. 143.

11. Shiji (53) mentioned a Yangshan mountain. Today there is a Yangshan county (see Fig. 54) which is identified as one of the passes in the Nanling mountain range Zhao Tuo closed. It is close to Qitian mountain, one of the five mountains in this range just north in Hunan province.

12. Sima Qian, & translated by Phan Ngọc. (2018). *Sử ký Tư Mã Thiên : (trọn bộ hai tập)* (Vol. 1, 2). Văn học. , p. 129.

13. Archaeologists identified Zhao Mo as the same as Zhao Hu cited in Shiji. See note 53, p. 9 of Shiji(53).

14. *Western Han Nanyue King Museum.* (2020?). www.gznywmuseum.org, http://en.gznywmuseum.org/product/list?categoryId=3&pageIndex=1#

15. Ibid.

16. Lary, D. (1996, January 1996). The tomb of the king of Nanyue - the contemporary agenda of history : scholarship and identity. *Modern China, Vol. 22 No. 1*, 3-27. , p. 5.

17. *Western Han Nanyue King Museum.* www.gznywmuseum.org, http://en.gznywmuseum.org/product/list?categoryId=3&pageIndex=1#

18. Photo by Pubuhan, CC BY-SA 2.5 - https://commons.wikimedia.org/w/index.php?curid=717654',. (2006). Si lü yu yi (silk thread jade burial suit), at the Museum of the Western Han Dynasty Mausoleum of the Nanyue King, Guangzhou.

19. Lary, D. (1996, January 1996). The tomb of the king of Nanyue - the contemporary agenda of history: scholarship and identity. *Modern China, Vol. 22 No. 1*, 3-27. , p. 7, "*From Beijing, the South starts with the Yangtze Valley and covers all of the southern half of China.*".

20. Ibid., p. 23.

21. Ibid., p. 7.

22. Translated from Sima Qian, & translated by Phan Ngọc. (2018). *Sử ký Tư Mã Thiên : (trọn bộ hai tập)* (Vol. 1, 2). Văn học. , Vol. 2, p. 223. Also see Chinese Text Project. (2006-2020). *Shiji-Historical Records- [Western Han] 109 BC-91 BC Sima Qian.* https://ctext.org/shiji, Chapter 97, Li Sheng Biography of Lu Jia, Paragraph 11.

23. Gu, B. (111). *Han shu - Book of Han.* https://ctext.org/han-shu/zh , https://ctext.org/han-shu/xi-nan-yi-liang-yue-zhao , Volume 95, Traditions of the Yi of the southeast, the two Yue, and Chosun (Korea) – Nanyue and Min Yue, Paragraph 16.

24. Western Ou (Guangxi) to the west , Min yue (Fujian) and Changsha (Hunan)– Shiji did not mention Changsha but Ou Lac instead.

25. Gu, B. (111). *Han shu - Book of Han.* https://ctext.org/han-shu/zh , https://ctext.org/han-shu/xi-nan-yi-liang-yue-zhao , Volume 95, Traditions of the Yi of the southeast, the two Yue, and Chosun (Korea) – Nanyue and Min Yue, Paragraph 17.

26. Chinese Text Project. (2006-2020). *Shiji-Historical Records- [Western Han] 109 BC-91 BC Sima Qian.* https://ctext.org/shiji, https://ctext.org/shiji/nan-yue-lie-zhuan, Chapter 113, Treatise on the Nanyue , paragraph 3.

27. According to SKTT, Vol. 1, p. 143, the exchange of letters took place in 179 BCE. So, 49 years earlier is 228 BCE which is seven years earlier than the year the Qin started their campaign against Bai-yue countries. Zhao Tuo died in 137 BCE. According to SKTT, Vol. 1, p. 141, he was 121 years old when he died in 137 BCE.

28. Châu, H. Đ. (2018). *An Nam Truyện - Ghi chép về Việt Nam trong chính sử Trung Quốc xưa.* Hội Nhà Văn. , p. 184. Gu, B. (111). *Han shu - Book of Han.* https://ctext.org/han-shu/zh , Volume 95, Traditions of the Yi of the southeast, the two Yue, and Chosun (Korea) – Nanyue and Min Yue, Paragraph 17 reads "a pair of white jade, thousand kingfishers, ten rhino horns, five hundred purple shells, a pair of Guiyu, forty pairs of green jade, two pairs of peacocks".

29. Shijij (53), p. 8.

30. Chinese Text Project. (2006-2020). *Shiji-Historical Records- [Western Han] 109 BC-91 BC Sima Qian.* https://ctext.org/shiji, https://ctext.org/shiji/nan-yue-lie-zhuan, Chapter 113, Treatise on the Nan-yue , paragraph 1. Also Shiji(53), p. 18.

31. Ibid., https://ctext.org/shiji/nan-yue-lie-zhuan, Chapter 113, Treatise on the Nan-yue , paragraph 8. Also Shiji(53), p. 13.

32. Shiji (53), p. 16 but in another chapter of Shiji, a total force of 200,000 was cited, see Sima Qian, & translated by Phan Ngọc. (2018). *Sử ký Tư Mã Thiên : (trọn bộ hai tập)* (Vol. 1, 2). Văn học. , Vol. 1,

p. 159 and Chinese Text Project. (2006-2020). *Shiji-Historical Records- [Western Han] 109 BC-91 BC Sima Qian.* https://ctext.org/shiji, https://ctext.org/shiji/ping-zhun-shu, Chapter 30, Equalization Level Book, Paragraph 43.

33. The first type of ship appeared to be armed with "*Qua*" or "*Ge*" halberds and the second type was used to descend over waterfalls or rapids. Refer SKTT, Vol. 1, p. 153. Also, the Pole-ax ship was so-called as it was armed with Ge halberds as a way to fight off divers as the Yue were reputedly very good at attacking ships from below the water line, see Kiều, T. H. (2016). *Góp phần nghiên cứu lịch sử văn hóa Việt Nam - Thời kỳ thiên niên kỷ đầu công nguyên.* NXB Thế Giới. , p. 481.

34. "*Ge*" is the same as the Ge type halberds discussed earlier (see 7.7.4).

35. SKTT, Vol. 1, p. 153, named these two Yue generals as Giáp (for Pole-ax) and Quý (for Descending rapids), Shiji (53), p. 17, noted them as Cheng Yen (Zheng Yan) and T'ian Chia (Tian Jia).

36. Gu, B. (111). *Han shu - Book of Han.* https://ctext.org/han-shu/zh , Chapter 65, "Xinan Yi Liang Yue Biography", (or 95) Traditions of the Yi of the southeast, the two Yue, and Chosun (Korea) – Nanyue and Min Yue, paragraphs 26, 27.

37. "*The flames had been so ferocious that they even burnt the stone sides of a canal.*" Brindley, E. (2018). *Ancient China and the Yue : perceptions and identities on the southern frontier, c.400 BCE - 50 CE.* , p. 228, footnote 17.

38. Shiji (53), p. 18: Su Hung (or Su Hong) captured the king, Zhao Jiande, Tu Chi (or Du Ji) or sometimes known as Sun Tu (Sun Du) caught Lu Jia, also see SKTT, Vol. 1, p. 153 (Tô Hoằng and Đô Kê or Tôn Đô respectively).

39. Sima, Q., & Chan, C. M. (2016). *The Grand Scribe's Records, Volume X : Volume X: The Memoirs of Han China, Part III* [Book]. Indiana University Press. , Memoirs 54, The Eastern Yue, p. 37.

40. Shiji (53) noted this location to be in Xiangzhou County, Laibin, Guangxi, near Liuzhou. Kuei-lin is Guilin.

41. A similar passage in Han shu gave a figure of 400,000 "mouths" from Western Ou and Lou surrendered, see Gu, B. (111). *Han shu - Book of Han.* https://ctext.org/han-shu/zh , Chapter 95, paragraph 27.

42. Maspero, H. (1918). Etudes d'histoire d'Annam. *Bulletin de l'Ecole française d'Extrême-Orient*, 1-36. https://www.persee.fr/doc/befeo_0336-1519_1918_num_18_1_5888 , p. 11.

43. TKCS, Book 37, p. 423.

44. SKTT Vol. 1, p. 153.

45. *The Cambridge History of China: Volume 1: The Ch'in and Han Empires, 221 BC–AD 220.* (1986). (D. Twitchett & M. Loewe, Eds. Vol. 1). Cambridge University Press. https://doi.org/DOI: 10.1017/CHOL9780521243278 , p. 126, p. 157.

46. Chinese Text Project. (2006-2020). *Shiji-Historical Records- [Western Han] 109 BC-91 BC Sima Qian.* https://ctext.org/shiji, Chapter 30, Level (stabilization) book, Paragraph 46. Translated from Sima Qian, & translated by Phan Ngọc. (2018). *Sử ký Tư Mã Thiên : (trọn bộ hai tập)* (Vol. 1, 2). Văn học. , Vol.1, p. 161.

47. Aurousseau, L. (1923). La première conquête chinoise des pays annamites (IIIe siècle avant notre ère). http://www.persee.fr/web/revues/home/prescript/article/befeo_0336-1519_1923_num_23_1_5933 , p. 185.

CHAPTER 12

1. Phan, H. L. (2018). *Lịch sử và văn hóa Việt Nam tiếp cận bộ phận* (P. T. Phan, Ed. 4th ed.). NXB Đại Học Quốc Gia Hà Nội., p. 127.

2. Nguyễn, T. D. (2018). *Văn hóa Việt Nam thường thức*. NXB Hà Nội., p. 72.

3. Lê, M. T., & Viện nghiên cứu Phật học Việt Nam. (2005). *Lục độ tập kinh và lịch sử khởi nguyên của dân tộc ta*. NXB Tổng hợp thành phố Hồ Chí Minh., p. 169.

4. SKTT, Vol 1, p. 147.

5. Such as *Đền thờ Triệu Đà* at Xuân Quan village, Văn Giang district, Hưng Yên province.

6. Ngô, T. S. N. P. (2001). *Việt sử tiêu án* (Hội Việt Nam nghiên cứu liên lạc văn hóa Á châu, Trans.). Văn sử (1991), digitised by Công Đệ, Doãn Vượng, Lê Bắc. (1775), p. 9.

7. Kiều, T. H. (2016). *Góp phần nghiên cứu lịch sử văn hóa Việt Nam - Thời kỳ thiên niên kỷ đầu công nguyên*. NXB Thế Giới., p. 106.

8. Allard, F. (2000). Frontiers and Boundaries: The Han Empire From its Southern Periphery. 233-254., p. 235.

9. Lữ Gia street in District 10 of Ho Chi Minh City.

10. VSTA, p. 13.

11. Đào, D. A. (2005). *Lịch sử cổ đại Việt Nam* NXB Văn Hóa Thông Tin., Chapter 6, p. 94.

12. Kiều, T. H. (2016). *Góp phần nghiên cứu lịch sử văn hóa Việt Nam - Thời kỳ thiên niên kỷ đầu công nguyên*. NXB Thế Giới., pp. 98-127.

13. Đào, D. A. (2006). *Lịch sử Việt Nam - Từ nguồn gốc đến thế kỷ XIX*. NXB Văn Hóa Thông Tin. (1957), p. 49. Đào believed that Qin forces probably reached as far as Thái Nguyên and Bắc Giang (see Fig. 49) but they were fiercely resisted by the Lạc people and withdrew; their newly conquered commandery of Xiang never extended to Vietnam. His view supports that of Henri Maspero whereby Xiang was completely inside the border of China, occupying part of Guangxi and Guangdong provinces only. On the other hand, Aurousseau took a different view; he suggests Qin forces occupied most of northern and central Vietnam, including Quang Nam province, and possibly as far south as Cape Varella, (see Fig. 3) as the southernmost border of Xiang commandery. One can find an excellent summary of various arguments in Kiều, T. H. (2016). *Góp phần nghiên cứu lịch sử văn hóa Việt Nam - Thời kỳ thiên niên kỷ đầu công nguyên*. NXB Thế Giới., pp. 48-68, who sided with Aurousseau that Xiang included a significant part of Vietnam. Aurousseau, L. (1923). La première conquête chinoise des pays annamites (IIIe siècle avant notre ère). http://www.persee.fr/web/revues/home/prescript/article/befeo_0336-1519_1923_num_23_1_5933, pp. 153, 154.

14. Over one thousand years later, troops from Đại Việt and Champa would use the coastal route, and not the land route, along central Vietnam to attack one another.

15. *The Cambridge History of China: Volume 1: The Ch'in and Han Empires, 221 BC–AD 220*. (1986). (D. Twitchett & M. Loewe, Eds. Vol. 1). Cambridge University Press. https://doi.org/DOI: 10.1017/CHOL9780521243278, Map 2, p.41.

16. SKTT, Vol. 1, p. 138.

17. Phan, H. L. (2018). *Lịch sử và văn hóa Việt Nam tiếp cận bộ phận* (P. T. Phan, Ed. 4th ed.). NXB Đại Học Quốc Gia Hà Nội., p. 107.

18. Đào, D. A. (2005). *Lịch sử cổ đại Việt Nam* NXB Văn Hóa Thông Tin., Chapter 6, p. 100

19. Shiji (53), footnote 7, p. 2.

20. *The Cambridge History of China: Volume 1: The Ch'in and Han Empires, 221 BC–AD 220*. (1986). (D. Twitchett & M. Loewe, Eds. Vol. 1). Cambridge University Press. https://doi.org/DOI: 10.1017/CHOL9780521243278 , Map 8.

21. Phan , H. L. (2018). *Lịch sử và văn hóa Việt Nam tiếp cận bộ phận* (P. T. Phan, Ed. 4th ed.). NXB Đại Học Quốc Gia Hà Nội. , p. 111

22. Ibid. p. 127

23. Ibid. p. 111

24. Gu, B. (111). *Han shu - Book of Han*. https://ctext.org/han-shu/zh , Chapter 95, paragraph 17.

25. SKTT, Vol. 1, p. 141

26. Shiji (53), footnote 51, p. 8

27. According to CM, Vol.1, p. 89, Cửu Chân was the Xiang commandery under the Qin dynasty. It had 12 prefectures, at 111 BCE, under the Han, it was divided into two: five prefectures (Tị Ảnh, Lư Dung, Tây Quyển, Tượng Lâm and Chu Ngô) formed Nhật Nam, the other seven (Tư Phố, Cư Phong, Đô Bàng, Dư Phát, Hàm Hoan, Vô Thiết and Vô Biên) remained Cửu Chân. The whole region covered Thanh Hóa, Nghệ An, Hà Tĩnh, Quảng Bình, Quảng Trị and Thừa Thiên.

28. Phan, H. L. (2018). *Di sản văn hóa Việt Nam dưới góc nhìn lịch sử*. NXB Đại Học Quốc Gia Hà Nội. , p. 939.

CHAPTER 13

1. Ba Dội pass is Tam Điệp pass between Thanh Hóa and Ninh Bình provinces.

2. The original version was written in Hán Nôm (using Chinese script) and translated into Vietnamese as below (taken from Dương Văn Thâm et al. (2005). *Hồ Xuân Hương - Thơ và Đời*. NXB Văn Học. , p. 55, replacing "Cửa con" with "Cửa son" which is used in other versions):

Một đèo, một đèo, lại một đèo,
Khen ai khéo tạc cảnh cheo leo.
Cửa son đỏ loét tùm hum nóc,
Hòn đá xanh rì lún phún rêu.

Another translation is as follows:

"A pass, another pass, and another
What exquisite talent has created all that!
The virgin gate, crimson hued, densely crested
The rock, dark green colored, thinly mossed".

As translated by Trần, M.-V. (2002). 'Come on, Girls, Let's Go Bail Water': Eroticism in Hồ Xuân Hương's Vietnamese Poetry. *Journal of Southeast Asian Studies, 33*(3), 471-494. www.jstor.org/stable/20072448 , p. 479. Befitting the poet as well-known for writing erotic poems, this poem is read by some as a description of a naked female body. See Hoàng, P. T. (2014). Phân tích tác động thẩm mỹ của văn bản thơ Đèo ba dội từ góc độ Mỹ học tiếp nhận. http://phebinhvanhoc.com.vn/phan-tich-tac-dong-tham-my-cua-van-ban-tho-deo-ba-doi-tu-goc-do-my-hoc-tiep-nhan/

3. Thái, V. C. (2009). *Nghiên cứu chữ viết cổ trên bia ký ở Đông Dương*. NXB Khoa Học Xã Hội. , p. 175.

4. Archaeologists also refer to another civilization, Đồng Nai, in the vicinity formed by Saigon, Đồng

Nai and Vàm Cỏ Đông rivers all the way down to the sea including Tây Ninh, Ho Chi Minh city and Bà rịa Vũng Tàu.

5. Phan, H. L. (2018). *Lịch sử và văn hóa Việt Nam tiếp cận bộ phận* (P. T. Phan, Ed. 4th ed.). NXB Đại Học Quốc Gia Hà Nội. , pp. 181-182

6. Map based on Lâm, T. M. D. (2018). *Sa Huỳnh - Lâm Ấp - Chămpa: Thế kỷ 5 trước công nguyên đến thế kỷ 5 sau công nguyên (một số vấn đề khảo cổ học) = Sa Huynh - Linyi - Champa: 5th century BC - 5th century AD: some archaeological issues*. NXB Thế Giới. , p. 47.

7. Photo by Zwegers, A. (2007). *Nha Trang, Po Nagar Cham, North Tower.* https://commons.wikimedia.org/wiki/File:Nha_Trang,_Po_Nagar_Cham,_North_Tower_(6223880651).jpg

8. According to Schweyer, A.-V. (2019). *The Birth of Champa.* , p. 3, the southernmost prefecture of Nhật Nam commandery, called Xianglin (*Tượng Lâm*) is Thừa Thiên-Huế province thus the border would likely to be at Hải Vân pass. Đào had a different view; he believed Xianglin prefecture extended as far south as Cả pass which would have included two more southern provinces of Bình Định and Phú Yên. See Đào, D. A. (2005). *Đất nước Việt Nam qua các đời - Nghiên cứu địa lý học lịch sử Việt Nam.* NXB Văn Hóa Thông Tin. , p. 61. On the other hand, Ngô suggests Tượng Lâm prefecture would extend to Cù Mông pass and include Bình Định province only. See Ngô, V. D. (2002). *Văn hóa cổ Champa.* NXB Văn Hóa Dân Tộc. , p. 49.

9. Glover, I. (2012). *Champa and its relations to preceding iron age cultures - Văn hóa Champa và mối quan hệ với các nền văn hóa thời đại đồ sắt trước đó.* Perspectives on the archaeology of Vietnam International Colloquium, Hanoi 29th February - 2nd March 2012 = Toàn cảnh khảo cổ học Việt Nam, Hanoi, Vietnam. , p. 157. According to Glover, the *name Champa is ultimately derived from India, being the name of an early kingdom in the lower Ganges valley near modern Bhagalpur.*

10. Lâm, T. M. D. (2018). *Sa Huỳnh - Lâm Ấp - Chămpa: Thế kỷ 5 trước công nguyên đến thế kỷ 5 sau công nguyên (một số vấn đề khảo cổ học) = Sa Huynh - Linyi - Champa: 5th century BC - 5th century AD: some archaeological issues.* NXB Thế Giới. , p. 38.

11. Phú Khương is the name of a hamlet at Phổ Khánh village, Đức Phổ District, Quang Ngãi province. The site is on a sand dune by An Khê lagoon. There are two other sites located at Thạnh Đức hamlet and Long Thạnh hamlet, both are in Phổ Thạnh village, Đức Phổ District, Quang Ngãi province by Nước Mặn Lagoon (about seven kilometres south of An Khê Lagoon). See Lê, H. K. (2019). *Đầm An Khê - Một di sản thiên nhiên quý báu.* http://baoquangngai.vn/channel/2047/201911/dam-an-khe-mot-di-san-thien-nhien-quy-bau-2976505/

12. Notably Phạm Thị Ninh, Nguyễn Kim Dung, Bùi Chí Hoàng, Henri Fontaine, Ian Glover, Andreas Reinecke and Mariko Yamagata and Lâm Thị Mỹ Dung.

13. Solheim, W. G. (1959). Introduction to Sa-huynh. *Asian Perspectives, 3*(2), 97-108. , p. 100.

14. Lâm, T. M. D. (2018). *Sa Huỳnh - Lâm Ấp - Chămpa: Thế kỷ 5 trước công nguyên đến thế kỷ 5 sau công nguyên (một số vấn đề khảo cổ học) = Sa Huynh - Linyi - Champa: 5th century BC - 5th century AD: some archaeological issues.* NXB Thế Giới. , p.49.

15. At Nghi Xuân district, by Cả river, north of Ngang pass.

16. Giồng Cá Vồ was excavated in 1993. It is located at Hòa Hiệp hamlet, Long Hòa village, Cần Giờ district, Hồ chí Minh city.

17. Excavated in 2002 and 2005. Located at thôn 3 Rạch Già, xã Đảo Long Sơn, Bà Rịa Vũng Tàu

18. Nguyễn, K. D. (2017). The Sa Huynh Culture in Ancient Regional Trade Networks: A Comparative Study of Ornaments. 311-332. , p.314.

19. Lockhart, B. M., & Phuong, T. K. (2011). *The Cham of Vietnam : History, society and art.* Singapore University Press.

20. Trà Kiệu hamlet, Duy Sơn village, Duy Xuyên district, Quảng Nam province.

21. Yamagata, M., & Matsumura, H. (2017). Austronesian Migration to Central Vietnam: Crossing over the Iron Age Southeast Asian Sea. 333-355. , p. 337.

22. Nguyễn, K. D. (2017). The Sa Huynh Culture in Ancient Regional Trade Networks: A Comparative Study of Ornaments. 311-332. , p. 313.

23. At Gò Mả Vôi site located at Duy Trung hamlet, Duy Xuyên district, Quảng Nam province, 22 iron objects were found including axes, hoes, knives, machetes and spearheads. There were also 29 bronze axes and spearheads of different design, see Nguyễn, C. (2011). *Di tích văn hóa Sa huỳnh ở Gò Mả Vôi (Quảng Nam) qua 3 lần khai quật*. https://123doc.net/document/2571704-di-tich-van-hoa-sa-huynh-o-go-ma-voi-quang-nam-qua-3-lan-khai-quat-pdf.htm, p. 183.

24. Bellwood, P. (1993). Southeast Asia before History. In N. Tarling (Ed.), *The Cambridge History of Southeast Asia: Volume 1: From Early Times to c.1800* (Vol. 1, pp. 51-136). Cambridge University Press. https://doi.org/DOI: 10.1017/CHOL9780521355056.004 , p. 130.

25. Phan , H. L. (2018). *Lịch sử và văn hóa Việt Nam tiếp cận bộ phận* (P. T. Phan, Ed. 4th ed.). NXB Đại Học Quốc Gia Hà Nội. , p. 151.

26. Nguyễn, K. D. (2017). The Sa Huynh Culture in Ancient Regional Trade Networks: A Comparative Study of Ornaments. 311-332. , p. 322.

27. Điện Nam village, Điện Bàn district, Quảng Nam province. See Hồ, X. T. (2017?). *Bảo Tàng Quảng Nam - 20 năm nghiên cứu khảo cổ học*. http://baotang.quangnam.gov.vn/Default.aspx-?tabid=63&Group=51&NID=1826&bao-tang-quang-nam--2-nam-nghien-cuu-khao-co-hoc

28. Nguyễn, K. D. (2017). The Sa Huynh Culture in Ancient Regional Trade Networks: A Comparative Study of Ornaments. 311-332. , p. 323.

29. Hung, H.-c., Nguyen, K. D., Bellwood, P., & Carson, M. T. (2013). Coastal Connectivity: Long-Term Trading Networks Across the South China Sea. *The Journal of Island and Coastal Archaeology, 8*(3), 384-404. , p. 390

30. Apostol, V. M. (2012). Way of the Ancient Healer : Sacred Teachings from the Philippine Ancestral Traditions. http://www.myilibrary.com?id=488055 , p. 202.

31. Nguyễn, K. D. (2017). The Sa Huynh Culture in Ancient Regional Trade Networks: A Comparative Study of Ornaments. 311-332. , p. 321.

32. Hung, H.-c., Nguyen, K. D., Bellwood, P., & Carson, M. T. (2013). Coastal Connectivity: Long-Term Trading Networks Across the South China Sea. *The Journal of Island and Coastal Archaeology, 8*(3), 384-404. , p. 390

33. Nguyễn, K. D. (2017). The Sa Huynh Culture in Ancient Regional Trade Networks: A Comparative Study of Ornaments. 311-332. , p. 322.

34. Ibid. p. 328.

35. Tràng Kênh, Minh Đức, Thủy Nguyên, Hải Phòng.

36. Hung, H.-c. (2014). Jade in Southeast Asia. 1-8. , p.4.

37. Hung, H.-c., Nguyen, K. D., Bellwood, P., & Carson, M. T. (2013). Coastal Connectivity: Long-Term Trading Networks Across the South China Sea. *The Journal of Island and Coastal Archaeology, 8*(3), 384-404. , p. 386

38. There are also sites north of Đèo Ngang at Hà Tĩnh but there are different opinions as to whether they belong to Sa Huỳnh (see p. 49 of reference below).

39. Lâm, T. M. D. (2018). *Sa Huỳnh - Lâm Ấp - Chămpa: Thế kỷ 5 trước công nguyên đến thế kỷ 5 sau công nguyên (một số vấn đề khảo cổ học) = Sa Huynh - Linyi - Champa: 5th century BC - 5th century AD: some archaeological issues*. NXB Thế Giới. , p 47.

40. Bellwood, P. (1993). Southeast Asia before History. In N. Tarling (Ed.), *The Cambridge History of Southeast Asia: Volume 1: From Early Times to <I>c.</I>1800* (Vol. 1, pp. 51-136). Cambridge University Press. https://doi.org/DOI: 10.1017/CHOL9780521355056.004 , p. 130.

41. There are Austroasiatic, Austronesian, Dravidian, Hmong-Mien, Indo-Aryan, Sino-Tibetan, Tai-Kadai, in the language phyla covering the region of Indian subcontinent, Southeast Asia and Indonesian Archipelago. See Coupe, A. R., & Kratochvíl, F. Asia before English, Pre-publication draft. *Handbook of Asian Englishes, Bolton, Kingsley, Kirkpatrick, Thomas A. and Botha, Werner (eds).* , p. 2.

42. Bellwood, P. (2012). *Vietnam and the Prehistory of Eastern Asia – A multidisciplinary perspective on the Neolithic - Việt Nam và tiền sử Đông Á - một hướng tiếp cận đa ngành về thời kỳ đồ đá mới* Perspectives on the archaeology of Vietnam International Colloquium, Hanoi 29th February - 2nd March 2012 = Toàn cảnh khảo cổ học Việt Nam, Hanoi, Vietnam. , p. 54.

43. Bulbeck, D. (2014). Island Southeast Asia: Neolithic. In C. Smith (Ed.), *Encyclopedia of Global Archaeology* (pp. 4090-4096). Springer New York. https://doi.org/10.1007/978-1-4419-0465-2_866

44. Hòa Diêm, Hòa Sơn hamlet, Cam Thịnh Đông commune, Cam Ranh city, Khánh Hòa province.

45. Yamagata, M., & Matsumura, H. (2017). Austronesian Migration to Central Vietnam: Crossing over the Iron Age Southeast Asian Sea. 333-355. , p. 346.

46. Meteorological Service Singapore. *Winds*. http://www.weather.gov.sg/learn_winds/

47. During the war between the Nguyễn and the Tây Sơn at the end of the 17th century (see Chapter 2), Nguyễn's navy would sail up from Saigon to attack Tây Sơn fortress at Quy Nhơn in Bình Định province during the months of Nồm winds (from the south) then withdraw during the months of Bắc winds (from the north).

48. Lâm, T. M. D. (2018). *Sa Huỳnh - Lâm Ấp - Chămpa: Thế kỷ 5 trước công nguyên đến thế kỷ 5 sau công nguyên (một số vấn đề khảo cổ học) = Sa Huynh - Linyi - Champa: 5th century BC - 5th century AD: some archaeological issues*. NXB Thế Giới. , p.35

49. Photo taken by author on 11 December 2019, National History of Vietnam, Hanoi.

50. Photo taken by author on 11 December 2019, National History of Vietnam, Hanoi.

51. Photo taken by author on 11 December 2019, National History of Vietnam, Hanoi.

52. Rotated by 180 degrees from photo taken by HappyMidnight, & BY-SA, C. (2012). Three node pendant. https://upload.wikimedia.org/wikipedia/commons/e/e6/Three_node_pendant_%-28Jade%29%2C_Artefacts_of_Phu_Hoa_site%28Dong_Nai_province%29.JPG

53. Photo taken by author on 11 December 2019, National History of Vietnam, Hanoi.

54. Photo taken by author on 4 July 2019 at the History Museum, Ho Chi Minh City.

55. Photo taken by author on 11 December 2019, National History of Vietnam, Hanoi.

CHAPTER 14

1. Around Việt Trì, Sơn Tây and Vĩnh Yên.
2. Census by the Han as of 2 CE, there were 92,440 (H=hearths), 746,237 (P=people) in Giao Chỉ, 35,743 H, 166,013 P for Cửu Chân and 15,460 H, 69,486 P for Nhật Nam. See Taylor, K. W. (1983). *The Birth of Vietnam*. Berkeley : University of California Press. , p 55. Also refer Gu, B. (111). *Han shu - Book of Han*. https://ctext.org/han-shu/zh , https://ctext.org/han-shu/di-li-zhi , paragraphs 33 to 39, Volume 28, Treatise of Geography.
3. SKTT, Vol.1, p. 135.
4. More Vietnamese folk tales can be found in Nguyen, N. C., & Sachs, D. (2003). *Two cakes fit for a king : folktales from Vietnam*. University of Hawai`i Press.

APPENDIX I

1. Officially, the Former Han dynasty divided Vietnam into three commanderies, not provinces or districts.
2. Sima Qian, & translated by Phan Ngọc. (2018). *Sử ký Tư Mã Thiên : (trọn bộ hai tập)* (Vol. 1, 2). Văn học.
3. Sima, Q., & Chan, C. M. (2016). *The Grand Scribe's Records, Volume X : Volume X: The Memoirs of Han China, Part III* [Book]. Indiana University Press.
4. Gu, B. (111). *Han shu - Book of Han*. https://ctext.org/han-shu/zh
5. Lịch Đạo Nguyên, (Li Daoyuan), Dương Thủ Kính, (Yang, Shoujing), Hùng Hội Trinh, (Xiong, Huizhen), Đoàn Huy Trọng, (Duan, Xizhong), Trần Kiều Dịch, (Chen, Qiaoyi), & Nguyễn Bá Mão. (2005). *Thủy kinh chú sớ* (Nguyễn Bá Mão, Trans.). NXB Thuận Hóa ; Trung tâm văn hóa ngôn ngữ Đông Tây. (Giang Tô, China 1999), Vol. 37, p. 427, or Shui Jing Zhu Shu (Additional notes on the commentary on the water classic) which is a 19th-century annotation of Shui Jing Zhu.
6. Chinese Text Project. (2006-2020). *Shui Jing Zhu, Wei, Jin, and North-South, Waterways*. https://ctext.org/han-shu/zh - Shui Jing Zhu (Commentary on the water classic).
7. Nguyễn, H. T. (2019). *Thư tịch cổ Trung quốc viết về Văn Lang, Âu Lạc, An Dương Vương, thành Cổ Loa*. Thời đại Hùng Vương trong tiến trình lịch sử Việt Nam - Kỷ yếu hội thảo khoa học quốc gia., Hanoi, 9-2019.
8. Such as *The Cambridge History of China: Volume 1: The Ch'in and Han Empires, 221 BC–AD 220*. (1986). (D. Twitchett & M. Loewe, Eds. Vol. 1). Cambridge University Press. https://doi.org/DOI: 10.1017/CHOL9780521243278
9. Kiều, T. H. (2016). *Góp phần nghiên cứu lịch sử văn hóa Việt Nam - Thời kỳ thiên niên kỷ đầu công nguyên*. NXB Thế Giới.
10. Such as Vietnam Academy of Social Sciences, Institute of Archaeology. (2018). *Tuyển tập 50 năm khảo cổ học Việt Nam 1968-2018*. NXB Khoa Học Xã Hội.
11. *Khâm Định*, Imperially ordered.
12. *Việt Sử*, History of Viet.
13. *Cương Mục*, Outline, summary and expanded details.
14. Quốc sử quán triều Nguyễn, & Viện sử học. (1998). *Khâm định Việt sử thông giám cương mục* (Hoa Bằng, Phạm Trọng Điềm,,Trần Văn Giáp (1957), Trans.). Giáo dục.

15. Trần, T. P. (2011). *Lĩnh nam chích quái* (restored and edited by Vũ Quỳnh and Kiều Phú, Đinh Gia Khánh, Nguyễn Ngọc San, Trans.). NXB Trẻ; Hồng Bàng. (1492)

16. Translation by Taylor, K. W. (1983). *The Birth of Vietnam*. Berkeley : University of California Press.

17. Ngô Sĩ Liên. (1998). *Đại Việt Sử Ký Toàn Thư* Khoa Học Xã Hội (Social Science) (1998). (Chính Hòa version (1697).)

18. Lịch Đạo Nguyên, (Li Daoyuan), Dương Thủ Kính, (Yang, Shoujing), Hùng Hội Trinh, (Xiong, Huizhen), Đoàn Huy Trọng, (Duan, Xizhong), Trần Kiều Dịch, (Chen, Qiaoyi), & Nguyễn Bá Mão. (2005). *Thủy kinh chú sớ* (Nguyễn Bá Mão, Trans.). NXB Thuận Hóa ; Trung tâm văn hóa ngôn ngữ Đông Tây. (Giang Tô, China 1999), Vol. 37, p. 427. Or Shui Jing Zhu Shu (Additional notes on the commentary on the water classic) which is a 19th century annotation of Shui Jing Zhu.

19. Unknown, translated by Trần Quốc Vượng (1959), & compared and corrected by Đinh Khắc Thuân. (2005). *Việt Sử Lược*. Thuận Hóa. (1377)

20. Ngô, T. S. N. P. (2001). *Việt sử tiêu án* (Hội Việt Nam nghiên cứu liên lạc văn hóa Á châu, Trans.). Văn sử (1991), digitised by Công Đệ, Doãn Vượng, Lê Bắc. (1775)

21. *Lüshi Chunqiu*. (2020). https://en.wikipedia.org/wiki/L%C3%BCshi_Chunqiu

22. Yanjun Lan.

23. *Huainanzi*. (2020). https://en.wikipedia.org/wiki/Huainanzi

24. Renjian – In the world of man (or people's leisure training).

25. *Records of the Grand Historian*. (2020). https://en.wikipedia.org/wiki/Records_of_the_Grand_Historian

26. Marquis of P'ing-chin and Chu-fu [Yen], Memoir 52, translated by Christiane Haupt.

27. There are 12 Annals, 10 Tables, 8 Treaties, 30 Genealogies, 70 Biographies (or Memoirs) in Shiji. Depending on the indexing methods, if the first annal is indexed as 1, then Memoir 53 would be indexed as 113 by the time the Tables, Treaties, Genealogies and Biographies are added. But if the 1st Biography is indexed as 1 then Memoir 53 would be indexed at 53.

28. The Southern Yüeh,1 Memoir 53, translated by William H. Nienhauser, Jr.

29. The Eastern Yüeh,1 Memoir 54, translated by William H. Nienhauser, Jr.

30. [The Kings of] Huai-nan and Heng-shan, Memoir 58, translated by Marc Nürnberger.

31. Treatise – Equalization.

32. House of King Goujian of Yue, Genealogies.

33. Genealogies (or Family), House of Zhao.

34. Li Sheng Biography of Lu Jia or Biographies of Li Yiji and Lu Gu.

35. *Book of Han*. (2020). https://en.wikipedia.org/wiki/Book_of_Han

36. Annals of Emperor Zhao, 86–74 BCE.

37. Treatise of Geography, Gu, B. (111). *Han shu - Book of Han*. https://ctext.org/han-shu/zh , https://ctext.org/han-shu/zh , paragraphs 33 to 39.

38. Biography of Yan Zhu.

39. Biography of *"Traditions of the Yi of the Southeast, the two Yues, and Chosun (Korea) – Nanyue and Min Yue"*

40. Fan Ye. (2020). *Book of the Later Han*. https://en.wikipedia.org/wiki/Book_of_the_Later_Han

41. Ma Yuan Biography (Chapter 14 or 24 if number 1 biography is counted as 11).
42. *Commentary on the Water Classic.* (2020). https://en.wikipedia.org/wiki/Commentary_on_the_Water_Classic
43. Lịch Đạo Nguyên, (Li Daoyuan), Dương Thủ Kính, (Yang, Shoujing), Hùng Hội Trinh, (Xiong, Huizhen), Đoàn Huy Trọng, (Duan, Xizhong), Trần Kiều Dịch, (Chen, Qiaoyi), & Nguyễn Bá Mão. (2005). *Thủy kinh chú sớ* (Nguyễn Bá Mão, Trans.). NXB Thuận Hóa ; Trung tâm văn hóa ngôn ngữ Đông Tây. (Giang Tô, China 1999), p.5.

APPENDIX 2

1. Lê, Q. Đ. (2007). *Đại Việt thông sử* (T. L. Ngô, Trans.). NXB Văn hóa - Thông tin. (1759), p. 121.
2. The Vietnamese term is *Văn Hiến* which directly translates as 'Books and Learned People'.
3. Lê, Q. Đ. (2007). *Đại Việt thông sử* (T. L. Ngô, Trans.). NXB Văn hóa - Thông tin. (1759), p. 123.
4. 110 books included 16 Hiến Chương type (charters, regulations, decrees, geography), 9 of which were no longer available - 67 Văn Thơ (literature and poetry) type - 19 Truyện ký (story, diary, history) type, one was no longer in existence – 14 Phương Kỹ (Buddhist Scripture, geography, medicine).
5. As a matter of contrast, around Lê Quý Đôn's time, thousands of miles away, King George III of Great Britain in 1760 purchased a private collection of 6,000 books from the library of Joseph Smith. After his death in 1820, King George IV donated these and other books, totalling 65,000 to the British Museum. See Nichols, T. (2010). *Handy-book of the British Museum, for every-day readers.* Nabu Press. , p. 396.
6. Lê, Q. Đ. (2007). *Đại Việt thông sử* (T. L. Ngô, Trans.). NXB Văn hóa - Thông tin. (1759), p. 124.
7. Lê Quý Đôn referred to *Chiếu*: decrees from the king,
8. Đặng, Đ. T. (2000). *Lịch sử sử học Việt Nam (từ thế kỷ XI đến giữa thế kỷ XIX)*. NXB Trẻ. , pp. 295-297.
9. It was made compulsory by the French colonial government in 1910 CE.
10. Nguyễn, P. P. Việt Nam, Chữ viết, Ngôn ngữ và Xã hội – Chương 1 – Cái nhìn đối chiếu giữa hai chữ tiếng Việt (Vietnam, Writing, Language and Society – Chapter 1 – A view of the comparison between two forms of Vietnamese writing). http://www.namkyluctinh.com/a-ngonngu/nphuphong-vnchuvietngonngu.pdf , p. 5.
11. Phan, H. C. (2014). *Lịch triều hiến chương loại chí – Tập 5 – Binh chế chí–Văn tịch chí–Bang giao chí* (Vol. 39 to 49). NXB Trẻ. (1819)
12. 207 included 27 Hiến Chương type (charters, regulations, decrees, geography), - 104 Thi Văn (literature and poetry) type - 52 Truyện ký (story, diary, history) type, 24 – Kinh Sử (scripture, history)
13. 429 included 166 in history, 37 in geography, ten in technical, fourteen in linguistics, 151 in literature, fourteen in religion, 20 in philosophy and seventeen in miscellaneous subjects. See Đặng, Đ. T. (2000). *Lịch sử sử học Việt Nam (từ thế kỷ XI đến giữa thế kỷ XIX)*. NXB Trẻ. , p. 12.
14. *"Null part on n'a vu le patrimoine intellectuel d'un peuple fondre avec une telle rapidité"*. See Pelliot, P., & Cadière, L. (1904). Première étude sur les sources annamites de l'histoire d'Annam. *Bulletin de l'Ecole française d'Extrême-Orient, 4*, 617-671. http://www.persee.fr/web/revues/home/prescript/article/befeo_0336-1519_1904_num_4_1_1360 , p. 617.

15. Ủy Ban Phiên Dịch Sử Liệu Việt Nam

16. Hán Nôm is now a bachelor study program of the Faculty of Sciences of Hue University

17. *Hán Nôm.* (2020?). http://khoavanhoc-ngonngu.edu.vn/gioi-thieu/cac-bo-mon-2/bộ-môn-hán-nôm.html

18. *Viện Hàn Lâm Khoa Học Xã Hội Việt Nam, Viện Nghiên Cứu Hán Nôm,* 漢喃研究院 *Institute of Sino-Nom studies.* (2020?). http://www.hannom.org.vn/

19. Chu, T. L. (2004, 12-13 tháng 11, 2004). *Số hóa để bảo quản và khai thác di sản Hán Nôm Việt Nam: triển vọng và thách thức. Digitisation to preserve and exploit the heritage of Hán Nôm Vietnam: Prospects and Challenges) – International Conference on Nôm language* Hội nghị quốc tế về chữ Nôm Thư viện quốc gia Việt Nam – Hà Nội , p. 1.

20. Vietnamese Khánh or Biên Khánh,

21. Trần, N., Gros, F., Viện Nghiên Cứu Hán Nôm, & École française, d. E.-O. (1993). *Di Sản Hán Nôm Việt Nam: Thư mục đề yếu.* . NXB Khoa Học Xã Hội.

22. Viện Nghiên Cứu Hán Nôm. (2007). *Thư mục thác bản văn khắc Hán Nôm Việt Nam = Catalogue des inscriptions du Viet-nam = Catalogue of Vietnamese inscriptions.* . NXB Văn hóa - Thông tin.

23. Lafont, P.-B. (2014). *The kingdom of Champa : geography, population, history.* International Office of the Champa. , p. 132.

24. SKTT, Vol 1, p. 15.

25. Lê, T. (2002). *An Nam Chí Lược* (Ủy ban phiên dịch sử liệu Việt Nam của Viện Đại Học Huế (1961), Trans.). Thuận Hóa. (1285)

26. Neither Lê Quý Đôn nor Phan Huy Chú included An Nam Chí Lược in their records.

27. Lê, T. (2002). *An Nam Chí Lược* (Ủy ban phiên dịch sử liệu Việt Nam của Viện Đại Học Huế (1961), Trans.). Thuận Hóa. (1285), p. 8

28. Ibid. – p 348.

29. Unknown, translated by Trần Quốc Vượng (1959), & compared and corrected by Đinh Khắc Thuân. (2005). *Việt Sử Lược.* Thuận Hóa. (1377)

30. Vietnamese (Tứ Khố Toàn Thư). The catalogue of the collection shows 10,680 titles along with a compendium of 3,593 titles.

31. Guy, R. K. (1987). *The Emperor's four treasuries: scholars and the state in the late Ch'ien-lung era.* Mass. ; Harvard University Press.

32. Taylor, K. W. (1983). *The Birth of Vietnam.* Berkeley : University of California Press. , p. 152.

33. Lý, T. X. (2012). *Việt điện u linh* (Đ. R. Trịnh & G. K. Đinh, Trans.). NXB Hồng Bàng. (1329)

34. Taylor, K. W. (1983). *The Birth of Vietnam.* Berkeley : University of California Press. ,pp. 353-354.

35. Lý, T. X. (2012). *Việt điện u linh* (Đ. R. Trịnh & G. K. Đinh, Trans.). NXB Hồng Bàng. (1329), p. 45.

36. Lê, T. (2002). *An Nam Chí Lược* (Ủy ban phiên dịch sử liệu Việt Nam của Viện Đại Học Huế (1961), Trans.). Thuận Hóa. (1285)

37. Lý, T. X. (2012). *Việt điện u linh* (Đ. R. Trịnh & G. K. Đinh, Trans.). NXB Hồng Bàng. (1329), p. 107.

38. Appointed in 877 CE as the Protector General of An Nam (previously Giao Chỉ) under Tang dynasty. See Lê, T. (2002). *An Nam Chí Lược* (Ủy ban phiên dịch sử liệu Việt Nam của Viện Đại Học Huế (1961), Trans.). Thuận Hóa. (1285), p. 205.

39. SKTT, Vol. 1, p. 201.

40. Trần, V. G. (1966). Sách "Vĩnh-Lạc đại điển bản Giao-Châu ký" mới bị phát hiện là một ngụy thư (sách giả tạo). *Tạp chí Nghiên cứu Lịch sử, Số 84 (Tháng 3)*, 26-28. (Viện Khoa học Xã hội Việt Nam) , p. 28.

41. Trần, T. P. (2011). *Lĩnh nam chích quái* (restored and edited by Vũ Quỳnh and Kiều Phú, Đinh Gia Khánh, Nguyễn Ngọc San, Trans.). NXB Trẻ; Hồng Bàng. (1492)

42. LNCQ, p. 29, p. 30.

43. Ngô Sĩ Liên. (1998). *Đại Việt Sử Ký Toàn Thư* Khoa Học Xã Hội (Social Science) (1998). (Chính Hòa version (1697).)

44. SKTT- Vol 1, p. 39.

45. Chính Hòa is the niên hiệu (age) of King Lê Hy Tông (1680-1705)

46. SKTT-Vol. 1, p. 63.

47. SKTT-Vol. 1, p. 6.

48. Ngô, T. S. N. P. (2001). *Việt sử tiêu án* (Hội Việt Nam nghiên cứu liên lạc văn hóa Á châu, Trans.). Văn sử (1991), digitised by Công Đệ, Doãn Vượng, Lê Bắc. (1775)

49. Quốc sử quán triều Nguyễn, & Viện sử học. (1998). *Khâm định Việt sử thông giám cương mục* (Hoa Bằng, Phạm Trọng Điềm,, Trần Văn Giáp (1957), Trans.). Giáo dục.

APPENDIX 3

1. Ibid., p. 12.

2. Ngô Sĩ Liên. (1998). *Đại Việt Sử Ký Toàn Thư* Khoa Học Xã Hội (Social Science) (1998). (Chính Hòa version (1697)), p. 153.

3. Đàm Thành is now known as Việt Thành, Cửu Nghi is now known as Mạnh Chử (see Kiều, T. H. (2016). Góp phần nghiên cứu lịch sử văn hóa Việt Nam - Thời kỳ thiên niên kỷ đầu công nguyên. NXB Thế Giới. , p. 36.

APPENDIX 5

1. LNCQ, p. 38.

2. SKTT, Vol. 1, p. 133

3. CM, pp. 74-75.

4. Đào, D. A. (2005). *Đất nước Việt Nam qua các đời - Nghiên cứu địa lý học lịch sử Việt Nam*. NXB Văn Hóa Thông Tin. , p. 19.

5. Ibid., p. 19.

6. Ibid., p. 99.

7. Maspero, H. (1918). Etudes d'histoire d'Annam. *Bulletin de l'Ecole française d'Extrême-Orient*, 1-36. https://www.persee.fr/doc/befeo_0336-1519_1918_num_18_1_5888 , p. 2.

APPENDIX 6

1. Đào, D. A. (2006). *Lịch sử Việt Nam - Từ nguồn gốc đến thế kỷ XIX*. NXB Văn Hóa Thông Tin. (1957), p. 37.

2. Others have suggested *crane egrets*, see Higham, C. F. W. (2012). The Đông Sơn chiefdom. , p. 35.

3. Ancient Chinese dynasty (2070-1600 BCE), Henan province, west of Shanghai.

4. Kiều, T. H. (2016). *Góp phần nghiên cứu lịch sử văn hóa Việt Nam - Thời kỳ thiên niên kỷ đầu công nguyên*. NXB Thế Giới. , p. 351.

5. Taylor, K. W. (1983). *The Birth of Vietnam*. Berkeley : University of California Press.

6. Brindley, E. (2018). *Ancient China and the Yue : perceptions and identities on the southern frontier, c.400 BCE - 50 CE*.

7. Nguyễn, K. V. (2015). *Viet Nam: a long history*. Thế Giới.

8. Kelley, L. C. (2015). Inventing traditions in fifteenth-century Vietnam. *Imperial China and Its Southern Neighbours*. (edited by Victor H. Mair and Liam C. Kelley (Singapore - Institute of Southeast Asian Studies, 2015).) , p. 183.

9. For example, the story of the gold turtle (see 9.9.1).

APPENDIX 7

1. Information from Kim, N. C. (2015). *The Origins of Ancient Vietnam*. Oxford University Press. , p. 106, shows a slightly different set of dates: Hòa Bình: 27,000-6,000 BCE; Bắc Sơn: 9,000-5,000 BCE; Đa Bút: 4,500-2,700 BCE, Phùng Nguyên: 2,000-1,500 BCE; Đồng Đậu: 1,500-1,100 BCE; Gò Mun: 1,100-700 BCE; Đông Sơn: 600 BCE-200 CE.

2. In Vietnamese *"Mái đá Ngườm"*

3. Nguyễn, D. H. (2013). *Văn minh Lạc Việt*. NXB Văn Hóa Thông Tin. , p. 255.

4. Nguyễn Thị Thanh Hiền, Bùi Thị Luận, Lê Hồng Sử, Đường Thị Ngọc Hóa, & Lê Thùy Dung. (2019). *Văn vật xứ Thanh - Thanh Hóa's material culture - Bảo tàng Thanh Hóa - Thanh Hoa Provincial Museum* NXB Thế Giới - World Publishers. , p. 43

5. Moser, J. (2012). The Hoabinhian Definition In the Past and Today: A Short Historical Review of Defining the Hoabinhian. 3-12.

6. Nguyễn, L. C. (2019). Những nghiên cứu cổ nhân học quan trọng của Việt Nam (1906-2018). *Tạp chí khoa học Đại học Đà Lạt, 9, số 3*, 17-55. , p. 47.

7. Hung, H.-c., Nguyen, K. D., Bellwood, P., & Carson, M. T. (2013). Coastal Connectivity: Long-Term Trading Networks Across the South China Sea. *The Journal of Island and Coastal Archaeology, 8*(3), 384-404. , p.386

8. Hà, V. T. (2018). *The making of Việt Nam*. Thế Giới. , p. 35.

9. Đặng, V. T. (2016). Nghiên cứu văn hóa Óc Eo sau 30 năm đổi mới (1986-2016). *Vietnam Academy of Social Sciences, Institute of Archaeology. (2018). Tuyển tập 50 năm khảo cổ học Việt Nam 1968-2018*. NXB Khoa Học Xã Hội, 888-901. Information from Kim, N. C. (2015). *The Origins of Ancient Vietnam*. Oxford University Press. , p. 106, shows a slightly different set of dates: Hòa Bình: 27,000-6,000 BCE; Bắc Sơn: 9,000-5,000 BCE; Đa Bút: 4,500-2,700 BCE, Phùng Nguyên: 2,000-1,500 BCE; Đồng Đậu: 1,500-1,100 BCE; Gò Mun: 1,100-700 BCE; Đông Sơn: 600 BCE-200 CE.

APPENDIX 8

1. Shiji(53), footnote 34 on p. 6 explains: *"The Western Ou were located in modern Kwangsi extending into what is now northern Vietnam. Lo (also Ou Lo) very likely refers to the kingdom of Au Lac in the Red River delta (modern Vietnam)"*. See also on p. 8, where Lo Lo is translated as Naked Lo, and p. 19.

2. Gu, B. (111). *Han shu - Book of Han*. https://ctext.org/han-shu/zh , Chapter 95 (or 65), paragraphs 17, 36.

3. Phan , H. L. (2018). *Lịch sử và văn hóa Việt Nam tiếp cận bộ phận* (P. T. Phan, Ed. 4th ed.). NXB Đại Học Quốc Gia Hà Nội. , p. 111.

4. Đào, D. A. (2005). *Đất nước Việt Nam qua các đời - Nghiên cứu địa lý học lịch sử Việt Nam*. NXB Văn Hóa Thông Tin. , p. 27.

5. Đinh, V. N. (1980). Đất Mê Linh - Trung tâm chính trị, quán sự và kinh tế của huyện Mê Linh thời Hai Bà Trưng. *Nghiên Cứu Lịch Sử - Viện Sử Học, 1*, 35-53. , p. 37.

6. Bộ Quốc Phòng - Viện Lịch Sử Quân Sự Việt Nam, Trần, Q. V., & Lê, Đ. S. (2001). *Lịch Sử Quân Sự Việt Nam - Tập 2 - Đấu tranh giành độc lập tự chủ (từ năm 179 TCN đến năm 938)*. NXB Chính Trị Quốc Gia. , p. 26.

7. Maspero, H. (1918). Etudes d'histoire d'Annam. *Bulletin de l'Ecole française d'Extrême-Orient*, 1-36. https://www.persee.fr/doc/befeo_0336-1519_1918_num_18_1_5888 , p. 11.

8. Chinese Text Project. (2006-2020). *Shiji-Historical Records- [Western Han] 109 BC-91 BC Sima Qian*. https://ctext.org/shiji, Table 20, "Yearly table of the officials who became Marquises since the Jianyuan period", https://ctext.org/shiji/jian-yuan-yi-lai-hou-zhe, paragraph 2.

9. Gu, B. (111). *Han shu - Book of Han*. https://ctext.org/han-shu/zh , Volume 17, (Table 5), Table of meritorious officials during the reigns of (Emperors) Jing, Wu, Zhao, Xuan, Yuan and Cheng, https://ctext.org/han-shu/jing-wu-zhao-xuan-yuan-cheng, paragraph 4.

10. Maspero, H. (1918). Etudes d'histoire d'Annam. *Bulletin de l'Ecole française d'Extrême-Orient*, 1-36. https://www.persee.fr/doc/befeo_0336-1519_1918_num_18_1_5888 , p. 18.

BIBLIOGRAPHY

Allard, F. (1994). Interaction and Social Complexity in Lingnan during the First Millennium B.C. *Asian Perspectives, 33*(2), 309-326. HTTP://WWW.JSTOR.ORG/STABLE/42928324

Allard, F. (2000). Frontiers and Boundaries: The Han Empire From its Southern Periphery. 233-254.

Alves, M. J. (2001). *What's so Chinese about Vietnamese?* Ninth Annual Meeting of the Southeast Asian Linguistics Society, Arizona State University, Program for Southeast Asian Studies.

Apostol, V. M. (2012). Way of the Ancient Healer : Sacred Teachings from the Philippine Ancestral Traditions. HTTP://WWW.MYILIBRARY.COM?ID=488055

Arpon, J. (2012). *Warriors formation from backwards. Xi'an, China.* HTTPS://COMMONS.WIKIMEDIA.ORG/WIKI/FILE:TERRACOTA_WARRIORS_002.JPG

Arpon, J. (June 2012). *Terracota warrior. Archer close-up (inside glass). Xi'an, China.* HTTPS://COMMONS.WIKIMEDIA.ORG/WIKI/FILE:TERRACOTA_WARRIOR_CLOSE-UP.JPG

Aurousseau, L. (1923). La première conquête chinoise des pays annamites (IIIe siècle avant notre ère). HTTP://WWW.PERSEE.FR/WEB/REVUES/HOME/PRESCRIPT/ARTICLE/BEFEO_0336-1519_1923_NUM_23_1_5933

Avibase. (2020). *Avibase - Bird Checklists of the World Vietnam.* HTTPS://AVIBASE.BSC-EOC.ORG/CHECKLIST.JSP?REGION=VN

Backus, C. (1981). *The Nan-chao kingdom and T'ang China's southwestern frontier.* Cambridge University Press.

Bellwood, P. (1993). Southeast Asia before History. In N. Tarling (Ed.), *The Cambridge History of Southeast Asia: Volume 1: From Early Times to c.1800* (Vol. 1, pp. 51-136). Cambridge University Press. https://doi.org/doi: 10.1017/CHOL9780521355056.004

Bellwood, P. (2012). *Vietnam and the Prehistory of Eastern Asia – A multidisciplinary perspective on the Neolithic - Việt Nam và tiền sử Đông Á - một hướng tiếp cận đa ngành về thời kỳ đồ đá mới* Perspectives on the archaeology of Vietnam International Colloquium, Hanoi 29th February - 2nd March 2012 = Toàn cảnh khảo cổ học Việt Nam, Hanoi, Vietnam.

Bình Giang - Public domain. (2009). *A bronze dagger, Dong Son Culture.*

Bình Giang. (2009). *The trigger portion of a Dong Son crossbow dating from 500 BCE-0.* https://commons.wikimedia.org/wiki/file:dong_son_crossbow_trigger.jpg

Bộ Quốc Phòng - Viện Lịch Sử Quân Sự Việt Nam, Trần, Q. V., & Lê, Đ. S. (2001). *Lịch Sử Quân Sự Việt Nam - Tập 2 - Đấu tranh giành độc lập tự chủ (từ năm 179 TCN đến năm 938)*. NXB Chính Trị Quốc Gia.

Book of Han. (2020). https://en.wikipedia.org/wiki/book_of_han

Brindley, E. (2018). *Ancient China and the Yue : perceptions and identities on the southern frontier, c.400 BCE - 50 CE.*

Bronze Age,. (2020). https://en.wikipedia.org/wiki/bronze_age#cite_note-35

Bulbeck, D. (2014). Island Southeast Asia: Neolithic. In C. Smith (Ed.), *Encyclopedia of Global Archaeology* (pp. 4090-4096). Springer New York. https://doi.org/10.1007/978-1-4419-0465-2_866

The Cambridge History of China: Volume 1: The Ch'in and Han Empires, 221 BC–AD 220. (1986). (D. Twitchett & M. Loewe, Eds. Vol. 1). Cambridge University Press. https://doi.org/doi: 10.1017/CHOL9780521243278

Cartwright, M. (2017). *Crossbows in Ancient Chinese Warfare.* https://www.ancient.eu/article/1098/crossbows-in-ancient-chinese-warfare/

Charles, F. W. H., Katerina, D., & Thomas, F. G. H. (2015). A New Chronology for the Bronze Age of Northeastern Thailand and Its Implications for Southeast Asian Prehistory [article]. *PLoS ONE*(9), e0137542. https://doi.org/10.1371/journal.pone.0137542

Châu, H. Đ. (2018). *An Nam Truyện - Ghi chép về Việt Nam trong chính sử Trung Quốc xưa.* Hội Nhà Văn.

Chế Lan Viên, & selected by Vũ Tuấn Anh. (2009). *Chế Lan Viên, tác phẩm chọn lọc.* NXB Giáo dục Việt Nam.

Chen, L. (2018). *Complete book of Chinese knotting: a compendium of techniques and variations.* TUTTLE Publishing.

Chinese Text Project. (2006-2020). *Shiji-Historical Records- [Western Han] 109 BC-91 BC Sima Qian.* https://ctext.org/shiji

Chinese Text Project. (2006-2020). *Shui Jing Zhu, Wei, Jin, and North-South, Waterways.* https://ctext.org/han-shu/zh

Chinese Text Project. (2006-2020). *Huainanzi, Western Han (206 BC-9)* https://ctext.org/huainanzi/ren-xian-xun/ens

Chu, T. L. (2004, 12-13 tháng 11, 2004). *Số hóa để bảo quản và khai thác di sản Hán Nôm Việt Nam: triển vọng và thách thức*.

Digitisation to preserve and exploit the heritage of Hán Nôm Vietnam: Prospects and Challenges) – International Conference on Nôm language Hội nghị quốc tế về chữ Nôm Thư viện quốc gia Việt Nam – Hà Nội

Climate in Hanoi (Ha Noi Municipality), Vietnam. (2020). HTTPS://WEATHER-AND-CLIMATE.COM/AVERAGE-MONTHLY-RAINFALL-TEMPERATURE-SUNSHINE,HANOI,VIETNAM

Commentary on the Water Classic. (2020). HTTPS://EN.WIKIPEDIA.ORG/WIKI/COMMENTARY_ON_THE_WATER_CLASSIC

Compiled by World Heritage Encyclopedia™ licensed under CC BY-SA 3.0. *Đạo Mẫu*. HTTP://COMMUNITY.WORLDHERITAGE.ORG/ARTICLES/RELIGION_IN_VIETNAM

Coupe, A. R., & Kratochvíl, F. Asia before English, Pre-publication draft. *Handbook of Asian Englishes, Bolton, Kingsley, Kirkpatrick, Thomas A. and Botha, Werner (eds)*.

Daaé Public domain via Wikimedia Commons. (2010). *Co Loa bronze drum at the Hanoi Museum*. HTTPS://UPLOAD.WIKIMEDIA.ORG/WIKIPEDIA/COMMONS/5/50/CO_LOA_DRUMS.JPG

Đặng, Đ. T. (2000). *Lịch sử sử học Việt Nam (từ thế kỷ XI đến giữa thế kỷ XIX)*. NXB Trẻ.

Đặng, H. S. (2019). *Nước Âu Lạc thời An Dương Vương* Thời đại Hùng Vương trong tiến trình lịch sử Việt Nam - Kỳ yếu hội thảo khoa học quốc gia, Hanoi, 9-2019.

Đặng, V. T. (2016). Nghiên cứu văn hóa Óc Eo sau 30 năm đổi mới (1986-2016). *Vietnam Academy of Social Sciences, Institute of Archaeology*. (2018). *Tuyển tập 50 năm khảo cổ học Việt Nam 1968-2018*. NXB Khoa Học Xã Hội, 888-901.

Đào, D. A. (2006). *Lịch sử Việt Nam - Từ nguồn gốc đến thế kỷ XIX*. NXB Văn Hóa Thông Tin. (1957)

Đào, D. A. (2005). *Đất nước Việt Nam qua các đời - Nghiên cứu địa lý học lịch sử Việt Nam*. NXB Văn Hóa Thông Tin.

Đào, D. A. (2005). *Lịch sử cổ đại Việt Nam* NXB Văn Hóa Thông Tin.

Depts.Washington.Edu. *Crossbows*. HTTPS://DEPTS.WASHINGTON.EDU/CHINACIV/MILTECH/CROSSBOW.HTM

Đinh, N. V. (2019). *Vấn đề nhà nước Nam Cương và nguồn gốc của Thục Phán*. Thời đại Hùng Vương trong tiến trình lịch sử Việt Nam - Kỳ yếu hội thảo khoa học quốc gia, Hanoi, 9-2019.

Đinh, V. N. (1980). Đất Mê Linh - Trung tâm chính trị, quân sự và kinh tế của huyện Mê Linh thời Hai Bà Trưng. *Nghiên Cứu Lịch Sử - Viện Sử Học, 1*, 35-53.

Discott, CC BY-SA (HTTPS://CREATIVECOMMONS.ORG/LICENSES/BY-SA/3.0),. (2011). *A statue of a man, dating from the State of Yue, located in the State Museum of Zhejiang province, Hangzhou, Zhejiang, China*. HTTPS://COMMONS.WIKIMEDIA.ORG/WIKI/FILE:YUE_STATUE.JPG

Đỗ, B. (2005). *Những khám phá về Hoàng Đế Quang Trung* (IV ed.). NXB Thuận Hóa.

Đoàn, T. Đ. (2013). *Truyền kỳ tân phả* (L. C. Ngô & V. G. Trần, Trans.). NXB Trẻ, NXB Hồng Bàng. (1811)

Dror, O. (2007). *Cult, Culture, and Authority : Princess Lieu Hanh in Vietnamese History*. University of Hawaii Press.

Dương, H. (2013). *Bronze lamp in the shape of a kneeling man (Lsb.1391)*. http://baotanglichsu.vn/en/articles/1004/13779/bronze-lamp-in-the-shape-of-a-kneeling-man-lsb-1391.html

Dương Văn Thâm et al. (2005). *Hồ Xuân Hương - Thơ và Đời*. NXB Văn Học.

Dutton, G. E. (2006). *The Tây Sơn uprising: society and rebellion in eighteenth-century Vietnam*. University of Hawai'i Press.

Ebrey, P. B. *A Visual Sourcebook of Chinese Civilization, China proper*. https://depts.washington.edu/chinaciv/geo/proper.htm

Fan Ye. (2020). *Book of the Later Han*. https://en.wikipedia.org/wiki/book_of_the_later_han

FAO. (2011). *AQUASTAT Country Profile – Viet Nam*. http://www.fao.org/3/ca0412en/ca0412en.pdf

French Indochina c. 1930. (2013). https://commons.wikimedia.org/wiki/file:french_indochina_c._1930.jpg

General Statistics Office of Viet Nam. (2018). *Land use (As of 31 Februarry 2017) by Type of land and Use - Number of administrative units as of 31 December by province by Cities, provincies, Years and Administrative units (2018)*. https://www.gso.gov.vn/default_en.aspx?tabid=773

Glover, I. (2012). *Champa and its relations to preceding iron age cultures - Văn hóa Champa và mối quan hệ với các nền văn hóa thời đại đồ sắt trước đó*. Perspectives on the archaeology of Vietnam International Colloquium, Hanoi 29th February - 2nd March 2012 = Toàn cảnh khảo cổ học Việt Nam, Hanoi, Vietnam.

Grossin, P. (1926). *La Province Muong de Hoa-Binh*. 2e édition. Impr. d'Extrême-Orient ;.

Gryffindor - CC BY-SA 3.0. (2008). *Lamp base in the shape of a kneeling man*. https://upload.wikimedia.org/wikipedia/commons/d/df/national_museum_vietnamese_history_28.jpg

Gu, B. (111). *Han shu - Book of Han*. https://ctext.org/han-shu/zh

Gunn, G. C. (2011). The Great Vietnamese Famine of 1944-45 Revisited.

Guy, R. K. (1987). *The Emperor's four treasuries: scholars and the state in the late Ch'ien-lung era*. Mass. ; Harvard University Press.

Hà, V. T. (2018). *The making of Việt Nam*. Thế Giới.

Hà, V. T. (2019). *Chữ trên đá, chữ trên đồng, minh văn và lịch sử*. NXB Trí Thức.

Hán Nôm. (2020?). http://khoavanhoc-ngonngu.edu.vn/gioi-thieu/cac-bo-mon-2/bộ-môn-hán-nôm.html

Han, X. (1998). The Present Echoes of the Ancient Bronze Drum: Nationalism and Archeology in Modern Vietnam and China. *Explorations in Southeast Asian studies*, *2*(2), 27-46.

HappyMidnight, & BY-SA, C. (2012). *Three node pendant*. https://upload.wikimedia.org/wikipedia/commons/e/e6/three_node_pendant_%28jade%29%2c_artefacts_of_phu_hoa_site%28dong_nai_province%29.jpg

Heger, F. (1902). *Alte Metalltrommeln aus Sudost-Asien*. Leipzig.

Helliwell, J., Layard, R., & Sachs, J. (2019). *World Happiness Report 2019*. New York: Sustainable Development Solutions Network.

Higham, C. F. W. (2012). The Đông Sơn chiefdom.

Higham, C. F. W. (2012). *The Đông Sơn chiefdom - Lãnh địa Đông Sơn*. Perspectives on the archaeology of Vietnam international colloquium, Hanoi 29th February - 2nd March 2012 = Toàn cảnh khảo cổ học Việt Nam, Hanoi, Vietnam.

Hồ, X. T. (2017?). *Bảo Tàng Quảng Nam - 20 năm nghiên cứu khảo cổ học*. http://baotang.quangnam.gov.vn/default.aspx?tabid=63&group=51&nid=1826&bao-tang-quang-nam--2-nam-nghien-cuu-khao-co-hoc

Hoàng, P. T. (2014). Phân tích tác động thẩm mỹ của văn bản thơ Đèo ba dội từ góc độ Mỹ học tiếp nhận. http://phebinhvanhoc.com.vn/phan-tich-tac-dong-tham-my-cua-van-ban-tho-deo-ba-doi-tu-goc-do-my-hoc-tiep-nhan/

Hoàng, T. T., & Nguyen, T. T. (2008). *The history of Buddhism in Vietnam*. Institute of Philosophy, Vietnamese Academy of Social Sciences.

Hoàng, X. C. (2012). *Đồ đồng văn hóa Đông Sơn - The bronze artifacts of Dong Son culture*. NXB Văn hóa thông tin.

Huainanzi. (2020). https://en.wikipedia.org/wiki/Huainanzi

Hubei Provincial Museum. *The sword of Goujian*. http://www.hbww.org/views/e_artgoodsdetail.aspx?pno=e_collection&no=e_gzzq&guid=ebc8eff0-8a90-4d27-a0ef-5915247ba857&type=detail

Hung, H.-c. (2014). Jade in Southeast Asia. 1-8.

Hung, H.-c., Nguyen, K. D., Bellwood, P., & Carson, M. T. (2013). Coastal Connectivity: Long-Term Trading Networks Across the South China Sea. *The Journal of Island and Coastal Archaeology, 8*(3), 384-404.

Imamura, K. (2010, 01/01). The Distribution of Bronze Drums of the Heger I and Pre-I Types: Temporal Changes and Historical Background.

Jack. (2013). *Lac Long Quan and Au Co – The Vietnam's ancient legend*. http://vietnamsurprise.com/2013/02/lac-long-quan-and-au-co-the-vietnams-ancient-legend.html

Johnlemon (Flickr) / CC BY-SA (https://creativecommons.org/licenses/by-sa/2.0). (2008). https://upload.wikimedia.org/wikipedia/commons/1/1a/%c4%90%e1%bb%81n_h%c3%b9ng%2c_ph%c3%ba_th%e1%bb%8d_%281%29.jpg

Kelley, L. C. (2015). Inventing traditions in fifteenth-century Vietnam. *Imperial China and Its Southern Neighbours*. (edited by Victor H. Mair and Liam C. Kelley (Singapore - Institute of Southeast Asian Studies, 2015).)

Kelly, L. (2013). Tai words and the place of the Tai in the Vietnamese past. *Journal of the Siam Society, 101*, 55-84.

Kiều, T. H. (2016). *Góp phần nghiên cứu lịch sử văn hóa Việt Nam - Thời kỳ thiên niên kỷ đầu công nguyên*. NXB Thế Giới.

Kim, N. C. (2015). *The Origins of Ancient Vietnam*. Oxford University Press.

Kutschke, B., & Norton, B. (2014). *Music and Protest in 1968*. Cambridge University Press. https://books.google.co.nz/books?id=nxj_oqeacaaj

L'Illustration : journal universel. (1862). L'Illustration : journal universel. *40 no. 1031 - 29 Novembre 1862*.

Lafont, P.-B. (2014). *The kingdom of Champa : geography, population, history*. International Office of the Champa.

Lại, V. T. (2012). *Cổ Loa: the capital of the Âu Lạc kingdom in the 3rd and 2nd centuries BCE - Cổ Loa: kinh thành của nhà nước Âu Lạc vào thế kỷ 3-2 tr CN*. Perspectives on the Archaeology of Vietnam International Colloquium, Hanoi 29th February - 2nd March 2012 = Toàn cảnh khảo cổ học Việt Nam, Hanoi, Vietnam.

Lâm, T. M. D. (2018). *Sa Huỳnh - Lâm Ấp - Chămpa: Thế kỷ 5 trước công nguyên đến thế kỷ 5 sau công nguyên (một số vấn đề khảo cổ học) = Sa Huynh - Linyi - Champa: 5th century BC - 5th century AD: some archaeological issues*. NXB Thế Giới.

Lary, D. (1996, January 1996). The tomb of the king of Nanyue - the contemporary agenda of history: scholarship and identity. *Modern China, Vol. 22 No. 1*, 3-27.

Lê, H. K. (2019). *Đầm An Khê - Một di sản thiên nhiên quý báu*. http://baoquangngai.vn/channel/2047/201911/dam-an-khe-mot-di-san-thien-nhien-quy-bau-2976505/

Lê, M. T., & Viện nghiên cứu Phật học Việt Nam. (2005). *Lục độ tập kinh và lịch sử khởi nguyên của dân tộc ta*. NXB Tổng hợp thành phố Hồ Chí Minh.

Lê, Q. Đ. (2007). *Đại Việt thông sử* (T. L. Ngô, Trans.). NXB Văn hóa - Thông tin. (1759)

Lê, T. (2002). *An Nam Chí Lược* (Ủy ban phiên dịch sử liệu Việt Nam của Viện Đại Học Huế (1961), Trans.). Thuận Hóa. (1285)

Lê, T. K. (2018). *Lịch sử Việt Nam từ nguồn gốc đến giữa thế kỷ XX* (N. Nguyễn & T. H. Nguyễn, Trans.; Vol. Nhã Nam, NXB Thế Giới). (1955, 1982)

Lê, V. S. (2003). *Việt Nam văn minh sử: lược khảo, tập thượng, từ nguồn gốc đến thế kỷ thứ X*. Lao Động.

Li Jinhui. (2003). *Stunning Capital of Xia Dynasty Unearthed*. http://www.china.org.cn/english/2003/nov/79635.htm

Lịch Đạo Nguyên, (Li Daoyuan), Dương Thủ Kính, (Yang, Shoujing), Hùng Hội Trinh, (Xiong, Huizhen), Đoàn Huy Trọng, (Duan, Xizhong), Trần Kiều Dịch, (Chen, Qiaoyi), & Nguyễn Bá Mão. (2005). *Thủy kinh chú sở* (Nguyễn Bá Mão, Trans.). NXB Thuận Hóa ; Trung tâm văn hóa ngôn ngữ Đông Tây. (Giang Tô, China 1999)

Linhcandng (thảo luận) CC BY-SA 3.0. (2016). *Hoành Sơn Quan*. https://commons.wikimedia.org/wiki/file:ho%c3%a0nh_s%c6%a1n_quan_5.jpeg

Lockhart, B. M., & Duiker, W. J. (2006). *Historical dictionary of Vietnam*. Scarecrow Press.

Lockhart, B. M., & Phuong, T. K. (2011). *The Cham of Vietnam : History, society and art*. Singapore University Press.

Lu Bu-wei. (247-239 BCE). *Lü Shi Chun Qiu*. https://ctext.org/lv-shi-chun-qiu/ens

Lüshi Chunqiu. (2020). https://en.wikipedia.org/wiki/l%c3%bcshi_chunqiu

Lý, T. X. (2012). *Việt điện u linh* (Đ. R. Trịnh & G. K. Đinh, Trans.). NXB Hồng Bàng. (1329)

Macholdt, E., Arias, L., Duong, N. T., Ton, N. D., Van Phong, N., Schröder, R., Pakendorf, B., Van Hai, N., & Stoneking, M. (2020, 2020/05/01). The paternal and maternal genetic history of Vietnamese populations. *European Journal of Human Genetics, 28*(5), 636-645. https://doi.org/10.1038/s41431-019-0557-4

Maspero, H. (1918). Etudes d'histoire d'Annam. *Bulletin de l'Ecole française d'Extrême-Orient*, 1-36. https://www.persee.fr/doc/befeo_0336-1519_1918_num_18_1_5888

Mattet, L., Barbier, J. P., Menz, C., Amiet, P., Chamay, J., Studio Ferrazzini, B., Musée d'art et, d. h., Musée, B.-M., & Museo Barbier-Mueller de Arte, P. (2008). *Le profane et le divin : arts de l'Antiquité de l'Europe au Sud-est asiatique : fleurons du Musée Barbier-Mueller*. Hazan ; Musées d'art et d'histoire : Musée Barbier-Mueller.

Meteorological Service Singapore. *Winds.* http://www.weather.gov.sg/learn_winds/

MikeHS CC BY-SA 3.0. (2009). *Tambor de la cultura Dong Son, de Vietnam (800 BC) al Museu Guimet, de París.* https://upload.wikimedia.org/wikipedia/commons/b/be/trong_dong_dong_son_guimet.jpg

mindat.org. (2020). *Núi Châu Sơn, Tỉnh Bắc Ninh, Vietnam.* https://www.mindat.org/feature-9871431.html

Minh Thư. (2007). *Tuyển chọn ca dao hay nhất.* NXB Văn hóa dân tộc

Ministry of Culture-Sport and Tourism. (2018). *Bảo Tàng Lịch Sử Quốc Gia, Vietnam National Museum of History.* http://baotanglichsu.vn/en

Moser, J. (2012). The Hoabinhian Definition In the Past and Today: A Short Historical Review of Defining the Hoabinhian. 3-12.

Mote, F. W. (2003). *Imperial China, 900-1800.* Harvard University Press.

Musée Guimet. *Tambour du Sông Dà dit «tambour Moulié».* https://www.guimet.fr/collections/asie-du-sud-est/tambour-du-song-da-dit-tambour-moulie/

New Economics Foundation. (2016). *Happy Planet Index Score.* http://happyplanetindex.org/countries/vietnam

Ngô Sĩ Liên. (1998). *Đại Việt Sử Ký Toàn Thư* Khoa Học Xã Hội (Social Science) (1998). (Chính Hòa version (1697).)

Ngô, T. S. N. P. (2001). *Việt sử tiêu án* (Hội Việt Nam nghiên cứu liên lạc văn hóa Á châu, Trans.). Văn sử (1991), digitised by Công Đệ, Doãn Vượng, Lê Bắc. (1775)

Ngô, V. D. (2002). *Văn hóa cổ Champa.* NXB Văn Hóa Dân Tộc.

Ngô, V. H. H. (2019). *Quan điểm của các nhà nghiên cứu sử học miền Bắc về thời đại Hùng Vương từ năm 1967 đến nay* Thời đại Hùng Vương trong tiến trình lịch sử Việt Nam - Kỷ yếu hội thảo khoa học quốc gia, Hanoi, 9-2019.

Nguyễn, C. (2011). *Di tích văn hóa Sa huỳnh ở Gò Mã Vôi (Quảng Nam) qua 3 lần khai quật.* https://123doc.net/document/2571704-di-tich-van-hoa-sa-huynh-o-go-ma-voi-quang-nam-qua-3-lan-khai-quat-pdf.htm

Nguyễn, D. C. (2019). *Hoa Văn Việt Nam - Từ thời tiền sử đến nửa đầu thời kỳ phong kiến*. NXB Hồng Đức. (2003)

Nguyễn, D. H. (2013). *Văn minh Lạc Việt*. NXB Văn Hóa Thông Tin.

Nguyễn, Đ. T. (1998). *Lịch sử tư tưởng Việt Nam* (Vol. 1). NXB TP. Hồ Chí Minh.

Nguyễn, G. H., & Trịnh, N. C. (2014). Đông Sơn culture – 90 years of discovery and research *Vietnam Archeology No. 9/2014*, 2-17.

Nguyễn, H. T. (2019). *Thư tịch cổ Trung quốc viết về Văn Lang, Âu Lạc, An Dương Vương, thành Cổ Loa*. Thời đại Hùng Vương trong tiến trình lịch sử Việt Nam - Kỷ yếu hội thảo khoa học quốc gia., Hanoi, 9-2019.

Nguyễn, K. D. (2017). The Sa Huynh Culture in Ancient Regional Trade Networks: A Comparative Study of Ornaments. 311-332.

Nguyễn, K. T., & Vương, L. (1974). Thử tìm nguồn gốc ngữ nghĩa của từ tố "Lạc". Hùng Vương dựng nước - Kỷ yếu của hội nghị nghiên cứu thời kỳ Hùng Vương lần thứ 4, tháng 4 năm 1974, Hanoi.

Nguyễn, K. V. (2015). *Viet Nam: a long history*. Thế Giới.

Nguyễn, L. C. (2019). Những nghiên cứu cổ nhân học quan trọng của Việt Nam (1906-2018). *Tạp chí khoa học Đại học Đà Lạt, 9, số 3*, 17-55.

Nguyễn, M. L. (1974). Cương vực nước Văn Lang. Hùng Vương dựng nước - Kỷ yếu của hội nghị nghiên cứu thời kỳ Hùng Vương lần thứ 4, tháng 4 năm 1974, Hanoi.

Nguyen, N. C., & Sachs, D. (2003). *Two cakes fit for a king : folktales from Vietnam*. University of Hawai`i Press.

Nguyễn, N. T. (2011). *Văn hóa Bách Việt vùng Lĩnh Nam trong quan hệ với văn hóa truyền thống ở Việt Nam - Luận án tiến sĩ văn hóa học* Đại Học Quốc Gia Tp. Hồ Chí Minh, Trường Đại Học Khoa Học Xã Hội và Nhân Văn,. goo.gl/5G33JN

Nguyễn, P. P. *Việt Nam, Chữ viết, Ngôn ngữ và Xã hội – Chương 1 – Cái nhìn đối chiếu giữa hai chữ tiếng Việt (Vietnam, Writing, Language and Society – Chapter 1 – A view of the comparison between two forms of Vietnamese writing)*. HTTP://WWW.NAMKYLUCTINH.COM/A-NGONNGU/NPHUPHONG-VNCHUVIETNGONNGU.PDF

Nguyễn, T. D. (2018). *Văn hóa Việt Nam thường thức*. NXB Hà Nội.

Nguyễn, T. Đ. (2017). *Vua nào nước ta đánh tan 50 vạn quân của Tần Thủy Hoàng?* HTTPS://BAOMOI.COM/VUA-NAO-NUOC-TA-DANH-TAN-50-VAN-QUAN-CUA-TAN-THUY-HOANG/C/22423045.EPI

Nguyễn Thị Thanh Hiền, Bùi Thị Luận, Lê Hồng Sử, Đường Thị Ngọc Hóa, & Lê Thùy Dung. (2019). *Văn vật xứ Thanh - Thanh Hóa's material culture - Bảo tàng Thanh Hóa - Thanh Hoa Provincial Museum* NXB Thế Giới - World Publishers.

Nguyễn, T. P. C. (2019). *Nghiên cứu về thời đại Hùng Vương của các tác giả ở miền nam Việt Nam trước 1975* Thời đại Hùng Vương trong tiến trình lịch sử Việt Nam - Kỷ yếu hội thảo khoa học quốc gia, Hanoi, 9-2019.

Nguyen, V. (2009-2020). *The Center for Southeast Asian Prehistory (CESEAP)*. HTTP://WWW.DRNGUYENVIET.COM/

Nichols, T. (2010). *Handy-book of the British Museum, for every-day readers.* Nabu Press.

Peak Advisor. *Nanling Mountains.* https://peakvisor.com/range/nanling-mountains.html

Pelliot, P., & Cadière, L. (1904). Première étude sur les sources annamites de l'histoire d'Annam. *Bulletin de l'Ecole française d'Extrême-Orient, 4,* 617-671. http://www.persee.fr/web/revues/home/prescript/article/befeo_0336-1519_1904_num_4_1_1360

Perlin, J. (2017). Peak wood and the Bronze Age. *Pacific Standard,* (June 14).

Phạm, Đ. M. (2014). Đông Sơn Signs in Southern Vietnam *Vietnam Archeology No. 9/2014.*

Phạm, H. (2008). *Do You Know How Vietnamese People Cultivate Wet Rice?* http://thingsasian.com/story/do-you-know-how-vietnamese-people-cultivate-wet-rice

Phạm, Q. Q. (2019). *Về những cây đèn đồng hậu Đông Sơn.* http://baotanglichsu.vn/vi/articles/3101/69641/ve-nhung-cay-djen-djong-hau-djong-son.html

Phan, H. C. (2014). *Lịch triều hiến chương loại chí – Tập 5 – Binh chế chí–Văn tịch chí-Bang giao chí* (Vol. 39 to 49). NXB Trẻ. (1819)

Phan, H. L. (2018). *Di sản văn hóa Việt Nam dưới góc nhìn lịch sử.* NXB Đại Học Quốc Gia Hà Nội.

Phan, H. L. (2018). *Lịch sử và văn hóa Việt Nam tiếp cận bộ phận* (P. T. Phan, Ed. 4th ed.). NXB Đại Học Quốc Gia Hà Nội.

Phan, H. L., Bùi, Đ. D., Doãn, P. Đ., Phạm, T. T., & Trần, B. C. (2019). *Một số trận quyết chiến chiến lược trong lịch sử dân tộc.* NXB Hồng Đức.

Quốc Hội. *Hiến Pháp nước Cộng Hoà Xã Hội Chủ Nghĩa Việt Nam năm 1980.* https://thuvienphapluat.vn/van-ban/bo-may-hanh-chinh/hien-phap-1980-cong-hoa-xa-hoi-chu-nghia-viet-nam-36948.aspx

Quốc Hội. (2013). *Hiến Pháp nước Cộng Hoà Xã Hội Chủ Nghĩa Việt Nam.* https://m.thuvienphapluat.vn/van-ban/bo-may-hanh-chinh/hien-phap-nam-2013-215627.aspx

Quốc sử quán triều Nguyễn, & Viện sử học. (1998). *Khâm định Việt sử thông giám cương mục* (Hoa Bằng, Phạm Trọng Điềm,,Trần Văn Giáp (1957), Trans.). Giáo dục.

Records of the Grand Historian. (2020). https://en.wikipedia.org/wiki/Records_of_the_grand_historian

Reinecke, A. (2012). *Insights into the archaeological research of Vietnam - Những góc nhìn về nghiên cứu khảo cổ học Việt Nam.* Perspectives on the Archaeology of Vietnam, International Colloquium, Hanoi 29th February - 2nd March 2012 = Toàn cảnh khảo cổ học Việt Nam, Hanoi, Vietnam.

Rummel, R. J. (1998). *Statistics of democide : genocide and mass murder since 1900.* LIT ; Distributed in North America by Transaction Publishers, Rutgers University. https://www.hawaii.edu/powerkills/sod.tab6.1b.gif

Sadalmelik - Public domain. (2007). *Topographic map of Vietnam. Created with GMT from publicly released GLOBE data.* https://commons.wikimedia.org/wiki/file:vietnam_topography.png

Schweyer, A.-V. (2019). *The Birth of Champa.*

Shi Jia. (2018). *Exhibition of unearthed artifacts reveal life and times of Zhejiang's historical past.* https://www.shine.cn/feature/art-culture/1806180236/

Sima, Q., & Chan, C. M. (2016). *The Grand Scribe's Records, Volume X : Volume X: The Memoirs of Han China, Part III* [Book]. Indiana University Press.

Sima, Q., Farmer, J. M., & Nienhauser, W. H. (2010). *The Grand Scribe's Records, Volume IX : The Memoirs of Han China, Part II* [Book]. Indiana University Press.

Sima Qian, & translated by Phan Ngọc. (2018). *Sử ký Tư Mã Thiên : (trọn bộ hai tập)* (Vol. 1, 2). Văn học.

Siyuwj. (2019). *Sword of Goujian, / CC BY-SA* (HTTPS://CREATIVECOMMONS.ORG/LICENSES/BY-SA/4.0) HTTPS://COMMONS.WIKIMEDIA.ORG/WIKI/FILE:SWORD_OF_GOUJIAN,_2019-06-15_07.JPG

Solheim, W. G. (1959). Introduction to Sa-huynh. *Asian Perspectives, 3*(2), 97-108.

Southworth, W. A. (2004). The coastal states of Champa. In B. P. IGlover I (Ed.), *Southeast Asia: from prehistory to history.* (pp. 209-233). Routledge Curzon.

Tạ, Đ. (2017). *Nguồn gốc và sự phát triển của trống đồng Đông Sơn - Sách chuyên khảo.* NXB Trí Thức.

Tana, L. (2002). *Nguyễn Cochinchina: southern Vietnam in the seventeenth and eighteenth centuries* (Second ed.). Southeast Asia Program Publications.

Taylor, K. W. (1983). *The Birth of Vietnam.* Berkeley : University of California Press.

Taylor, K. W. (2014). *A History of the Vietnamese.* Cambridge University Press.

Thái, V. C. (2009). *Nghiên cứu chữ viết cổ trên bia ký ở Đông Dương.* NXB Khoa Học Xã Hội.

The Met Fifth Avenue in Gallery 244. *Dagger 500 B.C.–A.D. 100 Vietnam.* HTTPS://WWW.METMUSEUM.ORG/ART/COLLECTION/SEARCH/60866

Tống, T. T. (2012). *A general outline on the history of archeology in Vietnam - Vài nét về lịch sử khảo cổ học Việt Nam.* Perspectives on the archaeology of Vietnam International Colloquium, Hanoi 29th February - 2nd March 2012 = Toàn cảnh khảo cổ học Việt Nam, Hanoi, Vietnam.

Trần, M.-V. (2002). 'Come on, Girls, Let's Go Bail Water': Eroticism in Hồ Xuân Hương's Vietnamese Poetry. *Journal of Southeast Asian Studies, 33*(3), 471-494. www.jstor.org/stable/20072448

Trần, N., Gros, F., Viện Nghiên Cứu Hán Nôm, & École française, d. E.-O. (1993). *Di Sản Hán Nôm Việt Nam: Thư mục đề yếu.* . NXB Khoa Học Xã Hội.

Trần, Q. V. (1995). The legend of Ông Dóng from the text to the field. *Essays into Vietnamese Pasts,* 13-41.

Trần, T. K. (1999). *Việt Nam Sử Lược.* Văn Hóa Thông Tin. (1921)

Trần, T. P. (2011). *Lĩnh nam chích quái* (restored and edited by Vũ Quỳnh and Kiều Phú, Đinh Gia Khánh, Nguyễn Ngọc San, Trans.). NXB Trẻ; Hồng Bàng. (1492)

Trần, V. G. (1966). Sách "Vĩnh-Lạc đại điển bản Giao-Châu ký" mới bị phát hiện là một ngụy thư (sách giả tạo). *Tạp chí Nghiên cứu Lịch sử, Số 84 (Tháng 3),* 26-28. (Viện Khoa học Xã hội Việt Nam)

Trịnh Đình Dương, Trương Thị Lan, Hoàng Thị Vân, Dương Thị Mỹ Dung, Lê Thùy Dung, Trần Thị Nga, & Trương Thị Phương Thảo. (2019). *Sưu tập cổ vật tiêu biểu văn hóa Đông Sơn - Bảo tàng Thanh Hóa - The collection of Dong Son culture typical artifacts - Thanh Hoa Provincial Museum* NXB Thanh Niên - Youth Publishing House.

Trịnh, H. H. (2019). *Kết quả nghiên cứu thành Cổ Loa (giai đoạn 2007-2014)*. Thời đại Hùng Vương trong tiến trình lịch sử Việt Nam - Kỳ yếu hội thảo khoa học quốc gia, Hanoi, 9-2019.

Trương, T. D. (2018). *Khảo chứng tiền sử Việt Nam - Researching of Vietnam prehistory*. NXB Tổng Hợp Thành Phố Hồ Chí Minh.

TUBS / CC BY-SA (https://creativecommons.org/licenses/by-sa/3.0). (2011). https://upload.wikimedia.org/wikipedia/commons/3/31/jiangsu_in_china_%28%2ball_claims_hatched%29.svg

Ulrich Theobald. (2011). *Ailao*. ChinaKnowledge.de, An Encyclopaedia on Chinese History, Literature and Art. http://www.chinaknowledge.de/history/altera/ailao.html

UNHCR, T. U. R. A. (2000). *The State of The World's Refugees 2000 - Chapter 4*. https://www.unhcr.org/3ebf9bad0.html

Unknown, translated by Trần Quốc Vượng (1959), & compared and corrected by Đinh Khắc Thuân. (2005). *Việt Sử Lược*. Thuận Hóa. (1377)

Unknown (18??–18??) - Public domain. (2007). *Qin Shi Huang's imperial tour across his empire. Depiction in an 18th century album. Source: Portal, Jane (Ed.). The first emperor: China's Terracotta Army. Cambridge, Massachusetts: Harvard University Press, 2007 ISBN 978-0-674-02697-7 Invalid ISBN (p.112)*. https://upload.wikimedia.org/wikipedia/commons/4/47/qin_shi_huang_imperial_tour.jpg

Văn, T. (2007). *Thời đại Hùng Vương: lịch sử, kinh tế, văn hóa, xã hội*. NXB Văn Học.

Viện Hàn Lâm Khoa Học Xã Hội Việt Nam, Viện Nghiên Cứu Hán Nôm, 漢喃研究院 Institute of Sino-Nom studies. (2020). http://www.hannom.org.vn/

Viện Nghiên Cứu Hán Nôm. (2007). *Thư mục thác bản văn khắc Hán Nôm Việt Nam = Catalogue des inscriptions du Viet-nam = Catalogue of Vietnamese inscriptions*. . NXB Văn hóa - Thông tin.

Viện Sử Học, & Quốc Sử Quán Triều Nguyễn. (2002). *Đại Nam Thực Lục* (T. Á. Ngô, D. T. Vũ, Đ. C. Trần, & Đ. H. Lê, Eds. Vol. 1 to 9). NXB Giáo Dục.

Vietnam Academy of Social Sciences, Institute of Archaeology. (2018). *Tuyển tập 50 năm khảo cổ học Việt Nam 1968-2018*. NXB Khoa Học Xã Hội.

Vũ, D. M., Trần, T. V., Tạ, N. L., Trương, T. Y., Võ, K. C., Tạ, T. T., Đinh, T. T. C., Nguyễn, V. N., Trần, Đ. C., Nguyễn, N. M., & Viện Sử Học. (2017). *Lịch sử Việt Nam* (Vũ Duy Miên, Ed.). NXB Khoa Học Xã Hội.

Vu, H. L., & Sharrock, P. D. (2014). *Descending dragon, rising tiger: a history of Vietnam*.

Vũ Tiến Lâm / CC BY-SA (https://creativecommons.org/licenses/by-sa/4.0). (2017). *Lễ hội Phủ Dầy*. https://upload.wikimedia.org/wikipedia/commons/a/af/l%e1%bb%85_h%e1%bb%99i_ph%e1%bb%a7_d%e1%ba%a7y.jpg

Vũ, V. L. (2008). *Tìm về nơi an nghỉ cuối cùng của các nữ sĩ Đoàn Thị Điểm, Hồ Xuân Hương và Bà Huyện Thanh Quan*. http://antg.cand.com.vn/tu-lieu-antg/tim-ve-noi-an-nghi-cuoi-cung-cua-cac-nu-si-doan-thi-diem-ho-xuan-huong-va-ba-huyen-thanh-quan-292394/

Washington State University College of Pharmacy. (2006). *Shen Nung 2696 BCE*. https://www.asmalldoseoftoxicology.org/shen-nung

Western Han Nanyue King Museum. (2020?). WWW.GZNYWMUSEUM.ORG, HTTP://EN.GZNYWMUSEUM.ORG/PRODUCT/LIST?CATEGORYID=3&PAGEINDEX=1#

Wilpers, M. (2018). *The Smithsonian's Biggest Drum*. HTTPS://MUSIC.SI.EDU/STORY/SMITHSONIAN%E2%80%99S-BIGGEST-DRUM

Xiu, O., & Davis, R. L. (2004). *Historical Records of the Five Dynasties*. Columbia University Press.

Yamagata, M., & Matsumura, H. (2017). Austronesian Migration to Central Vietnam: Crossing over the Iron Age Southeast Asian Sea. 333-355.

Yprpyqp - Own work CC BY-SA 4.0. (2014). HTTPS://COMMONS.WIKIMEDIA.ORG/W/INDEX.PHP?CURID=67546191

Yprpyqp. (2011). *Han crossbow trigger components*. HTTPS://COMMONS.WIKIMEDIA.ORG/WIKI/FILE:HAN_CROSSBOW_TRIGGER_COMPONENTS.JPG#/MEDIA/FILE:HAN_CROSSBOW_TRIGGER_COMPONENTS.JPG

Yu, N. (2005). *CC BY-SA 3.0*, HTTPS://COMMONS.WIKIMEDIA.ORG/W/INDEX.PHP?CURID=305427. HTTPS://COMMONS.WIKIMEDIA.ORG/WIKI/FILE:QIN_EMPIRE_210_BCE.JPG

Zeng Gongliang, Ding Du, & Weide, Y. (1044). *Wujing Zongyao or 'Collection of the Most Important Military Techniques'*.

Zhao Ying, Liu Xu, Zhang Zhao, Jia Wei, & Zhao Xi. (941-945). *Old Book of Tang* HTTPS://CTEXT.ORG/WIKI.PL?IF=GB&RES=456206

Zwegers, A. (2007). *Nha Trang, Po Nagar Cham, North Tower*. HTTPS://COMMONS.WIKIMEDIA.ORG/WIKI/FILE:NHA_TRANG,_PO_NAGAR_CHAM,_NORTH_TOWER_(6223880651).JPG

www.ingramcontent.com/pod-product-compliance
Lightning Source LLC
Chambersburg PA
CBHW051209290426
44109CB00021B/2396